Antislavery, Abolition, and the Atlantic World
R. J. M. Blackett and James Brewer Stewart, Editors

CARIBBEAN SLAVE REVOLTS

AND THE

BRITISH ABOLITIONIST movement

GELIEN MATTHEWS

LOUISIANA STATE UNIVERSITY PRESS)((BATON ROUGE

Published by Louisiana State University Press

Copyright © 2006 by Louisiana State University Press
All rights reserved
Manufactured in the United States of America
Louisiana Paperback Edition, 2012

Designer: Michelle A. Garrod
Typeface: Sabon
Typesetter: The Composing Room of Michigan, Inc.

Library of Congress Cataloging-in-Publication Data
    Matthews, Gelien, 1965–
  Caribbean slave revolts and the British abolitionist movement / Gelien Matthews.
        p. cm.
    Includes bibliographical references.
    ISBN 0-8071-3131-8 (cloth : alk. paper)
      1. Slavery—Caribbean Area—History. 2. Slave insurrections—Caribbean
  Area—History. 3. Antislavery movements—Great Britain—History. I. Title.
  HT1071.M38 2006
  306.3'6209729—dc22

                                                                    2005023669

  ISBN 978-0-8071-5008-5 (pbk.: alk. paper) — ISBN 978-0-8071-4890-7 (pdf) —
  ISBN 978-0-8071-4891-4 (epub) — ISBN 978-0-8071-4892-1 (mobi)

This study is dedicated to Aisha, Tewana, Coreisha, Abiola, Sabrina, Orlanda, Avril, Kizzy, and also Fana Zulu, 1997–1999 5C students of the Success Laventille Composite School of the Republic of Trinidad and Tobago.

CONTENTS

PREFACE

Caribbean Slave Revolts and the British Abolitionist Movement studies the British antislavery movement and the major nineteenth-century slave revolts in the English colonies, particularly those in Barbados (1816), Demerara (1823), and Jamaica (1831–1832). It examines the links that abolitionist discourse established between British antislavery and slave revolts in the colonies. A study of this nature bears on the long-standing historical debate concerning the primacy of various agencies in achieving slave emancipation.[1] Although this book focuses on British abolitionists' commentary on West Indian slave revolts, it does not seek to overthrow other explanations that historians have advanced to explain abolition. Factors such as the growth of public support and agitation in Britain against slavery; political reform in the British Parliament; the planters' recalcitrance about slavery amelioration; persecution of sectarian missionaries in the colonies; the financial difficulties facing the West Indian planters as a result of duties paid on sugar exported to Britain; hurricanes in the colonies and soil exhaustion, among other hardships; as well as the culminating effects of slave revolts all contributed to the dismantling of the servile regime. Principles of humanity, justice, and Christianity, as well as economic, political, and social developments in Britain and in the colonies impacted the attack on British West Indian slavery. However, while these factors feature prominently in discussions of British abolitionism, the slave-revolt theme is conspicuously absent. This book rescues slave rebellion from its obscurity in historical accounts of the British antislavery struggle. It seeks to broaden the circumference of the British antislavery

---

1. This debate has emerged from the works of Reginald Coupland, Frank Klingberg, G. R. Mellor, Seymour Drescher, Roger Anstey, C. L. R. James, Eric Williams, Richard Hart, Hilary Beckles, and James Walvin, among other historians who insist that either religious and humanitarian factors, economic interests, or the self-liberating efforts of the slaves were primary in achieving the abolition of slavery. A more detailed discussion of this debate will be presented in chapter 1.

argument without claiming that slave rebellion was more important than any other dimension. Consequently, the book fills a gap left in mainstream narratives on the history of antislavery in Britain by demonstrating that slaves in rebellion commandeered humanitarian attention. Rebels led abolitionists to carve out a narrative best defined as the slave rebellion discourse of British abolitionism. The experiences of the colonized on one side of the Atlantic shaped a significant strand of the discourse of the colonizers on the other side. The most depressed subjects in the slave plantation colonies provided distinguished metropolitan spokesmen with a discourse, which, while hidden from history, ought to be regarded as a dynamic episode in the making of the Atlantic world.

Although there exists no other full-scale treatment of the impact of slave rising in the West Indies on the discourse of abolitionists' thought in Britain, this study is comparable to Hogendorn and Lovejoy's treatment of the end of slavery in Northern Nigeria.[2]

2. Paul Lovejoy and Jan Hogendorn, *Slow Death for Slavery: The Course of Abolition in Northern Nigeria, 1897–1936* (Cambridge: Cambridge University Press, 1993).

ACKNOWLEDGMENTS

First, I must express my deepest gratitude to my supervisor at the University of Hull, Professor David Richardson. I deeply appreciate his unfailing concern for my well-being, his support of every academic adventure I embarked on during my three years at Hull, his patient, candid, and useful criticism, and his astute suggestions for surmounting the challenges that I faced as a research student. I am also grateful for the meticulous scrutiny with which Professor David Eltis, Queens University of Canada, perused early drafts of these chapters. To the ever efficient Gill Craig and the very pleasant and helpful Vikki Magee at Hull, I say thank you.

I am indebted to the University of Hull for the Black Diaspora Scholarship and to the School of Economics, University of Hull, which also contributed to my financial support. I say thanks to the trustees of the Phillip Reckitt Trust Fund for sponsoring part of my research trip to Barbados, Jamaica, and Guyana in 2000 and to the directors of Arnold Matthew Publications, who also contributed generously to that trip. My gratitude goes to the David Nicholls Memorial Trust Fund for making it possible for me to conduct research at the Bodleian Library in Oxford and the Angus Library at Regent's College, Oxford. I am thankful to Dr. Diana Paton, Mrs. Marjorie Davis, and others at the Society for Caribbean Studies for two bursaries that enabled me to attend and present papers at their seminars and conferences in 2000 and 2001.

To the many families who accommodated me in their homes during my research trips, thank you very much. These families are Margaret and Owen Minnot of Hope Pastures, Jamaica; Margaret and Anthony Christy of St. Phillip, Barbados; Janice and John Woolford of Demerara, Guyana; Dr. Christine Ayorinde of Jack Straw Lane, Oxford, England; and Chris Essilfie of Hillsborough Court, London, England.

I am especially thankful to Professor Bridget Brereton of the University of the West Indies, St. Augustine Campus, who first believed in my ability to make some useful contribution to this body of scholarship and who took the first steps in making my studies at Hull a reality. And, of course, I must say thanks to God Almighty, the one who orchestrates from the beginning to the end my every endeavor. I give him the highest praise for the favor he has bestowed on me.

CARIBBEAN SLAVE REVOLTS
AND THE BRITISH ABOLITIONIST MOVEMENT

INTRODUCTION

This book analyzes four aspects of the British antislavery discourse on the slave rebellions that erupted in the British West Indies in the first three decades of the nineteenth century. Chapter 2 focuses on the abolitionists' denial that antislavery agitation prompted slave revolts and their attempts to understand revolt from the slaves' perspectives. Chapter 3 discusses how British abolitionists interpreted and described the suppression of these revolts, portraying slaves as both victims of slavery and agents of antislavery. Chapter 4 shows how abolitionists validated slave rebels as instruments advancing the antislavery campaign, for the slaves' suffering following crushed rebellions revealed some of the corruption of colonial society. Finally, chapter 5 shows how abolitionists presented continual servile warfare as a threat to the survival of the plantation empire and how they used slave revolts as a rationale for extensive imperial intervention in a slave colonial system that made revolt almost inevitable.

Each chapter furnishes a fresh abolitionist perspective on the significance of various aspects of the slave revolts in Barbados (1816), Demerara (1823), and Jamaica (1831–1832). While there are repeated references to these revolts, a measure of repetition is unavoidable in a study of this nature. This approach provides a clear identification of the nature and composition of a discourse that has for too long been shielded from history and makes it possible to illustrate that the abolitionists were sharp in perceiving the diverse significance of the slaves' revolts to their antislavery struggle. The book's methodology also produces a sense of the progression over time of the abolitionists' intellectual handling of the slave rebellion issue. This strand of their debate spanned roughly from 1816 to 1832 and moved from a defensive posture to an aggressive justification for demanding slave emancipation.

Eric Williams provided one of the earliest indications that the historiography of British West Indian slavery is faulty in its discussion of the British antislavery movement. Williams has commented that "most writers on the period of slavery have ignored the slaves."[1] He, however, does not explore in depth the role that the slaves played, but his brief observations have added fuel to the current controversy among historians regarding the appropriateness of widening the discussion of the British antislavery movement to include slave rebellions. The most telling of Williams's comments on this subject is, "In 1833 . . . the alternatives were clear: emancipation from above, or emancipation from below. But EMANCIPATION."[2] Williams's interpretation of the thesis of "emancipation from below" has its shortcomings. It gives credit to the fact that slaves were active agents of their own emancipation but ignores the crucial point that abolitionists were the ones who converted servile warfare into antislavery propaganda. The thesis needs to be expanded to explore how the actions of rebel slaves impacted upon and interacted with the intellectual battle that abolitionists waged against slavery in the British West Indies.

Historian Michael Craton has written extensively on slave resistance and esteems slave revolts as a dynamic force in the local plantation scene. He confidently asserts that "one of my basic assumptions is that the slave system was shaped largely by the slaves. But one must not underestimate the complexity of that shaping."[3] While Craton postulates that slaves shaped the slave system in the colonies, he cannot reconcile himself to the notion that the rebel slaves helped shape abolitionist commentary on slavery in Britain. Craton objects to Williams's suggestion that emancipation may very well have come from below: "It would be perverse to claim that slaves actually achieved their own emancipation by resistance."[4] Craton claims that "slave rebellions were counter productive to the anti-slavery cause."[5] With each fresh outbreak up to 1823, "no one dared to defend in public the action of the slaves."[6] Craton also highlights antislavery's

1. Eric Williams, *Capitalism and Slavery* (London: Andre Deutsch, 1964), 197.

2. Ibid., 208.

3. Michael Craton, *Testing the Chains: Resistance to Slavery in the British West Indies* (London: Cornell University Press, 1982), 14.

4. Ibid., 242, 295.

5. Michael Craton, *Empire, Enslavement and Freedom in the Caribbean* (Jamaica: Ian Randle Publishers, 1997), 309.

6. Michael Craton, "Emancipation from Below? The Role of the British West Indian Slaves in the Emancipation Movement, 1816–1834," in *Out of Slavery: Abolition and After,* ed. Jack Hayward (London: Frank Cass and Co., 1985), 119.

abhorrence of revolutionary methods when he observes that "slave rebellion was never to be condoned, least of all by the emancipationists and
the missionaries."[7] Consequently, Craton notes that after the 1816 Barbados rebellion, the "saints" thought it best to "rest on their oars."[8] The
merit of Craton's interpretation is that it underscores the denunciatory dimension of the abolitionist response to the slaves' violent attempts at self-
liberation. It also draws attention to the British government's tendency to
withdraw its support from the abolitionists whenever slaves revolted.
Craton gives the misleading impression, however, that the revolts retarded
the abolitionists' commitment to the antislavery cause. Abolitionists' attitude to slave revolts was far more complex than Craton seems to appreciate. It was a double-edged attitude of fear and denunciation as well
as a renewed and expanded attack on the servile regime. It is interesting to
note how Craton interprets the 1831–1832 Jamaican slave revolt, which
almost coincided with the abolitionists' adoption of immediate slave
emancipation: "In the early phase of British anti-slavery, slave resistance
was intentionally resisted by humanitarians . . . in the latter phase, slave
resistance and emancipation were clearly intertwined."[9] Craton's general
analysis of the two themes suggests that the abolitionists succeeded in ignoring the rebels for the greater period of the struggle against slavery. This
book presents the alternative interpretation that while abolitionists were
discomforted by the slaves' rebellion, from the outset they had little choice
but to accommodate it in their campaign.

The idea that the abolitionists were discomforted by evidence of slave
agency and were thus incapable of providing a discourse to counter the
planter's negative depiction of slave insurrection is emphasized in the
work of Clare Midgley. She insists that Elizabeth Heyrick from Leicester
was the earliest and lone delineator of an alternative antislavery vision of
slave rebellion. Midgley comments that while other abolitionists shrank
back from the violence and destruction of revolts, Heyrick boldly portrayed slave rising as "self-defence from the most degrading, intolerable
oppression."[10] As early as 1824 Heyrick distinguished herself in stoutly

7. Ibid., 125.
8. Ibid., 115.
9. Ibid., 125.
10. Clare Midgley, *Women Against Slavery: The British Campaigns, 1780–1870* (London: Routledge, 1992), 105–106.

opposing the conservative policy of amelioration and gradual emancipa-tion espoused by the vanguard of the "saints."[11] Heyrick offended the leading male abolitionists in two ways; she was female, and she was openly radical. Among the abolitionists, however, Heyrick was not alone in challenging the "Negrophobic" planter commentary on slave rebel-lions. In fact, the male leaders of the British antislavery movement did Heyrick the injustice of adopting the very views on slave rebellions that she had expressed in her book, which they had banned among their cir-culation of antislavery pamphlets, without acknowledging her contribu-tion. As shall become evident, some leading male abolitionists also adopted Heyrick's positive portrayal of slave rebellion.

A panoramic survey of the secondary literature reveals the common perception that revolts were of no value or were only a nuisance to the emancipation cause.[12] Lowell Ragatz believes that "slave revolts were mi-nor setbacks to be expected, though nevertheless, severely suppressed."[13] While he admits that later outbreaks were questioned in the motherland, he does not examine the nature or value of that questioning. His account of slavery in *Fall of the Planter Class* focuses on the economic and social factors that led to the decline in wealth, influence, and power of the "West India Interest." For him, as for several historians of the British antislav-ery movement, the subject of slave revolts is a passing concern. Ronald Kent Richardson makes a statement that epitomizes the marginal role of revolts vis-à-vis the attack on slavery: "The British humanitarians did not step forward to implement a social programme put forward by the Afro-

11. In addition to *Immediate and Not Gradual Emancipation of Slavery* (London, 1824), Elizabeth Heyrick wrote two pamphlets reinforcing her opposition to the main anti-slavery support for gradual slave emancipation: *An Enquiry Into Which of the Two Parties is Best Entitled to Freedom? The Slave or the Slave Holder?* (London: Baldwin, Cradock, and Joy, 1824) and *Letters on the Necessity of a Prompt Extinction of British Colonial Slav-ery* (London, 1826).

12. Elsa Goveia, *Amelioration and Emancipation in the British Caribbean* (St. Augus-tine: University of the West Indies, 1977), 34; Reginald Coupland, *The British Anti-Slavery Movement* (London: Thorton Butterworth, 1933), 130; Reginald Coupland, *Wilberforce: A Narrative* (Oxford: Clarendon, 1923), 456; David Geggus, "Haiti and the Abolitionists: Opinion, Propaganda and International Politics in Britain and France, 1804–1838," in *Abo-lition and Its Aftermath: The Historical Context, 1790–1916,* ed. David Richardson (Lon-don: Frank Cass and Co., 1985), 113–114.

13. Lowell Joseph Ragatz, *The Fall of the Planter Class in the British Caribbean, 1763–1833: A Study in Social and Economic History* (New York: Octagon, 1963), vii.

Caribbean slaves; nor did they consult black people when formulating their anti-slavery programme."[14] This might be true, but had it not been for the slaves and their experiences, the British antislavery campaign would have been nonexistent. The divergence in the methods and objectives of black and British antislavery do not justify dismissing the impact revolts had on the movement. The revolts of the slaves arrested the attention of the abolitionists and were described in antislavery speeches. Richardson later mentions, "It was the slaves who by their behaviour created the problems of slavery with which the abolitionists grappled."[15] If Richardson is suggesting that slave rebellions impeded the pace of the abolitionist program, then he has missed the fact that the conservative nature of British abolitionism was primarily a direct reflection of British political and social culture. The general tone of the British antislavery movement would not have been less gradualist had slaves not revolted. Indeed, had slaves not revolted, the pace of the antislavery program might have been even slower than it was. Like Ragatz, however, the bulk of Richardson's work on slavery history is not concerned with revolt; rather, it focuses on the antagonism that existed between the colonial legislature and the British parliament.

James Walvin, Andrew Lewis, Richard Hart, and Hilary Beckles have made partial inroads into the skepticism of the critics who have rejected Williams's construct of emancipation from below and into the narrow context in which slave revolts have been traditionally considered. Walvin and others have emphasized how the self-determining slaves made themselves allies of the humanitarians.[16] In one sense, Walvin takes the examination a little further. He is certain that planter hostility to the rebel

14. Ronald K. Richardson, *Moral Imperium: Afro Caribbeans and the Transformation of British Rule, 1776–1838* (New York: Greenwood, 1987), 13.

15. Ibid., 98.

16. Andrew Lewis, "An Incendiary Press: British West Indian Newspapers During the Struggle for Abolition," *Slavery and Abolition* 16, no. 3 (1995): 348, 351; Hilary Beckles, *Black Rebellion in Barbados: The Struggle Against Slavery, 1627–1838* (Bridgetown, Barbados: Carib Research and Publications, 1987), 3, 9; Hilary Beckles, "Emancipation by War or Law? Wilberforce and the 1816 Barbados Slave Rebellion," in *Abolition and Its Aftermath: The Historical Context, 1790–1916,* ed. David Richardson (London: Frank Cass and Co., 1999), 81; James Walvin, "Freeing the Slaves: How Important Was Wilberforce?" in *Out of Slavery: Abolition and After,* ed. Jack Hayward (London: Frank Cass and Co., 1985), 30; Richard Hart, *Slaves Who Abolished Slavery: Blacks in Rebellion,* vol. 2 (Jamaica: Institute of Social and Economic Research, 1985), 335.

strengthened the humanitarian argument of the moral evils of the system. Walvin concludes that "slave revolts with their tales of persecution, reasonable slave claims and savage planter repression were grist to the abolitionist mill."[17] He also explains that "anti-slavery became the most popular political issue in these years."[18] Abolitionists held thousands of lectures throughout Britain between 1787 and 1833, and crowds thronged to the "town halls, guild halls, music halls, chapels, churches and the Leeds Coloured Cloth Hall."[19] William Wilberforce was the first to take the lead in the British antislavery movement, which attracted "forces which Wilberforce did not like, could not control and of which he would not approve."[20] Walvin denies that the movement's leaders established a direct and crucial link between antislavery and slave revolts. He argues that the antislavery struggle was sustained by a vast number of Britons who came to view slavery as an unacceptable evil in an age of social reform.[21] This focus snatches the initiative from the leaders and establishes a more direct connection between revolts, their outrageous suppression, and the British public. Walvin is convinced that "the slaves themselves were effectively ignored by Wilberforce and other humanitarians."[22] He distrusts the efforts to lodge the slaves' rebellion in the parliamentary campaign against slavery because, like Richardson, he realizes that the rebels' radical antislavery methods were contrary to the respectable conservatism of the leading "saints." What Walvin has perhaps overlooked, however, is that timing and expediency, not policy and principles, were the factors that bound the campaigners and the rebels together. The slaves' rebellion forced itself upon the attention of the abolitionists. Antislavery campaigners did not enthusiastically champion the rising of the slaves. Walvin believes that "there is a powerful case for arguing that the conduct of the slaves from the late eighteenth century helped shape and direct the debate about black freedom."[23] He admits,

17. James Walvin, *Questioning Slavery* (Kingston: Ian Randle Publishers, 1977), 122, 165.

18. Ibid., 35.

19. Ibid., 36.

20. Walvin (1985), 39.

21. James Walvin, *Slavery and the Slave Trade: A Short Illustrated History* (London: Macmillan, 1983), 87.

22. Ibid., 41.

23. Ibid.

however, that "it is difficult to know what priority to give to black resistance."[24] Walvin's suggestion for further investigation in this area echoes
other claims that a more thorough analysis of slave resistance history is
needed, paying particular attention to the dialectic between slave rebellions and antislavery in Britain."[25]

A few historians have undertaken to assess slave rebellion within the
broader context of the British antislavery movement but have restricted
their discussions to chapters or paragraphs within works with other foci
or to articles in historical journals. Almost invariably, these brief commentaries have also been limited to the Jamaican slave revolt of 1831–
1832. Barry Higman, for example, has commented that "in the political
arena in which the legislative decision to abolish slavery was made . . . the
rebellion [the Baptist War] strengthened the hand of the humanitarians
and their supporters."[26] Pointing less directly to the abolitionists themselves, Philip Curtin makes a similar but more general observation: "The
slave revolt impressed Britons and Jamaicans alike with the difficulty of
keeping a people subject against their will."[27] Gad Heuman notes that the
Jamaican rebellion has also been called the Christmas Rebellion or Baptist War. It "was a crucial event in the abolition of slavery."[28] W. L. Green
makes the bold assertion that "it was the Jamaican rebellion, not the new
vigour of the anti-slavery movement that proved a decisive factor in pre-
cipitating emancipation."[29] Mary Turner is also convinced that the fear of
rebellion fueled abolitionist conviction of the need for immediate abolition but that this conviction was cushioned by the persecution of sectarian missionaries.[30] While these observations are useful, abolitionists' ex-

24. Ibid., 117.

25. Kofi Argosah, ed., *Maroon Heritage: Archaeological, Ethnographic and Historical
Perspectives* (Barbados: Canoe Press, 1994), xii; Seymour Drescher, "The Historical Context of British Abolitionism," in *Abolition and Its Aftermath: The Historical Context, 1790–
1816,* ed. David Richardson (London: Frank Cass and Co., 1985), 13.

26. Barry Higman, *Slave Population and Economy in Jamaica, 1807–1834* (Manchester: Manchester University Press, 1976), 230.

27. Philip Curtin, *Two Jamaicas: The Role of Ideas in a Tropical Colony, 1830–1865*
(New York: Greenwood, 1968), 89.

28. Gad Heuman, "A Tale of Two Jamaican Rebellions," *Jamaican Historical Review*
19 (1996):1.

29. W. L. Green, *British Slave Emancipation, 1830–1865* (Oxford: Clarendon, 1976), 112.

30. Mary Turner, "The Baptist War and Abolition," *Jamaican Historical Review,* Sam
Sharpe Rebellion 150th Anniversary Issue, 13 (1982): 31–41.

tensive commentary upon and utilization of slave revolts makes it mandatory to devote more than cursory attention to the subject.

The polemical nature of the state of the debate concerning the connection between slave revolts and British antislavery is aggravated by the separate esteem that has been reserved for the persecution of the missionaries and the relative value of that persecution to antislavery. The angle from which missionary persecution has been assessed diminishes the influence of slave revolts on antislavery. Philip Wright calls the elevation of the missionary factor the act of "stealing the martyr's crown"[31] but makes no attempt at reconsidering this one-sided view. Northcott reinforces abolitionist Henry Brougham's opinion that there is no fault in christening John Smith the martyr of Demerara.[32] Indeed, the abolitionists did make deliberate and generous use of the persecution of missionaries in the West Indian slave plantations. It must not be overlooked, however, that the abolitionists saw missionary persecution as one part of a much larger question. Brougham himself declared in 1824 that "no man can cast his eye upon this trial [The Trial of the Reverend John Smith] without perceiving that it was intended to bring an issue between the system of the slave law and the instruction of the Negroes."[33] The abolitionists' perception of the missionaries' role in the slave rebellions needs to be reassessed and is examined to some extent in this book.

The major problem with the efforts made to date to integrate slave revolts and the British antislavery movement is that the angles from which these efforts have been made have been faulty. The focus has been oriented too narrowly toward assessing the value of slave revolts in the achievement of emancipation. This objective, while useful, has limited the historical research and squandered the opportunity to assess how the abolitionists' slave rebellion discussions emerged and reflected various dimensions. It was not until 1830 that abolitionists called for the immediate emancipation of slave children and not until 1832 that they first moved for general, complete, and immediate abolition of slavery. Obviously, straining the research in this direction would be productive of very little

31. Philip Wright, *Knibb "the Notorious": Slaves' Missionary, 1803–1845* (London: Sidgwick and Jackson, 1973).

32. Cecil Northcott's work in this area of scholarship is *Slavery's Martyr: John Smith of Demerara and the Emancipation Movement, 1817–1824* (London: Epsworth, 1976).

33. *Hansard's Parliamentary Debates*, new ser., 11 (June 1, 1824): 996.

in the way of integrating the themes of slave revolt and the British anti-slavery movement. Yet, there is some merit in this approach, and it should not be discarded altogether. When activists finally came to the decision that slavery ought to be abolished, rebellions acted to strengthen their resolve. Still, it is necessary to trace and investigate not merely the final outcome of the association between antislavery in Britain and slave rebellion in the colonies but also the form of that association itself. Historical explorations tracing cause and effect relationships are indeed interesting and often rewarding. It is equally the task of the historian, however, to investigate and analyze historical discourses shaped in less dramatic modes by those who have made history.

Another hindrance to understanding the relationship between antislavery in Britain and slave revolts in the colonies has been the attention given to the incongruent conservative reform methods of the former and the violent, destructive activities of the latter. This fundamental difference between the "saints" and the rebels should be regarded not as a stumbling block but as one of the factors that abolitionists absorbed despite their aversion to mass popular rising. Abolitionists denounced and lamented slave revolts but could not wash their hands clean of the rebels. The slaves seemed to make a point of identifying their overt resistance with the debates taking place in Britain on their behalf by timing their risings to follow each wave of abolitionist activity. Abolitionists succumbed to the pressure that rebellious slaves exerted on the metropolitan campaign in ways that were most advantageous to their movement. Renouncing violence as a means of effecting social change in the plantation societies was neither the final nor the most significant abolitionist pronouncement on slave rebellions. In fact, rebels forced British abolitionists to adopt some of the very revolutionary ideas that repulsed them. The image of the suppliant slave featured on a ceramic medallion by Josiah Wedgwood also promotes the notion that abolitionists essentially saw slaves as suffering objects to be pitied rather than individuals from whom they could draw materials for their attack on slavery.[34] Consequently, it seems impossible that activists could have ever contemplated a campaign against slavery in which they could advance some kind of useful and sympathetic case on behalf of rebels. However, rebelling slaves defied the docile perception

---

34. Howard Temperley, *British Antislavery, 1833–1870* (London: Longman, 1972), 3–4.

that abolitionists had of them and stretched the angles from which the metropolitan campaigners were prepared to fight the slavery cause. Over time, rebellious slaves in the British West Indies succeeded in shifting the abolitionists' conservative policy progressively to the left.

It is striking that the histories that have been written on slave rebellions and the antislavery movement in Britain have unfolded in two distinctly opposite directions, each resulting in an impression that misrepresents the essence of the last era of slavery. That rebels made it no secret that they regarded abolitionists' activities as fuel for their servile warfare is sufficiently documented.[35] Conversely, British antislavery activists worked during an era when slaves were especially prone to rebellion. It is highly improbable, therefore, that in conducting their campaign, abolitionists could have consistently and successfully ignored slave rebellions. Therefore this book provides the missing volume in the history of British abolitionism by examining the activist response to and utilization of the rebellion of nineteenth-century slaves in the English Caribbean.

To a degree, this book takes a relativist position to defend its hypothesis.[36] The emphasis in this work does not lie primarily on empirical evidence, for indeed there is little novelty about the discrete facts of British West Indian slavery history. What is required is a reexamination of historians' interpretations of these facts. To expose to the light of history the slave-rebellion discourse of British abolitionism, this book repositions, rejects, and replaces existing perspectives on the antislavery/slave-rebellion dialectic.

To an extent, this book builds on the Williams/Hart theory of "emancipation from below."[37] This theory presents two foci. First, it sets the slaves' agency against the abolitionists' in its analysis of the struggle against slavery. Second, the theory emphasizes that the major historical significance of slave rebellions was the achievement of emancipation. These foci are neither the only nor the most productive perspectives from which to gauge the relationship between revolts and the antislavery movement. One shortcoming in the theory of "emancipation from below" is

35. Walvin (1977), 122, 165.
36. See Edward H. Carr, *What is History?* (New York: Vintage, 1961), 13–14, 16, 22; K. Jenkins, *Rethinking History* (London: Routledge, 1991), for a discussion on the relativist position.
37. Williams (1964), 208; Hart (1985).

that it ignores that slavery was practically ended by British parliamentary legislation. The theory erroneously elevates slave rebellion above other factors in the achievement of emancipation. However, humanitarian, economic, social, and political factors rather than the primacy of any one agent effected the abolition of slavery. Another fundamental weakness in the theory of self-liberating slaves is that it concentrates twenty-odd years of abolitionism into the final act of emancipation. Such a concentration ignores significant dimensions of the abolitionist slave rebellion discourse, which was shaped long before the abolitionists were prepared to demand slave emancipation. In this study, therefore, the theory of self-liberating slaves is reshuffled. Although hidden from the history of the British abolitionist struggle, slaves in rebellion contributed to the metropolitan attack on colonial slavery. This book takes the broader view, however, that abolitionists took into account West Indian servile warfare and that such an account reinforced rather than superseded the role of humanitarian pressure in the slavery struggle. Furthermore, the slaves' rebellion not only contributed to the achievement of emancipation but also helped to shape the content of nineteenth-century antislavery narrative.

This book also rejects the idea that abolitionists treated slave rebellions as a taboo subject that was only a nuisance to the metropolitan campaign.[38] Such a claim ignores the abolitionists' counterarguments designed to refute the allegations of slavery advocates that antislavery activities exerted an incendiary influence upon the slaves. By focusing on abolitionists' counterarguments, this book proves that antislavery activists could not and did not remain mute on the slave violence issue. Campaigners realized that it was in their best interest to structure their defense so as to eliminate the nuisance value perception of slave revolts. Their counterarguments raise the important question as to whether commentary on slave rebellions was merely an abolitionist mechanism of defense. Following this inquiry it becomes clear that abolitionists did not solely attempt to refute proslavery allegations but also challenged their opponents' depiction of the nature of slave rebellions. To some extent, the abolitionists sympathized with, justified, and positively conceptualized and es-

---

38. This chapter refers to the views of Michael Craton, Reginald Coupland, and Elsa Goveia on attempts to integrate studies on slave rebellion in the broader context of the British antislavery movement.

teemed the slaves' overt resistance to enslavement. Through this line of investigating the slave revolt/British antislavery dialectic, the book demonstrates how this strand of the abolitionists' discourse progressed from one level to another.

To highlight and describe the changes over time of the British abolitionist slave rebellion discourse, to an extent this book shapes its discussion of the research along a chronological pattern. By mapping the chronological stages of the British antislavery movement to abolitionists' reflections upon various aspects of each of the major nineteenth-century slave revolts in the English colonies, this study reflects the differing dimensions of the abolitionists' slave rebellion discourse.

In spite of the relativist element of the methodology, scrupulous attention is given to empirical data. In this introduction is a broad overview of slave revolts and the British antislavery movement, consisting principally of a survey of the printed secondary sources. This overview demonstrates how historians generally perceive the two major themes discussed in this book. In remaining chapters, I present my interpretation of how an integration of slave revolts and British antislavery ought to be perceived. There, a greater reliance on primary resources, both printed material and unpublished manuscripts, is evident. The interplay between the secondary and primary materials reveals the extent to which studies in slave revolts and British antislavery need to be integrated. The primary sources consulted include *Hansard's Parliamentary Debates* of abolitionists on the subject of British West Indian slavery; *British Parliamentary Papers* with dispatches and other official records of the revolts in the colonies; Anti-Slavery Society pamphlets and other publications; unpublished antislavery papers of leading abolitionists, such as Thomas Clarkson, William Wilberforce, Henry Brougham, and Thomas Fowell Buxton; records of correspondence between government officials in the colonies during the time of the revolts and personnel at the Colonial Office in Downing Street, London; nineteenth-century magazines like the *Edinburgh Review* and *Quarterly Review;* the *London Times;* the reports of sectarian missionaries who were persecuted during slave revolts, such as the Baptists in Jamaica and the London Missionary Society missionaries in Demerara; and colonial newspapers such as the *Barbados Mercury and Bridgetown Gazette* and the *Jamaican Courant,* which published articles on the revolts and on abolitionist activities in Britain. I rely heavily on abolitionist source materials because the aim here is to delineate a particular aspect of British abolitionism.

The British debates on slavery centered principally among three groups. These were British government ministers, the West India "interest," and the abolitionist "party." Government personnel such as the Secretary of State for War and the Colonies, the Parliamentary Undersecretary, and officers serving in the capacity of civil servants from the Colonial Office at Downing Street in London were involved in the slavery debates. Government ministers mediated between the abolitionists and the West Indians in the parliamentary discussions on this question. Although the role played by the ministers of the crown and their views on slavery are evident, their position on the slavery question is only of secondary importance here. The powerful and very influential group commonly referred to as the West India interest represented the proslavery position. The West India interest included sugar colony agents and proprietors of West Indian concerns living in Britain. They often sat on the London-based West India Committee or the Society of West India Merchants and Planters established in the 1770s. The West India group also included some of the M.P.s representing English ports engaged in colonial trade. In Parliament, they spoke on behalf of their own interests and represented those of their overseas colleagues and dependents, overseers, managers, bookkeepers, resident planters, and colonial authorities. British abolitionists were the third group dominating the slavery debates and the group with which this book is principally concerned. They had advocated and succeeded in persuading Parliament of the necessity of abolishing the British slave trade. For most of the period when they attacked the system of slavery, however, they insisted that amelioration and not sudden abolition was their objective. Nevertheless, even during their campaign to mitigate slavery's evils rather than abolish the system altogether, they were still referred to as abolitionists. They have also been called antislavery campaigners or activists, emancipationists, and the "saints." The abolitionist "party" was characterized by a strong religious flavor. The abolitionists based their arguments on religious principles, justice, humanity, and commercial considerations, as well as on the threat that slave rebellion made it expedient to abolish slavery.[39]

39. *Anti-Slavery Monthly Reporter* 1, no. 14 (July 31, 1826): 197. For a discussion of

By 1833 when slavery was abolished, the ranks of antislavery supporters had swollen to include an extensive cross section of British society—religious men; humanitarian reformers; businessmen with links in
Brazil, Cuba, Mauritius, and India who would have benefited greatly from
free trade; industrialists and domestic consumers of sugar who cried out
for a cheaper supply of that commodity; and all those who felt outraged
for one reason or the other by the existence of West Indian slavery. According to Charles Buxton, son of abolitionist T. F. Buxton, "the strenuous efforts of many men, working in very different spheres [were involved
in the movement]."[40] This book does not extend its scope to include this
entire spectrum. Women, such as Heyrick, were also involved in the
British antislavery initiative. Unfortunately, however, they do not feature
here because they were slighted by their male counterparts. Additionally,
ex-slaves, such as Olaudah Equiano, who supported the struggle, are not
included, for their writings do not express views on the slave revolts that
are treated in this study.[41] This book focuses on male leadership in British
antislavery for two seemingly contradictory reasons. First, the leaders'
conservative, antirevolutionary dogma has been largely advanced to support the claim that no significant relationship could have possibly existed
between British antislavery and colonial slave revolts. The leading abolitionists, however, did not maintain an inflexible conservative policy during the duration of the antislavery campaign. They yielded sufficiently to
repeatedly raise the issue of rebellion, not only to condemn it but also to
defend the charge that they were influencing slave rebels, to challenge how
revolt was traditionally perceived, and to justify and invigorate the anti-
slavery position. Second, this study narrowly interprets its definition of
antislavery leadership because other than those discussed here—Wilberforce, Brougham, Mackintosh, Buxton, Clarkson, James Stephen, and, to
a lesser extent, Macaulay—few forcefully and positively appropriated the

---

the three groups that were locked in the debates on slavery, see also Izhak Gross, "The Abolition of Negro Slavery and British Parliamentary Politics, 1823–1833," *Historical Journal*
23, no. 1(1980): 63–85; Kathleen Mary Butler, *The Economics of Emancipation: Jamaica
and Barbados, 1823–1843* (Chapel Hill: University of North Carolina Press, 1995), 8–9.

40. Preface to Charles Buxton, ed., *Memoirs of Sir Thomas Fowell Buxton* (London:
John Murray, 1852).

41. See Olaudah Equiano, *The Interesting Narrative of the Life of Olaudah Equiano or
Gustavus Vassa, The African, Written by Himself* (London, 1789).

slaves' rebellion for the antislavery struggle. Indeed, the rebellion of the slaves ensured that the antislavery body in Britain was by no means a homogeneous entity, and yet a core of humanitarians operating mainly within the British Parliament emerged as spokesmen on slave revolts in the colonies.

The British antislavery movement was marked by four recognizable phases. The first began around 1783, when the initial attacks against the servile regime were heard in Britain, and included the period from 1787 to 1807, which concentrated on the abolition of the British slave trade.[42] During this time, the West India interest and their supporters charged that tampering with the institution of slavery would lead to rebellion. In the closing years of the eighteenth and the first decade of the nineteenth centuries, however, the slaves' conduct had not provided a solid enough basis to draw the abolitionists into a significant examination of the subject. Thus, the abolitionists fought the first leg of the campaign without having to be too seriously concerned about rebellious slaves. Consequently, the British antislave trade program, the first phase of the metropolitan attack against slavery, is of minor significance to this study.

The book is also only marginally concerned with the second phase of the British antislavery movement, from 1807 to about 1814, when the abolitionists determined to allow slave trade abolition to lead naturally to slave amelioration. They had calculated that as planters were now dependent on increased birth rate to boost slave populations instead of importation from Africa, laws would steadily improve until slavery gradually vanished.[43] These ambitions did not materialize. Higman has com-

---

42. For a discussion of early British attacks against the slave system, see Thomas Clarkson, *The History of the Rise, Progress, and Accomplishment of the Abolition of the Slave Trade by the British Parliament*, vol. 1 (1808; reprint, London: Frank Cass and Co., 1968); Ragatz (1963), 240, 244–248; Coupland (1933), 42, 45, 56–66; Temperley (1972), 1–3; F. J. Klingberg, *The Anti-Slavery Movement in England: A Study in English Humanitarianism* (New Haven: Yale University Press, 1926,) 40–41.

43. William Wilberforce, *A Letter on the Abolition of the Slave Trade; Addressed to the Freeholders and Other Inhabitants of Yorkshire* (London: T. Cadell and W. Davies, Strand; and J. H. Piccadilly, 1807), 248–251; Thomas Clarkson, *Thoughts on the Necessity of Improving the Condition of the Slaves in the British Colonies, with a View to Their Ultimate Emancipation; and on the Practicability, the Safety and the Advantages of the Latter Measure* (London: J. Hatchard and Son, 1824), 1; Henry Richard, *Memoirs of Joseph Sturge* (London: Patridge and Bennet, 1864), 74.

mented that this policy "derived from the fallacy that slavery was created and sustained by the slave trade."[44] By 1814, abolitionists realized that their post-1807 policy of inaction ought to be reconsidered. Slave masters continued to pursue policies contrary to humanity and even to their own interests.[45]

Between 1814 and slave emancipation in 1834, abolitionism entered its third and fourth phases, the phases upon which this study concentrates. By 1815, abolitionists advocated that some positive steps should be taken to ensure that the abolition of the slave trade fulfilled the slave ameliora-tion objectives they had anticipated. Abolitionists called on the ministers of the imperial government to enforce a compulsory registration of slaves and to encourage the local governments of crown and legislative colonies to ameliorate slave laws.[46] The colonists protested against these strategies, and in 1816 slave insurgents of Barbados demonstrated that they too were important participants in the discussions of the West India question. Af-ter the Barbados revolt, abolitionists found themselves unable to further their discussions without making reference to slave rebellion.

The rebels' presence in abolitionist discourse mounted in proportion to the degree of pressure that the humanitarians exerted on the servile regime. By 1823 antislavery activists stepped up their efforts. In that year the London-based Anti-Slavery Society was formed, and soon Thomas Clarkson led the campaign to establish branch societies throughout the kingdom. Many antislavery pamphlets were published, and for the first time the abolitionists stood up in the House of Commons and called for the gradual abolition of slavery.[47] Slavery advocates bitterly opposed the

44. Higman (1976), 231.

45. Temperley (1972), 9.

46. For a discussion of abolitionist strategies from 1812 to 1820, including the slave reg-istration issue, see Ragatz (1963), 390–393. Ragatz notes that in 1815 James Stephen pub-lished a pamphlet entitled *Reasons for Establishing a Registry of Slaves in the Colonies.* William Law Mathieson, *British Slavery and Its Abolition, 1823–1838* (New York: Long-man's, Green and Co., 1926), 27; Sir Alan Burns, *History of the British West Indies,* rev. 2d ed. (London: George Allen and Unwin, 1965), 611–612; Coupland (1933), 114–115. These sources also provide insight into the constitutional arrangements between Britain and her crown and legislative colonies.

47. For an insight into the growth of abolitionist support and activities by 1823, see Tem-perley (1972), 9–10; Mathieson (1926), 118; Ragatz (1963), 409–410. The full debate of May 15, 1823, in which the abolitionists first called for the gradual emancipation of the slaves, is recorded in *Hansard's Parliamentary Debates,* new ser., 9 (May 15, 1823): 257–360.

new direction that the campaigners were taking. Meanwhile, Demerara slaves ensured that the momentum of the abolitionist slave rebellion discourse begun seven years earlier by the slaves in Barbados did not lag. Notably, it was after the Demerara rebellion that the abolitionists insisted that slave reform in the colonies should no longer await the cooperation of the colonists. The British Parliament should enforce from above the laws the abolitionists suggested to improve the servile regime.[48] Slave rebellion was significant among the factors influencing the abolitionist policy of parliamentary intervention in colonial affairs. Demerara slave rebels widened the dimension of the already newly revised agenda of the 1823 abolitionist program.

The fourth and final stage of the attack on slavery in Britain began by about 1830, when the abolitionists abandoned their policy of reform and gradual abolition of slavery. They now demanded complete and immediate freedom for the servile laborers. The decision of slaves in Jamaica to rise just at the juncture of the abolitionist shift from gradualism to immediacy reinforced the bases upon which the campaigners demanded emancipation. Abolitionists argued that in addition to their view that slavery was repugnant to religion, humanity, and the British constitution, slave revolts demonstrated the expediency of abolishing a system fraught with danger to the well-being of all parties concerned.[49]

It is important to note that while this study seeks to integrate two subthemes in British West Indian slavery, it does not focus on how slave revolts were sparked in the colonies as a result of abolitionist agitation in Britain. Of course, this discussion surfaces in the body of the work. Incisive research, noted in the historiographical context in this chapter, has already been conducted in this area. It is thus appropriate only to acknowledge and not duplicate this scholarship here. My examination consequently gives attention to that neglected aspect of the connection between antislavery and slave revolts, concentrating on how the abolitionists assimilated into their campaign the rebellions of the slaves and not how the slaves fed off events taking place in Britain on their behalf.

Throughout the two hundred years of British West Indian slavery,

---

48. Mathieson (1926), 140.

49. See Buxton (1852), 286–292; Sir George Stephen, *Anti-Slavery Recollections in A Series of Letters Addressed to Mrs. Beecher Stowe,* 2d ed. (London: Frank Cass and Co., 1971), 121, for a discussion of the abolitionists' adoption of the policy of immediate emancipation.

slaves continually opposed the servile regime. This book is not concerned with the entire history of resistance but with the major slave rebellions of the nineteenth century. There is a considerable contemporary body of scholarship on slave resistance history. Very interesting themes about the slaves' opposition to their enslavement have emerged. First, historians have divided the slaves' struggle into the two categories of passive and active resistance. Some historians object to the use of the term *passive resistance,* regarding it as a contradiction in terms.[50] The term *covert acts of resistance* to slavery is preferred to *passive resistance.* Covert forms of resistance seldom included violence directed at oppressors and were seldom recognized by slave masters as acts of resistance. Slaves practiced disguised resistance almost on a daily basis, and it was certainly far more frequent than overt acts. Covert resistance included such behavior as suicide, infanticide, feigned laziness and stupidity, careless yet deliberate mishandling and destruction of plantation property, malingering or working slowly, stealing, and self-mutilation.[51] While it is useful that historians have defined and analyzed the nature of the slaves' covert resistance, such opposition escaped abolitionist attention and consequently is not examined in this study.

Active resistance to slavery, the type of resistance with which this study is concerned, was open, direct, violent, and destructive. Rebel slaves engaged in strike action against the labor regime, burnt plantation buildings and works, looted their masters' property, and took up arms with which they sometimes wounded and killed the managers and owners of the slave system. Far more slaves, however, were hurt or killed during and after slave rebellions than were whites. The themes that have emerged in the study of overt acts of rebellion include the endemic nature of the slaves'

50. See Barbara Bush, *Slave Women in Caribbean Society, 1650–1838* (Kingston: Ian Randle, 1990), 53. Bush points out that the term *passive resistance* was first made in pioneering studies of the Old South by Raymond and Alice Bauer and Kenneth Stampp.

51. For discussions on disguised acts of slave resistance, see Craton (1982), 24, 53. Craton uses the term *passive* resistance; Monica Schuler, "Day-to day Resistance to Slavery in the Caribbean During the Eighteenth Century," *African Studies Association of the West Indies Bulletin* 6 (Dec. 1973): 57–77; Gordon Lewis, *Main Currents in Caribbean Thought: The Historical Evolution of Caribbean Society in Its Ideological Aspects, 1492–1900* (Baltimore: Johns Hopkins University Press, 1983), 175–180; Bernard Marshall, "Maroons in Slave Plantation Societies: A Case Study of Dominica, 1785–1815," *Caribbean Quarterly* 22, nos. 2 and 3 (1976), 26–34; Williams (1964), 202.

resistance, which has led Beckles to speak of "The Two Hundred Years War"; the ethnicity and occupational status of the leadership and rank and file of the revolts; the factors that were responsible for and facilitated open slave rebellion; and the rebels' tactics and objectives.[52] Historians differentiate between slave revolts in the periods prior to and during the late-eighteenth/early-nineteenth centuries. The early slave revolts of the sixteenth and seventeenth centuries, and even the later 1739 and 1795 maroon wars in Jamaica and Tacky's 1760 slave revolt, fall outside of the formative period of the abolitionist era. They unfolded when the international voice of opposition to slavery was scarcely audible. Inevitably, these earlier episodes of open slave resistance have been perceived as events within the narrow confines of the British West Indian plantation setting. The pre-abolitionist era of slave revolts has not been considered in any great detail here.[53]

52. Hilary Beckles, "The Two Hundred Years War: Slave Resistance in the British West Indies: An Overview of the Historiography," *Jamaican Historical Review,* Sam Sharpe Rebellion 150th Anniversary Issue, 13 (1982): 1–10. For other discussions of the constant threat that slave rebels posed to the plantation societies of the British West Indies, see Orlando Patterson, "Slavery and Slave Revolts: A Socio-Historical Analysis of the First Maroon War, Jamaica, 1655–1740," *Social and Economic Studies* 19, no. 1 (1970): 289; Richard Price, ed., *Maroon Societies: Rebel Slave Communities in the Americas* (New York: Anchor/ Doubleday, 1973), 2; Barbara Kopytoff, "The Early Political Development of Jamaican Maroon Societies," *William and Mary Quarterly,* 3d ser., 35 (April 1978): 287; Melville Herskovits, *The Myth of the Negro Past* (Boston: Beacon, 1958), 93; James Walvin, *Slaves, Slavery and the British Colonial Experience* (Manchester: Manchester University Press, 1992), 75; Hilary Beckles, *A History of Barbados From Amerindian Settlement to Nation State* (Cambridge: Cambridge University Press, 1990), 35–40, 75–90. Historians also emphasize that open resistance to slavery began not just in the slave plantation societies of the New World but in the slaves' African homeland. For discussions of slave resistance in Africa and during the transatlantic crossing, see Herskovits (1958), 87–89; Barry Boubacar, *Senegambia and the Atlantic Slave Trade* (Cambridge: Cambridge University Press, 1998), 123; Vincent Bakpetu Thompson, *The Making of the African Diaspora in the Americas, 1442–1900* (Harlow, Essex: Longman, 1987), 110; Francis Dow George, *Slave Ships and Slaving* (Massachusetts: Maine Research Society, 1927), 121–131; Richard Rathbone, "Some Thoughts on Resistance to Enslavement in West Africa," in *Out of the House of Bondage: Runaways, Resistance, and Marronage in Africa and the New World,* ed. Gad Heuman (London: Frank Cass and Co., 1986), 11–12; David Richardson, "Shipboard Revolts, African Authority, and the Atlantic Slave Trade," *William and Mary Quarterly,* 3d ser., 58, no. 1 (2001): 69–92.

53. For an explanation of the term *marronage,* see Price (1973), 246–292; Hilary Beckles, "From Land to Sea: Runaway Barbados Slaves and Servants, 1630–1700," in Heuman

The first three decades of the nineteenth century was the only period when there coexisted a well-organized and recognized antislavery body in Britain and significant examples of slave revolts in the colonies. It was the only time when the slavery reform campaign of British abolitionists could have embroiled them in the tensions of balancing a conservative program alongside the conduct of rebellious slaves. Thus the Barbados revolt of 1816, the Demerara revolt of 1823, and the Jamaican revolt of 1831–1832 feature prominently here because these were the three that most often captured the attention of the abolitionists.

Slaves in Barbados rose on Sunday, April 4, 1816. The open rebellion was centered in the southeastern end of the island and encompassed the four parishes of St. Phillip, Christ Church, St. George, and St. John. The slaves most heavily involved belonged to Bailley's and Simmon's plantations in St. Phillip, which was the rebellion's starting point. Colonial authorities identified Bussa, a slave ranger on Bailley's plantation, as the leader. Other "elite" slaves in the St. Phillip's parish as well as some free colored men, such as Franklyn Washington and Sergeant, assisted Bussa in organizing the rebellion. Female slaves were also involved. Robert, a slave on Simmon's plantation, testified that a slave called Nanny Grigg encouraged others to fight to obtain freedom as had been done in St. Domingue. The slave rebels of Barbados in 1816 practiced arson and looting on a wide scale, but there was no deliberate attempt to take the lives of the white masters. Conflicting views concerning the causes of the rebellion arose. These views were polarized along lines that reflected pro- and antislavery positions. Defenders of slavery charged that the slaves rebelled because of the Registry Bill that the abolitionists had sponsored in the year just prior to the revolt. They explained that the slaves misinterpreted registration for abolition and rose to claim by war what

---

(1986), 79. For a general study of the maroons, see Patterson (1970); Monica Schuler, "Ethnic Slave Rebellion in the Caribbean and the Guianas," *Journal of Social History* 3, no. 4 (1970); Kopytoff (1978). Bryan Edwards's "Observations on the Disposition, Character, Manner and Habits of Life; and a Detail of the Origin, Progress and Termination of the Late War Between those People and the White Inhabitants," quoted in Price (1973), 230–245, is an extract from Edwards, *The History, Civil and Commercial of the British Colonies in the West Indies,* vol. 1, appx. 2 (London, 1807), 522–535, 537–545, which was first published separately in 1796. Much of the historical portion of this account is taken nearly verbatim from Edward Long (1774).

the colonists denied them by law. They argued that Barbadian slaves were
fighting for an imaginary emancipation decree; a notion that arose as a
result of abolitionists' activities in Britain.

The abolitionists, of course, denied these claims. They insisted that the
rumor circulating among the slaves about freedom granted but denied was
propagated by the colonists' careless talk of events taking place in Britain.
Abolitionists also insisted that the slaves in Barbados armed themselves
against the regime because of slavery's gross inhumanity. Slavery advocates used the revolt to demand a seizure of the slavery debates, while activists widened their humanitarian and religious attack against slavery as
well as demanded limited slave reform. The accusation that slave rebellions would be the natural consequence of tampering with the servile
regime had continually been a plantocratic ploy to stave off abolitionist
attacks. The 1816 rebellion in Barbados, however, provided both pro- and
antislavery advocates with the first concrete basis for examining the issue
of servile warfare within the context of abolitionism in Britain.[54]

Slaves in Demerara rose on August 18, 1823. The rebellion was confined to the East Coast of Demerara, encompassing the area just five miles
outside of Georgetown, the capital, to Mahaica. The slaves most heavily
involved belonged to Success and Le Resouvenir plantations. Quamina
Gladstone, a slave from Le Resouvenir, and his son Jack were the principal insurgents. Quamina was the chief deacon at Bethel Chapel, over
which John Smith of the London Missionary Society presided. As was the
case in Barbados in 1816, slaves in Demerara demonstrated no intention
whatsoever to take the lives of their masters in their revolt. They confined
white masters, overseers, managers, and bookkeepers in the slave stocks
and parleyed with the governor of the island and with the commander of
the troops about their rights to wages, days without labor, and freedom.
Unlike in Barbados, property destruction in Demerara in 1823 was negli-
gible. Despite the relatively peaceful nature of the revolt, the colonists brutally suppressed it. Hundreds of slaves lost their lives in the field of the
one-sided battle and in the courts-martial executions that followed.[55]

54. For analyses of the Barbados slave revolt of 1816, see Beckles (1987); Anthony Wiltshire, "The Reaction of the Barbadian Plantocracy to Amelioration, 1823–1833" (M.A. thesis, University of the West Indies, Cave Hill Campus, Barbados, 1983); Craton (1982), 254–
266.

55. For analyses of the Demerara slave revolt, see Joshua Bryant, *Accounts of the In-*

Again, the revolt was not ignored in the metropolis but rather polarized positions in the slavery debates. Antislavery activists were particularly bound to respond because the Demerara revolt came in the wake of measures taken by the British government to meet the 1823 call for the gradual abolition of slavery. Missionaries working among slaves in Demerara, Reverend Smith in particular, were seen as cohorts of the abolitionists and were also blamed for the revolt.[56] Abolitionists could not and did not fail to appreciate the bond that linked their activities in Britain with the rebellious slaves in the colonies.

The slaves of Jamaica staged the greatest of all rebellions in the British West Indies. The rising erupted on the night of December 27, 1831, at the Kensington plantation in the parish of St. James. Slaves had held several planning meetings at Plantation Retrieve, also located in the St. James district. Most of their rebellious activities were concentrated in the island's western region, in St. James, Trelawney, Hanover, Westmoreland, St. Elizabeth, and in the eastern parish of Portland. Jamaican colonial authorities charged Gardiner of Greenwich estate in Hanover, Dove of Belvidere in St. James, Johnson of Retrieve, and, above all, Samuel Sharpe of Craydon estate in St. James for leading the revolt. The slaves killed about a dozen whites, but the economic devastation they wreaked by arson was quite extensive. The flames dealt a severe blow to the Jamaican economy. The crushing of the rebellion was typically ruthless, and approximately five hundred slaves lost their lives.[57] Meanwhile, in Britain the abolition-

---

surrection of the Negro Slaves in the Colony of Demerara (Demerara: Guiana Chronicle Office, Georgetown), 1824; Northcott (1976); James Rodway, History of British Guiana from the Year 1682 to the Present Time, vol. 2, 1782–1833 (Demerara: J. Thompson, 1893); E. A. Wallbridge, The Demerara Martyr: Memoirs of the Reverend John Smith, Missionary to Demerara (Demerara: Charles Gilpin, 1848); Craton (1982), 267–290.

56. Emilia Da Costa objects to the fact that in the Demerara slave revolt "many of the records see the slaves as ciphers, as men and women who had risen either because they had been manipulated by devious missionaries or because they had been victimised by godless planters and managers." Crowns of Glory, Tears of Blood: The Demerara Slave Rebellion of 1823 (Oxford: Oxford University Press, 1994), xvi.

57. For analyses of the Jamaica slave revolt of 1831–1832, see John Howard Hinton, Memoir of William Knibb, Missionary in Jamaica (London: Houlston and Stoneman, 1847); Henry Bleby, Death Struggles of Slavery (London, 1853); Mary Reckford, "The Jamaican Slave Rebellion of 1831," Past and Present: A Journal of Historical Studies 40 (July 1968): 108–125; Stiv Jakobsson, Am I Not A Man And A Brother? British Missions and the Abo-

ists did not find it possible nor were they desirous by 1830 to ignore the impact of rebellions on their campaign. Jamaican slaves in rebellion succeeded in securing a firm place within British abolitionist attacks on colonial slavery.

While abolitionists' responses to the nineteenth-century revolts in Barbados, Demerara, and Jamaica are the focus of this study, some attention is given to the 1791 rebellion in French St. Domingue. British abolitionists' attitude to that rebellion laid the basis for the activist response to later uprisings in the English colonies. Proslavery advocates also made it almost impossible for British abolitionists to agitate without addressing the issue of St. Domingue.

The terms that have been used to describe the rising of the slaves against their bondage have been subjected to a puzzling variety of usages. It is evident that antislavery activists were particular in the terms they used to refer to the slaves' rising. They were hesitant in referring to slave resistance movements as *rebellions* or *revolts* or even *insurrections*. They believed that these terms denoted levels of violence and bloodshed that were markedly absent in the nineteenth-century rising of British West Indian slaves. They felt that it was more accurate to use more general and lenient, though often vague, terms such as *riot, commotion, disorders, disturbances, movement, transaction, events,* or *combination* in their commentary on the slaves' overt resistance. Historians have also contributed some ambiguity in the meaning of the names that have been ascribed to open slave resistance. Sometimes, the term *revolution,* as used in the St. Domingue slave rising of 1791, has been applied to the servile warfare in the British West Indies. The term *revolution,* however, cannot appropriately describe the events discussed here. David Close and Carl Bridge have pointed out that a revolution includes "rebellions or coups directed against individual holders of authority, but accepting the system through which they rule." Close and Bridge also insist that one requirement of a revolution is that it must involve some large-scale process of change.[58] Slave rising in the British West Indies did not directly produce this kind

lition of the Slave Trade and Slavery in West Africa and the West Indies, 1786–1838 (Uppsala: Gleerup, 1972), chap. 8.

58. David Close, "The Meaning of Revolution," in *Revolution: A History of the Idea,* ed. David Close and Carl Bridge (London: Croom Helm, 1985), 1–2.

of change. In this book, consequently, the term *revolution* is not used. The terms *revolt, rebellion,* and *insurrection* are used interchangeably to refer to slaves confronting their masters with arms in a bid for freedom. At the same time, wherever appropriate, it has been made evident that antislavery campaigners insisted on clearly distinguishing between the slave revolts that erupted prior to and during the era of British abolitionism.

Very little in the events unfolding in and impacting upon Britain in the late eighteenth and early nineteenth centuries could explain how and why leading abolitionists in Parliament spoke as extensively as they did on the revolts of Caribbean slaves. This was a period when the ruling classes in Britain felt threatened by the revolutionary ideas and the industrial unrest that swept over the plebeian orders of several European nations. To read only the history of the reaction of the upper and middle classes, to which British abolitionists generally belonged, to the assertiveness of the common people in this period will suggest the absurdity of searching for links between slave rebellion and British abolitionism. By 1760, George III had ascended the British throne, and until about 1790 the monarchy exerted its influence to the fullest to ensure that ministers of the crown in Parliament secured the royal prerogative and the privileges of the church. The king left little room for his subjects to exercise increased civil liberties. It was toward the end of George III's reign that antislavery organs in Britain were taking shape. The interaction between slave revolts and antislavery was not as yet evident, but the king's jealous regard for the status quo exerted some influence in setting the initial tone for a conservative antislavery program. Despite the royal prejudice, however, the antislavery position evolved to enable leading abolitionists to meet the challenge of slaves in rebellion. Britain's war with the thirteen colonies in North America, which ended with the declaration of American independence in September 1783, also did not augur well for a campaign on behalf of slaves who resorted to arms in a bid to obtain freedom. Britain's loss of America suggested that it was wise not to tamper with age-old institutions like slavery. Consequently, it would have been adding insult to injury to use slave revolts to justify antislavery strategies, however moderate, to regulate the master/slave relationship in the colonies.[59] This was another significant

59. See Stephen Conway, *The British Isles and the War of American Independence* (Oxford: Oxford University Press, 2000); Peter Linebaugh and Marcus Rediker, *The Many-Headed Hydra: Sailors, Slaves, Commoners, and the Hidden History of the Revolutionary Atlantic* (Boston: Beacon, 2000), chap. 7.

historical episode impinging on the British antislavery movement that the leading abolitionists managed to hurdle while defending rebellious slaves.

The French Revolution of 1789 and the ensuing French and Napoleonic wars directly and dynamically affected British abolitionists' narrative of slave rebellions. Britain's conflict with France and France's attempt to export revolutionary aims and ideas triggered a conservative reaction that attempted to counter the appeal of radical propagandists. In British political and national life, this reaction manifested itself in at least five distinct ways. The prime minister for most of this troubled period, the younger Pitt, who was regarded as the dupe of George III, harnessed his ministers and resources to defend the royal prerogative, support the privileges of the Church of England, cultivate strong patriotic sentiment in the nation at large, encourage militant loyalists, and suppress radical dissent. Between 1789 and 1815 habeas corpus was suspended, Combination Acts were passed, governmental prosecutions of cases of sedition abounded, and individuals branded as radicals by the government were continually subjected to unusually harsh sentences. The government took draconian measures to stamp out domestic radicalism.[60] Future leaders of the British abolitionist movement, especially William Wilberforce, supported the government's repressive measures in the wake of the French Revolution.[61] Their response to European radicalism from 1789 to 1815 did not measure up entirely to their later response to the rebellion of slaves in the colonies. To a certain extent, the same can be said of the abolitionists' response to the plight of the poor and of miserable workers in this period of Britain's

60. For an insight into domestic and international politics in Britain in the late eighteenth and early nineteenth centuries, see Harry Dickson, "The Impact on Britain of the French Revolution and the French Wars, 1789–1815," in *Britain and the French Revolution, 1789–1815*, ed. Harry Dickson (Basingstoke: Macmillan, 1989), 1–20; Frank O'Gorman, "Pitt and the 'Tory' Reaction to the French Revolution, 1789–1815," in Dickson (1989), 21–37; Macaulay Trevelyan, *British History in the Nineteenth Century and After, 1782–1919*, new ed. (London: Longmans, Green and Co., 1937), 35–77; Roger Wells, *Insurrection: The British Experience, 1795–1803* (Gloucester: Allan Sutton, 1983); Eric J. Evans, *William Pitt the Younger* (London: Routledge, 1999).

61. For discussions on Wilberforce's response to the repressive measures of the British government in the "age of revolution," see *Cobbett's Parliamentary History of England*, vol. 32: 293–294 (London: T. C. Hansard, 1795); Coupland (1923), 179, 265, 411–412; Patrick Cormack, *Wilberforce: The Nation's Conscience* (England: Pickering Paperbacks, 1983), 105.

industrial development. However, abolitionists were not completely oblivious and indifferent to the conditions under which poor children and adult workers subsisted in factories and mines. They supported a number of charitable organizations, and in Parliament they moved to improve the lot of chimney sweeps and cotton weavers. As middle-class reformers, however, antislavery activists supported the doctrine that the wealth of the propertied must be protected from the wanton destruction of workers.[62] Slaves in rebellion, however, forced British abolitionists to alter their own personal experiences with resistance in Europe and to look to the slaves on the other side of the Atlantic to structure their narrative on slave revolts. It was a narrative often tinged with some of the revolutionary concepts of the age.

It has been argued that slave rebellions retarded the objectives of the campaigners and stamped upon the movement its gradualist image. This charge, however, seems unfair considering that long before the abolitionists recognized slave revolts as significant in their program, they had openly avowed their commitment to a careful course. British abolitionists operated within a narrow political and civil culture, which they largely respected. Eighteenth- and nineteenth-century slavery opponents without exception took it for granted that freedom for slaves necessitated working through normal political and judicial channels. For the most part, the movement's leaders adhered to the practice of targeting the parliamentary class to effect the various changes in slavery that they advocated. They were less persistent in arousing public opinion in support of the cause, except during the slave-trade debates and in the very last years of the campaign. They preferred presenting reasoned arguments to the highest authority in the land. As Temperley has observed, abolitionists believed that "whatever the rights and wrongs of slavery, . . . changes . . . must come gradually, after full discussion and with due regard for the political pro-

62. For a discussion of the economic distresses of the poor during the industrial revolution, see Patricia Hollis, "Anti-Slavery and British Working Class Radicalism in the Years of Freedom," in *Anti-Slavery, Abolition and Reform: Essays in Memory of Roger Anstey,* ed. Christine Bolt and Seymour Drescher (England: William Dawson and Sons, 1980), 303; E. J. Hobsbawm and George Rude, *Captain Swing* (London: Lawrence and Wishart, 1969); Eric Evans, *Britain Before the Reform Act: Politics and Society, 1815–1832* (New York: Longman, 1989); William Molesworth, *History of England from the Year 1830–1874,* vol. 1 (London: Chapman and Hall, 1877).

prieties."[63] British abolitionists were bound to each other by factors generally unsuited to the establishment of a commentary on slave rebellions—religion, dislike of revolutionary methods, and middle-class and humanitarian ideals. Consequently, slaves in rebellion tested the legitimate limits to which abolitionists were prepared to go in agitating the West India question in Britain. Activists came to view the risks of slave rebellion as far more tolerable than the perpetual existence of slavery.

The findings of this study lead toward a major revision of how slave revolts and British antislavery are perceived. Revolts must be regarded as significant historical experiences beyond the confines of the local plantation. This book explains how British abolitionists were able to conduct a nonviolent campaign of social reform while making use of the combustible materials provided by slaves.

63. Howard Temperley, "Anti-Slavery," in *Pressure from Without in Early Victorian England,* ed. Patricia Hollis (London: Edward Arnold, 1974), 27–51. For discussions of the policies and methods of the British antislavery movement, see also Jack Gratus, *The Great White Lie: Slavery, Emancipation and Changing Racial Attitudes* (New York: Monthly Review Press, 1973), 200; David B. Davis, "The Emergence of Immediatism in British and American Anti-Slavery Thought," *Mississippi Valley Historical Review* 44, no. 2 (1962): 214–222; Gordon Lewis, *Slavery, Imperialism, and Freedom: Studies in English Radical Thought* (New York: Monthly Review Press, 1978), 53; David Turley, *The Culture of English Anti-Slavery, 1780–1860* (London: Routledge, 1991).

2

AGITATING THE QUESTION

This chapter examines the circumstances that cleared the path for the emergence of the British abolitionists' slave rebellion discourse. The slaves' decision to rebel just when abolitionists had begun to attack the institution of slavery itself unlocked an offensive and defensive pro- and anti-slavery debate that centered on slave revolts. The rebellion of the slaves fed accusations that abolitionist agitation prompted colonial servile warfare. Abolitionists, in turn, opened their commentary on slave rebellions by structuring a series of defensive arguments. This chapter looks at the three periods over which these defensive arguments were spread. First, the chapter considers the self-exculpatory positions that the abolitionists, led by William Wilberforce, took in the aftermath of the Barbados slave rebellion of 1816. Then the chapter traces the abolitionist attitudes to slave revolts that were presented by Thomas Fowell Buxton in the preamble of his House of Commons speech on slavery on May 15, 1823. Finally, the chapter examines the defense that the abolitionists put forward after slaves in Demerara in August 1823 confronted their masters with arms in a bid for freedom. The abolitionist response to rebellion following the Jamaican slave revolt of 1831–1832 is not considered here. By 1830, while planters persisted in accusing abolitionists of instigating servile violence, the abolitionists no longer felt pressured into providing a defense for the inflammatory effect of their agitation of the slavery question.

ON THE DEFENSIVE

Throughout the month of June 1816, the *Times* of London covered the Barbados slave rising in the form of reports from the governor, Sir James Leith, extracts from letters, editorials, and excerpts from the *Barbados Mercury and Bridgetown Gazette*. Proslavery items dominated the coverage. The abolitionists were severely attacked and were described as "men with diabolical motives."[1] Planters insisted that antislavery activities in Britain were responsible for the rebels who were "Negroes of the worst disposition."[2] Slavery supporters claimed that "the cause of the revolt in Barbados boils down to the early and fatal effects of the Registry Bill."[3] In another London *Times* article of the same date, critics of abolitionists asserted that the Registry Bill threatened "the peace and safety of the colonies" and was tantamount to "an impolitic interference by the home government between the local legislatures and the slaves."[4] These articles presented the connection between slave revolts and the British antislavery movement from a negative and damaging perspective.

The abolitionists' early responses were clearly self-defensive. William Wilberforce, still leading the humanitarian attack against slavery in Parliament by 1816, was the first to issue statements on the revolt and respond to the allegations of proslavery advocates. Wilberforce made a strenuous effort to disassociate the antislavery struggle in Britain from the counterproductive activities of the slaves in the colonies. Wilberforce declared that he "did not wish to agitate the subject or to enter fully into the state of the island."[5] In an unmistakably self-exculpatory manner, he declared that "whatever happened had no reference to himself or his friends, he had no share in creating the explosion that had been felt; he washed his hands clean of the blood that was spilt."[6] Notwithstanding the finality of the tone with which Wilberforce attempted to dismiss the perceived connection between British antislavery and colonial slave revolts, this was not the end of his reflections on the Barbados revolt. Wilberforce was haunted by the need to satisfactorily respond to the taunt that "they [the abolitionists] will never be able to persuade one man besides themselves of a statement so glaringly untrue . . . They may gloss it over to themselves as they do to others; but there will be a moment when that still, small voice; which is an inhabitant of every bosom, will be heard, and will tell

1. Comment by Sir Charles Brisbane, St. Vincent, in the *London Times,* June 20, 1816.

2. Account in the *London Times,* June 4, 1816, based on a private letter dated April 22, 1816, and on extracts from Barbados newspapers.

3. Ibid.

4. Ibid.

5. *London Times,* June 19, 1816.

6. Ibid.

them; this [revolt] has been your work."[7] The West India interest and their supporters rejected Wilberforce's disclaimer, although it was backed by arguments against the connections that slavery supporters drew between the abolitionist-sponsored slave registration scheme and the revolt.

Wilberforce insisted that the abolitionist scheme of slave registration could not have been responsible for instigating rebellion among the slaves. He viewed slave registration as a harmless measure that would improve and not destabilize the conditions under which slaves lived and labored in the colonies, and was surprised that the revolt had been attributed to "their unhappy registration bill."[8] James Stephen Sr., who by 1812 was a member of Parliament and a director of the African Institution, an anti-slavery committee formed in 1808, had devised the registration scheme. Using its prerogative to issue orders-in-council to colonies without legislative assemblies, the British government had directed the crown colony of Trinidad in March 1812 to create and maintain an annual census of the slave population based on Stephen's plan. The expense of the registry was to be met by the planters.[9] Slaves were to be identified by age, sex, stature, country, and personal marks, and births and deaths were also to be recorded. The register was to be transmitted to London in duplicate each year. One year after the scheme was introduced in Trinidad, it was found that the slave population had increased by more than 4,500 between 1811 and 1813.[10] Abolitionists naturally assumed that this proved that a contraband slave trade was taking place despite the colonists' repeated denials. Abolitionists rejected the explanation that the discrepancy in the figures was owing to the carelessness that prevailed in preparing the earlier census in comparison to the relatively more official report forwarded to London in 1813. Following this incident, James Stephen prepared and submitted to the African Institution a report calling for the establishment of a general registration of slaves in the British West Indies. He argued that slave registration was vital to the enforcement of the slave-trade abo-

7. *Hansard's Parliamentary Debates,* new ser., 34 (June 19, 1816): 1194.

8. Ibid., 1158.

9. See Ragatz (1963), chap. 11; Stephen (1971), 20–28; Mathieson (1926), 26; Burns (1965), 590, for discussions on the slave registration scheme. For structure of crown and legislative colonies, see *Hansard's Parliamentary Debates,* new ser., 10 (March 16, 1824): 1095.

10. Ragatz (1963), 390.

lition law and that Parliament should urge colonists to adopt the measure.[11]

The abolitionists as a body took action. First, in 1815 they promoted
an address to the crown stating that legislatures of crown and chartered
colonies should be encouraged to ameliorate their slave laws. Then, in
June of that year, Wilberforce presented in the House of Commons a bill
for slave registration along the same lines of the Trinidad order-in-council
of March 26, 1812. Both houses of Parliament agreed to forward the abolitionists' recommendations to the colonies.[12] The West Indians, in Britain
and the colonies, reacted bitterly, regarding this development as the penultimate step to the emancipation of the slaves. They saw it as a means of
unfair taxation since they enjoyed no direct representation in the British
Parliament but were required to bear the cost of the scheme. They insisted
that the charges of smuggling were totally unfounded. Above all, they re-
sented the measure as disregarding the rights they held over their private
property and violating their autonomy in colonial affairs.[13] Thus, when
the slaves in Barbados revolted one year after the registration controversy,
the colonists grabbed the opportunity to blame the revolt on the unpopular measure. Wilberforce and his supporters, however, rejected that such
a conservative measure of reform could have produced such a lamentable
consequence.

It was the colonists' reaction to the registration scheme, Wilberforce
insisted, and not the measure itself that goaded slaves to take up arms
against their masters. He said that slaves in Barbados rebelled on account
of the planters' misrepresentation of the objectives of the abolitionist campaign. Wilberforce reiterated that the registration measure mentioned
nothing about freedom. He argued that the colonial newspaper reports
and "the violence with which the proprietors expressed themselves on the
subject . . . and the heat with which persons talked, even in the presence
of their slaves, on the effects of the registry bill" created the Barbados ca-
tastrophe.[14] The planters had printed in their papers that the abolitionists

11. Ibid., 391. Ragatz notes that in 1815 James Stephen published a pamphlet entitled
Reasons for Establishing a Registry of Slaves in the Colonies.

12. Mathieson (1926), 27; Burns (1965), 611–612; Coupland (1933), 114–115.

13. Ragatz (1963), 393.

14. *Hansard's Parliamentary Debates,* new ser., 34 (June 19, 1816): 1158.

were "going to make the slaves free and suggested the possibility of black rising."[15] Other abolitionists supported Wilberforce's argument. Henry Brougham insisted that the harmless registration bill had been contaminated and made dangerous when "the registry was coupled with insurrection and emancipation when its motives were otherwise clearly stated."[16] Brougham also brought it to the attention of the House that "he held in his hands three Jamaican gazettes, in which it was openly avowed that registration was only a cloak for emancipation."[17] Jamaican slaves did not rise in rebellion in 1816. Brougham, nevertheless, was warning the colonists that slave revolts would become a more regular occurrence if they persisted in mismanaging news of the slavery debate. The anonymous author of *Remarks,* an abolitionist pamphlet reflecting views on the Barbados slave revolt, also supported Wilberforce's defensive arguments: "The planters have at all times expressed the fear that their gangs would be excited to insurrection by parliamentary discussions in the country. But their own conduct throughout the whole of the abolition controversy, flatly contradicts that profession, and proves it insincere; for these very discussions, of which the slaves could never hear without their help, have been regularly published by themselves in the colonial newspapers—or rather have been misrepresented by them in the way most likely to infuse dangerous ideas into the minds of the slaves, if they were thought susceptible of such impressions."[18]

To a degree, the abolitionists were correct in asserting that the planters had predicted their own ruin at the hands of their slaves. The abolitionists were discussing the subject of slavery thousands of miles away from the scene where the system was in operation. Whatever slaves learned about the parliamentary debates depended largely on how the colonists managed or mismanaged that information. The abolitionists were the authors, but they were not ultimately responsible for the circulation of their discussions in the colonies. The central point that the abolitionists were making here was that the planters had violated the very principle that they

15. Ibid.

16. Ibid., 1215.

17. Ibid., 1217.

18. Anonymous, *Remarks on the Insurrection in Barbados and The Bill for the Registration of Slaves* (London: Ellerton and Henderson, 1816), 4. (Hereafter this book is referred to as *Remarks.*)

had repeatedly espoused. The need for peace and safety in the colonies was one of the major factors upon which they had opposed the agitation of the slavery question. Yet, the colonists littered their newspapers with the incendiary material that they claimed was seized upon by the slaves to oppose slavery. Up to a point Wilberforce was correct in concluding, "the piece which they had overloaded against the advocates of the measure had burst upon themselves."[19]

There was, however, a greater irony in the abolitionist argument of blaming the colonists for the Barbados slave revolt. The abolitionists had undermined the basis upon which the validity of their argument rested. Wilberforce's line of reasoning pointed to the conclusion that the revolt took place because the slaves were not nearly as stupid as planters had assumed. Wilberforce's sons noted that their father had expressed the view that "the poor creatures, [the slaves] however, degraded, were not in such a state of absolute brutality as not to be operated upon by some of the passions that actuate the rest of the species. Though unable to read, the domestic slaves would obtain and promulgate the notion that their friends in Great Britain were labouring to give them liberty, while their masters were the only persons who opposed it."[20]

In comparison to other commentaries on the intellect of slaves, even abolitionists' commentaries, this was a fairly liberal position to take. Many racist conceptions were generated during slavery. Prominent among these was the belief in the abject stupidity of the "Negro." Eric Williams quotes the English philosopher Hume as stating about the "Negro": "their mind is in a continual state of depression, and if they have no expectation in life to awaken their abilities, and make them eminent, we cannot be surprised if a sullen stony stupidity should be the leading mark in their character."[21] Even some of the Christian missionaries working among the slaves to Christianize and civilize them imbibed the notion of the absolutely ignorant slave. The rector of St. Paul's Anglican Church in Antigua explained the slaves' low attendance at church by this logic. "Let it be remembered that the slaves are in a state of grossest ignorance; that

19. *Barbados Mercury and Bridgetown Gazette,* July 27, 1816.

20. Robert I. Wilberforce and Samuel Wilberforce, *The Life of William Wilberforce,* 5 vols., vol. 4 (London: J. Murray, 1838), 288.

21. Eric Williams, *British Historians and the West Indies* (London: Andre Deutsch, 1966), 23–24.

their minds are totally destitute of all cultivation."[22] Wilberforce's explanation that slaves had fed off the planters' discussion of the British antislavery campaign was an admission that slaves exercised thinking faculties. Wilberforce suggested that slaves had tuned in to the debate in Britain that concerned their status as slaves and that the role of ideas was influential in their rebellious action. The defensive arguments raised in the wake of the 1816 Barbados revolt revealed the ambivalence of the abolitionist concept of the intellectual capacities of slaves. Antislavery campaigners insisted that ideas for the rebellion emerged from the careless talk of the planters, but they denied that slaves were intelligent enough to be affected by abolitionists' discussion of their status. This ambivalence notwithstanding was to lead the abolitionists away from concentrating solely on the need to deflect blame to a more slave-centered depiction of the slaves' rising.

James Stephen, writing years later in 1830, revealed that he did not quite share the opinion that the overseas agitation of the slavery question was incapable of unsettling the slaves. He was in agreement with other abolitionists when he reasoned that "to deprecate discussions here, [in Britain] is in other words, to require the advocates of the slaves a final abandonment of this cause. But while we protest against any responsibility for such discussions, where [in the slave plantation colonies] they are utterly useless, we will never, desist from them here, where they are the only possible means by which we can hope to redeem our oppressed fellow subjects from bondage, or our country from guilt."[23] However, Stephen went on to contradict this view, which was held by many other abolitionists. "I am far from thinking that such long protracted discussions, even in the mother country, fruitless as they have hitherto been of reformation, are unaccompanied with danger."[24] It took fourteen years following the slave rebellion in Barbados for one abolitionist to admit openly that indeed the campaigners were aware of the incendiary effect of their debate on the slave population.

22. *Edinburgh Review* 40, no. 79 (March 1824): 229.
23. James Stephen, *Being a Delineation of the State in Point of Practice*, vol. 2 of *The Slavery of the British West India Colonies Delineated, as it Exists Both in Law and Practice, and Compared with the Slavery of Other Colonies, Ancient and Modern* (London: J. Hatchard and Son, 1830), 412.
24. Ibid., 413.

Another defensive tactic adopted by Wilberforce in the wake of the Barbados slave revolt was his reiteration of the conservative agenda of the abolitionists. To defend the good name of the humanitarians, Wilberforce reminded parliamentarians that although he and his friends were accused of instigating the slaves to fight for their freedom, they were not advocating emancipation at this stage of the campaign. He provided evidence of the cautious path that the movement's leaders had always taken to slavery reform. He recalled that in 1792, when Mr. Burke had called for bolder, more concrete slave legislation, he himself had opposed the suggestion since "the friends . . . had been satisfied with the general measure of abolition to which they looked as the grand object of their solicitude."[25] The sum of the plan embraced by 1815, Wilberforce asserted, was "the abolition of the slave trade with a view to produce the amelioration of the slaves; that we might see the West Indies cultivated by a happy peasantry, instead of being cultivated by slaves."[26] The changes in colonial society that the abolitionists had envisioned were to occur smoothly over a reasonable, unspecified period of time.

Wilberforce's defensive maneuvers in the wake of Barbados 1816 were not surprising. The radical, chaotic, and destructive dimensions of revolt ran counter to his campaign's judicious principles and methods. Historian David Turley notes that the abolitionists were the "middle-class, religious, liberal segment of the bourgeois by the nineteenth century. They had a sense of appropriateness in balancing liberty and control, civilisation and barbarism within England and the wider world."[27] Wilberforce's repudiation of the slaves' violent and destructive solution to the problem of slavery manifested the conservative principles to which he and his circle were committed. The abolitionists' dilemma was compounded by the fact that Barbados slaves rebelled at a time when official antislavery policy was that freedom should flow almost effortlessly from cooperative planters. With the forces of conservatism bearing so heavily against them, the initiative that Barbadian slaves took in attacking slavery may very well have rendered the metropolitan struggle a lost cause. The defensive positions that Wilberforce took in 1816, however, represented only a small fraction of the abolitionists' slave rebellion discourse.

25. *Hansard's Parliamentary Debates*, new ser., 34 (June 19, 1816): 1155–1156.
26. Ibid.
27. Turley (1991), 6.

THE WEIGHTY CHARGE

In the years between the 1816 Barbados revolt and that of Demerara in 1823, British abolitionists were realizing that a more decisive program against slavery was needed. The campaigners did give some thought to the possibility that slaves could rebel on the strength of the movement in Britain. They vacillated between accepting slave revolt as a necessary risk of their humanitarian campaign and rejecting altogether any responsibility for causing rebellion. The crisis of conscience that Thomas Fowell Buxton experienced prior to accepting Wilberforce's offer to take over the leadership of the antislavery movement in the British Parliament clearly reflects the dilemma that revolts presented to the abolitionists. Buxton did not follow entirely Wilberforce's defensive position but was more often inclined to take the view that if indeed slavery agitation in Britain brought insurrection in the colonies, then it was a worthwhile risk of the cause. Wilberforce had written to Buxton from London on May 24, 1821, "earnestly conjuring you to take most seriously into consideration the expediency of devoting yourself to this blessed service . . . I entreat you to form an alliance with me [for] I should not be able to finish it [this blessed service]."[28] Buxton's son Charles attested, "what chiefly led him to hesitate . . . was the fear that the discussion of abolition in England might lead to a servile insurrection in the West Indies."[29] Buxton was unable to either easily dismiss his fears or justify the cause. Charles reasoned that his father "deeply felt the weight of this responsibility and it was the subject of long and anxious thought."[30] It was not "till after long and mature deliberations that he accepted the weighty charge . . . Indeed he does not appear to have resolved upon undertaking it till a year and a half after the receipt of Wilberforce's letter."[31]

Buxton's resolution in this difficult matter was eventually based upon his willingness to accept responsibility for any adverse results of the campaign that he was requested to lead. In his attempt to quiet his apprehensions about taking over from Wilberforce, Buxton asked himself, "If a

28. Buxton (1852), 104.
29. Ibid., 107.
30. Ibid.
31. Ibid., 106.

servile war would break out, and 50,000 perish, how should I like that?"[32] His fairly honest attempt to eliminate the difficulty from his mind led him to flirt with the position that the end justified the means. His troubled conscience seemed to be appeased by his reasoning that "if I had two sons, I would choose to have one free and one dead than both being alive enslaved."[33] Buxton's resolution reflected the risks that he as an abolitionist was willing to take because of his personal revulsion at the unmitigated horror of British West Indian slavery, which he considered greater than that of slave rebellion itself. Making a choice on the issue of servile war was not something he could avoid. He was not allowed the luxury of entering into the struggle against slavery while ignoring the reality of slave revolts. In a letter written to a friend on February 24, 1825, Buxton stated, "the maxim I quote in our deliberations is that of the navy in the last war, 'Always Fight.'"[34]

Buxton was one among only a few abolitionists who spoke so forthrightly about the impact of slave revolts on the British antislavery program. Other leaders held serious reservations despite evidence that suggests that Buxton had at least considered that the threat of slave revolt was no obstacle to the antislavery cause. James Stephen's son George observed that the real or perceived dangers of tampering with the slave system acted as a forceful barrier to the emergence of a homogeneous abolitionist attitude to slave revolts: "The ablest and most zealous of the abolitionists . . . were well persuaded that . . . the bare suggestion of emancipating them, would create such a tumult in the country and in Parliament, as to defeat all their [the abolitionists'] future efforts for their protection . . . [thus] nothing was said about emancipation, or if said, it was in a whisper. Colonial abuses, colonial obduracy, colonial hypocrisy, were the only topics for agitation, but colonial castigation and colonial emancipation were tabooed."[35]

By the beginning of 1823, with the formal launching of the Anti-Slavery Society, the abolitionists broke their silence on the question of emancipation. In an extremely conservative manner, Buxton, now leading the

32. Ibid.
33. Ibid.
34. Ibid., 132.
35. Stephen (1971), 60.

antislavery campaign in Parliament, declared to the House of Commons that slavery was repugnant to the British Constitution and to Christianity and ought to be gradually abolished.[36] The demands made in this speech on behalf of the slaves were very limited. George Stephen observed, nevertheless, that even when Buxton was given the go-ahead to introduce in the House of Commons the conservative plan for gradual slave emancipation, several abolitionist leaders were skeptical of the consequences. Stephen wrote, "It cannot be doubted that Mr. Buxton's agitation of the question was still premature, and I have reason to believe that most of the leaders gave only a reluctant assent to it. The country was not prepared for such a decided course; an unreformed Parliament was not to be coerced into it, even had popular opinion been ripe to goad them on. Many feared, and my father was among the number, that in the then state of the slave population, a partial admission to their undoubted rights might lead to an insurgent movement to compel a full concession of them."[37] The campaigners had ushered British abolitionism into a new era. They were quite aware that the tensions between the struggle in Britain and the conduct of rebellious slaves were growing more apparent and less simple to ignore or resolve.

THE PREAMBLE TO BUXTON'S 1823 SPEECH

Slave rebellion was at the core of the preamble of Buxton's May 15, 1823, speech. The preamble occupied eight and one half pages of a speech just over seventeen pages long. Before formally divulging the "new" objectives of the antislavery lobbyists, Buxton felt bound to address the anxieties that he knew concerned every member of Parliament. On the evening before Buxton's speech, Mr. Baring, a proslavery M.P., reminded Buxton of the risks he was about to undertake. Mr. Baring claimed that he himself was an abolitionist and supported amelioration of slavery. However, "to bring forward the subject of the abolition of slavery in the House, was to shed blood in the West Indies and to cause rebellion."[38] The advocates of slavery did their part in ensuring that abolitionists were not oblivious to and silent about their role, secondary and indirect though it was, in stir-

36. See *Hansard's Parliamentary Debates,* new ser., 9 (May 15, 1823): 256, in reference to Buxton's May 15, 1823, speech on slavery.

37. Stephen (1971), 61.

38. *Hansard's Parliamentary Debates,* new ser., 9 (May 15, 1823): 256.

ring slave rebellion. Buxton's speech vacillated between views that accepted and rejected the charge that abolitionists' activities caused rebellion in the colonies, and he was less dogmatic than Wilberforce in rejecting the connection between the slaves' conduct and the abolitionists' activities.

Buxton's speech began "by referring to the warning he had received of dreadful evils likely to be produced in the West Indies by the agitation of this subject."[39] He did not lightly dismiss the warnings but agreed that the question was "a perilous one . . . It is no slight matter, I have been told, and I admit it, to agitate the question at all."[40] He even appeared willing to shoulder "the responsibility which I incur by the agitation of the question."[41] Buxton nevertheless rejected the accusations that the abolitionists' well-intentioned attempts to humanize British West Indian slavery were a call for "insurrection of all the blacks . . . murder of all the whites."[42] Just as Wilberforce had sought to defend the slave registration measure from the scourge of rebellion, so, too, Buxton insisted that the abolitionists' reform measures of 1823 were innocuous. Buxton was convinced that all the proposals the abolitionists had advanced for the improvement of West Indian slavery were gentle remedies for a harsh and inhumane system. In his maiden slavery speech of 1823, Buxton proposed that slaves should be attached to the soil and that they should no longer be viewed by the law as chattel. He asked that slave testimony be received; that obstructions to manumission be removed; that no governor, judge, or attorney general be a slave owner; that provisions be made for the religious instruction of slaves; that slave marriage be enforced and sanctioned; and that an alternative to the current method of punishing slaves be introduced with the complete abolition of flogging. Buxton asked rhetorically, "Is there anything irritating in this? What is there in all of this calculated to rouse the furious passions of the Negro?"[43] In response to his own rhetorical question, Buxton treated his opponents' propaganda on slave rebellions as baseless apprehensions. He observed that "no motion was ever made in this House on the subject of Negro slavery, which has not been met with

39. Mathieson (1926), 119; Northcott (1976), 54.
40. *Hansard's Parliamentary Debates*, new ser., 9 (May 15, 1823): 257.
41. Ibid., 258.
42. Ibid., 260.
43. Ibid., 267.

the same predictions."[44] He recalled that their opponents produced the bogey of slave rebellion in 1787 when abolitionists sought to lessen the sufferings of the Middle Passage and to end Britain's involvement in the foreign slave trade. The same outcry was made when it was proposed that it should be made a capital offense for a white man to murder a slave.[45] Buxton concluded that it was fantastic that proslavery forces could expect that the "Negro" slaves would be so lacking in common human sensitivity that they would revolt when measures were introduced to improve their condition. It was yet to be seen that indeed the planters were less illogical in pressing this point than the abolitionists had imagined or accepted. As far as Buxton and his circle were concerned, however, it was safe to proceed with the slavery discussions and suggest reforms since the objections raised against them were baseless and amounted to nothing.

Buxton and his colleagues were smug in the mistaken notion that it was possible to improve slavery and that slaves would gratefully welcome any change that appeared to mitigate their suffering. What the abolitionists did not seem to understand was that in the last years of slavery, improved conditions did not make contented slaves. The planters, in a desperate effort to hold the line against reform, were in a better position to appreciate this. Alexander Barclay, who had spent twenty-one years in Jamaica, hinted at this conclusion. "It has at least sometimes happened, that slaves have been found the foremost and most active in rebellion where the reigns of authority had been most slackened, and the greater indulgences had been granted to them . . . where order and subordination are not maintained, there will be found the greatest discontent among the slaves, the greatest trouble to the manager."[46]

This was not a perfect analysis, as Craton has noted, of nineteenth-century slave revolts in the British West Indies.[47] Slaves rebelling when the white forces of law and order had weakened tended to be more common during the eighteenth century and was particularly evident in Cuffee's Re-

44. Ibid., 260.

45. Ibid., 260–261.

46. Alexander Barclay, *Practical View of the Present State of Slavery in the West Indies or An Examination of Mr. Stephen's "Slavery of the British West India Colonies,"* 2d ed. (London: Smith Elder and Co., 1827), 251.

47. Craton (1982), 241.

bellion of 1763 in Dutch Berbice. The decimation by disease of the whites and the loss of their Indian allies, who were caught up in tribal warfare, encouraged the resistance of the slaves there in that year. Their leader Cuffee negotiated with the Dutch governor as an equal, and the slaves held control of Upper Berbice as well as the capital for little more than one year.[48] By the time slaves in Barbados, Demerara, and Jamaica rose in rebellion in the nineteenth century, the West Indian slave-plantation scenario was shaped by significantly different circumstances. Alexander Barclay, nevertheless, had pointed to a near enough approximation of the psyche of the slaves. Greater indulgences, in this case the 1823 amelioration proposals, encouraged slaves to make all-out freedom their ultimate aspiration. As Craton has noted, amelioration measures "did no more than refine, redefine, and whet that will [to be free]."[49]

Buxton went on in his preamble to defend his claim that his opponents' apprehensions were without substance by proudly asserting that "those twenty years, which, if the West Indians were true prophets, ought to have been marked with perpetual violence, bloodshed and desolation, were, in point of fact, remarkable for a degree of tranquillity in the British West Indies, unexampled in any other period of history."[50] It seemed that the abolitionists sincerely believed that their movement brought peace rather than servile war to the colonies and that their attempts to humanize slavery could not but make the slaves more contented with their lot. Buxton asserted that their campaign "declared to be so injurious in theory [has] never produced the slightest practical injury."[51] Reference to the record of slave revolts before and during the antislavery era attest somewhat to the validity of Buxton's conclusion. There certainly were far more uprisings in the pre-antislavery era than during the movement. What the abolitionists, perhaps, did not realize was that though fewer in number, the later revolts that took place during their agitation were more intense than the former ones.

Taking alone the figures for the three territories that constitute the core of this study, the frequency of uprisings just before the launching of the campaign against the slave trade are staggering. In British Guiana, slaves

48. Ibid., 270.
49. Ibid., 293.
50. *Hansard's Parliamentary Debates*, new ser., 9 (May 15, 1823): 261.
51. Ibid.

revolted in Berbice in 1733–1734, 1749, 1752, 1762, and 1763, and in Essequibo in 1732, 1744, and 1772.[52] After the establishment of the humanitarian campaign against the slave trade in 1787, however, only four significant uprisings were reported for British Guiana. These were the uprisings of 1795, 1802, 1804, and 1823 in Demerara.[53] In Barbados, because of geographical and other localized conditions unfavorable to the success of slave rebellions, such occurrences were comparatively rare. There were "no mountains, forests or great inequalities of surface in the island"[54] to facilitate retreat during and after struggles with the local militia or British military forces. Furthermore, the military force in that territory was reasonably strong, the ratio of whites to blacks was relatively high, and over the length and breadth of Barbados, there existed the concentrated development of the plantation system. Even in this colony, the figures on both sides of the records seem to bear out the narrow conclusion of the abolitionists. They seemed to have convincingly proven that their opponents had blundered when they associated abolitionism with episodes of slave unrest. Only two plots were uncovered in Barbados in the era of nineteenth-century slavery reform attempts, whereas, previously, slave insurrection against the system in that territory had erupted in 1675, 1683, 1692, and 1768.[55]

Even more supportive of this theory is the history of armed and violent slave resistance in the colony of Jamaica. James Walvin has commented that "the history of the island until freedom in 1838 could almost be written in terms of slave revolt and resistance."[56] This is no idle statement. Ragatz has calculated that "over a dozen outbreaks erupted in Jamaica alone in the eighteenth century."[57] By the time the Society for the Abolition of the Slave Trade was launched, however, revolts in Jamaica had been significantly reduced in number. After the occurrence of the 1776

52. Winston McGowan, "Christianity and Slavery," *History Gazette* (Guyana History Society) 24 (September 1990): 5.

53. Ibid.

54. *Hansard's Parliamentary Debates,* new ser., 34 (June 19, 1816): 1160.

55. Claude Levy, *Emancipation, Sugar, and Federalism: Barbados and the West Indies, 1833–1876* (Gainesville: University Presses of Florida, 1980), 28.

56. Walvin (1992), 53.

57. Ragatz (1963), 31.

Afro-Creole slave plot in the parish of Hanover in Jamaica, the 1831–1832 slave rebellion in that island was the next serious rising of the slaves.[58]

Indeed, the record is impressive. The agitators, however, were deceived into thinking that fewer slave revolts justified their conclusion that the slavery-reform measures ushered in a period of relative peace in the colonies. The spirit that informed the slave rebellions in Barbados (1816), Demerara (1823), and Jamaica (1831–1832), as opposed to Tacky's rebellion (1760) in Jamaica and Cuffee's (1763) in Berbice, again confirms that the abolitionists' superficial assessment of the situation was off target. As historians like Mary Turner, Walvin, and Williams have incisively commented, slaves by the nineteenth century were generally more restless, expectant, and politically curious about affairs concerning their status than were their predecessors.[59] They had a greater faith in the possibility that freedom could come in their lifetime. More significantly, while the pre-nineteenth-century generation of slave rebels aimed at overthrowing their masters, taking over the plantations, or living as outlaws in hardy and inaccessible terrain, the spirit that motivated the new generation was quite different and more dangerous. The later generation of rebels, especially their leaders, were among the slave "elite." They were headmen, drivers of gangs, craftsmen—confidential slaves whose masters afforded them the privileges of extra allowances of the primary necessities of life. Above all, they had achieved some level of basic literacy and grasped every opportunity to tap into any discourse that pertained however remotely to their situation. They took advantage of the chance to operate within a context of public discussion taking place locally and internationally, a context that was outside the reach of their predecessors. Like their forebears, they wanted to be free. Unlike their forebears, however, they were not struggling merely to be refugees from the law. The rebels of the "Emancipation Revolts" fought for what they considered to be rightfully theirs by law. They aspired to the status of freemen with the right to be

---

58. Craton (1982), 172.

59. Turner (1982), 48; Walvin (1992), 83–84; Eric Williams, *Documents on British West Indian History, 1807–1833 (Select Documents from the P.R.O., London, England, Relating to the Colonies of Barbados, Jamaica and Trinidad)* (Port-of-Spain: Trinidad Publishing Co., 1952), 179.

fairly compensated for their labor on the plantations or to have two or three days of leisure to use as they saw fit.

Nineteenth-century slave rebels in the British West Indies borrowed articulations from the British antislavery movement to make their demands. They recognized how the objectives of the movement bore some resemblance to their own basic aspiration to be free. Eugene Genovese fittingly observes in relation to the late slave revolts that "the goals of the revolts and the terms in which they were cast changed with the revolutionary events in . . . European and American society as a whole."[60] Slave rebellion informed by this kind of ideology was more contagious and dangerous to the preservation of British West Indian pre-emancipation society than uprisings led by African chieftains like Tacky and Cuffee. Walvin, drawing on the Craton/Genovese debate on this issue, has succinctly commented that "perhaps the most unusual aspect of the major slave revolts in the British islands was that the worst incidents erupted in the last years of slavery, not when slavery was at its worst, but in the years when the abolitionist campaigns in Britain were apparently making headway towards securing black freedom."[61]

This observation underscores the difficulty of separating the British antislavery struggle from the rebellious conduct of slaves. The metropolitan movement against slavery sharpened the slaves' tools of resistance. The insurgents in Demerara, for example, had a definite plan of action that reflected the influence of events taking place in the metropolis. "They were first to take all the arms, and then confine the white people in the stocks, for fear they should carry the news to town. In the morning the whites would all be sent to town, and the Negroes were then to arm themselves and await the Governor, whom they expected would come and ask the reasons for so acting, meanwhile they would remain on the estate without working."[62] This was a substantial leap in planning the course of

60. Eugene Genovese, *From Rebellion to Revolution: Afro-American Slave Revolts in the Making of the Modern World* (Baton Rouge: Louisiana State University Press, 1979), chap. 1.

61. Walvin (1992), 84. See also Michael Craton, "Proto-Peasant Revolts? The Late Slave Rebellions in the British West Indies, 1816–1832," *Past and Present* 85 (Nov. 1979): 99–126.

62. Rodway (1893), 227; *The London Missionary Society's Report of the Proceedings Against the Late Reverend John Smith of Demerara, Minister of the Gospel . . . and Including the Documentary Evidence Omitted in the Parliamentary Copy With an Appendix;*

rebellion from the days of the mid-eighteenth century. The objective of the slaves in sending the whites to town was to gain an update of news on the slavery question that was rumored to have arrived from England. Slaves were exercising political curiosity and seeking out their interests. They felt confident enough to discuss their condition with the chief political authority in the colony, and refusal to work had become part of their planned action of resistance. The colonists refused to believe that the rebels were responsible for such a sophisticated strategy. The editor of the *Demerara Gazette* concluded on August 28, 1823, that "the plans and arrangements of the rebels were most extensive and well made—too well made indeed to admit of a doubt but a superior order of people had laid the original foundation."[63] The editor went so far as to suggest that "perhaps the intriguing saints at home had a hand in it."[64]

Although not much attention has been paid in the records to the role of female slaves in the pre-emancipation revolts in the British West Indies, it is evident that women instigated and were active participants in them. In the Barbados revolt of 1816, the court-martial testimony of Robert, one of the captured male slaves accused of rebellion, asserted that a firebrand named Nanny Grigg was a leading propagandist for the revolt. According to Robert's testimony, Nanny insisted that the free paper of emancipation had arrived from Britain and that the slaves should refuse to continue to work. By the New Year when no emancipation proclamation was forthcoming, Nanny reputedly rebuked the slaves for passively accepting servitude and egged them on to burn the sugar cane plantations in a bid to achieve emancipation as had been done in St. Domingue.[65]

A similar attention to detailed planning was evident in the Jamaican slave rebellion of 1831–1832. Its leader Sam Sharpe confessed before he was executed that after Christmas all the slaves were to sit down and refuse to work unless their managers agreed to pay wages for their labor.[66]

Containing the Letters of and Statements of Mr. and Mrs. Smith, Mrs. Elliot, Mr. Arrindell, &C and Also, the Society's Petitions to the House of Commons. The whole published under the authority of the directors of the said society (London: F. Westley, 1824), 43, 83. Hereafter this item is referred to as *The London Missionary Society's Report.*

63. Rodway (1893), 240.

64. Ibid.

65. See chapter 1.

66. Baptist Missionary Society, *Facts and Documents Connected With the Late Insur-*

The editor of the *Demerara Gazette* was not totally wrong when he implicated the abolitionists in the 1823 slave rebellion. What he did not recognize was that the slaves were appropriating in their own way the events taking place in Britain on their behalf. The sophistication of their armed resistance by the nineteenth century represented the upward transition of warfare against slavery in which the slaves had matured considerably in their ideology of rebellion. This is a more reasonable explanation for the fewer number of revolts that occurred in this period than the apparent comparative passivity of the slaves. Buxton attempted to come to terms with the rebellion of the slaves, but his faulty reading of the slave revolt figures caused him to misunderstand to some extent the impact of the abolitionist campaign on the conduct of the slaves. The abolitionists did not fully grasp the level of consciousness that slaves in rebellion were manifesting by the turn of the nineteenth century in the English colonies.

In an argument that reflected less of the abolitionist desire to refute the allegations of proslavery advocates and more of the ambivalence with which the new leader regarded the issue of slave revolts, Buxton argued that the danger in slavery arose primarily from the system's hardships. "For I know," Buxton asserted in his preamble, "wherever there is oppression, there is danger, wherever there is slavery, there must be great danger."[67] As far as stirring rebellion was concerned, abolitionist activities were not nearly as great a threat as the unmitigated evils of slavery. Nevertheless, he was willing to consider that "even supposing the danger of giving to be as great as the danger of withholding, there may be danger in moving and danger in standing still—danger in proceeding and danger in doing nothing."[68] Buxton had come to the position that whether or not the question of slavery was agitated, slave rebellions were inevitable. Such being the case, Buxton felt compelled to ask the House "and to ask it seriously—whether it be not better for us to incur peril for justice and humanity, for freedom, and for the sake of giving happiness to millions hitherto oppressed; or whether it be better to incur peril for slavery, cruelty and for injustice—for the sake of destroying the happiness of

rection in Jamaica and the Violations of Civil and Religious Liberty arising out of it* (London: Holsworth and Ball, Anti-Slavery International, Broomsgrove Road, 1832), 23. Hereafter this item is referred to as *Facts and Documents*.

67. *Hansard's Parliamentary Debates,* new ser., 9 (May 15, 1823): 264.
68. Ibid.

those wretched beings, upon whom we have already showered every species of calamity."[69] This attitude to slave rebellion was a less outright rejection of culpability than had been made following the earlier rebellion in Barbados and was even less ambivalent than other aspects of Buxton's preamble. Buxton and his supporters were prepared to temporarily accommodate slave rebellion once the risk meant that measures were taken to alter the servile regime, and, eventually, to dismantle it altogether. This compromise was more attractive than the alternative of doing nothing in the misplaced belief that inaction would secure peace and security in the colonies.

In his 1823 speech, Buxton also vacillated between rejecting and accepting some responsibility for slave rebellion by emphasizing that abolitionists were neither the first nor the only group to have participated in discussions on British colonial slavery. If Buxton was reluctant to shoulder the entire blame for slave revolts, at least he expressed a willingness to share responsibility for any adverse effects produced by the abolitionist campaign on behalf of the slaves. Buxton stressed that the slavery question "had been debated again and again within these walls by the House of Commons, the House of Lords and the Privy Council, and it does so happen, that during those thirty years, every man of distinction in this House, without exception, has put forth his opinions on these subjects: not only the men professing to be the most eager for liberty, and who, therefore, might be supposed to overlook the danger in the pursuit of their favourite subject."[70] The attempt here was to infuse legitimacy into a debate that their opponents as well as conservative abolitionists regarded as impolitic. By referring to other authorities in varying branches of government who participated in the slavery debate, Buxton tried to reduce the proslavery antagonism that the abolitionists attracted. Their lobbying on behalf of slaves against vested colonial interests won them notoriety for sponsoring what were perceived as ill-conceived measures. Essentially, Buxton's reference to the broad-based nature of the slavery debate was a position of compromise. Buxton's boldest step in acknowledging the connection between slave rebellions and British antislavery was his declaration that he was not "opposed to the pursuit of the ideal good at the ex-

69. Ibid.
70. Ibid., 259.

pense of present danger."[71] This statement recalls the personal resolution Buxton made upon assuming leadership of the cause, when he embraced the view that whatever the danger, the end justified the means.

The defensive arguments of Buxton's maiden speech on the West India question in the House of Commons had slightly shifted the abolitionist slave rebellion discourse from the uncompromising position Wilberforce had taken in 1816. In the later period, Buxton reflected a tendency to share some responsibility for the occurrence of slave revolts. Such a considera-tion opened the way for abolitionists to consider revolts as a worthwhile risk factor in a metropolitan campaign geared to mitigate and eventually abolish the slavery regime. It is also significant that the position embraced by Buxton was a clear indication that abolitionists partially acknowl-edged the possibility that slaves might use the debates in Parliament as a cue to confront their masters with arms.

LOSS OF REPUTATION

The West India interest and their supporters were more vociferous in their accusations of the inflammatory effects of abolitionists' activities in the aftermath of the Demerara slave rebellion of 1823 than they had been af-ter the Barbados rebellion. An editorial in the London *Times* included an extract expressing proslavery views of the revolt. The consensus was that "they [the abolitionists] have put the knives at our throats, and if the blow is not struck, we shall not be indebted for our escape to either their good will or forbearance . . . for the chance of obtaining a possible good, they are promoting an immediate and positive evil.[72] Abolitionist leaders cringed under this attack. Charles Buxton observed that following the Demerara revolt the antislavery campaigners were painfully aware that they were "opposed by the West Indians, deserted by the government and deemed enthusiasts by the public."[73] They also realized that antislavery support dwindled as "their lukewarm partisans left them at once."[74] The Demerara rebellion ensured that the abolitionists' commentary on revolts, which Buxton had shaped just three months before, was open to expan-sion. More abolitionists now contributed to the planter accusation that

71. Ibid.
72. *London Times,* October 13, 1823.
73. Buxton (1852), 124.
74. Ibid., 122.

the agitation of the slavery question was setting off rebellion. The conduct of slaves in rebellion was attracting increasing abolitionist attention.

Zachary Macaulay was one of the abolitionists who looked back to the defensive position that Wilberforce had taken in 1816 to respond to the charge that antislavery agitation set off the Demerara rebels. Macaulay, however, took an even more cowardly step than Wilberforce. He did not blame the colonists' reaction to reform measures but rather the manner in which ministers of the imperial government attempted to implement these measures. Macaulay wrote to Buxton: "In whatever degree, therefore, the disturbances in Demerara are to be traced to England (and I do not believe that they are to be so traced) they must be considered as the work of Canning, Bathurst, Horton and company instead of that other reviled and calumniated firm [the abolitionists]."[75] Macaulay explained that the 1823 amelioration measures that set off the rebellion were sponsored by the British government and were not implemented according to "the cautious though firm spirit of the reforms propounded by the friends of abolition, but as a substitute for them, falling short in some respects, and in others going greatly beyond what they had suggested."[76] Macaulay's letter was clearly intended to reassure his friend at a time when proslavery advocates were unsparing in their attacks. The letter must have been little comfort after Buxton had accepted that slave violence was a possible corollary to his leadership of the antislavery struggle.

Thomas Clarkson was another abolitionist who expressed concern for the blow to the movement's reputation. He recorded that the campaigners were perceived as "traitors of our country . . . The planters had circulated the most furious and false publications throughout the whole kingdom; I found their books in the libraries and reading rooms, coffee houses and at some of the inns."[77] Clarkson questioned whether "it would be wiser to travel on in the teeth of these calumnies, or stop my journey for a few weeks and go home and write a pamphlet, and thus try to refute them."[78] Clarkson did stop, and his pamphlet *Thoughts on Negro*

75. Zachary Macaulay to Thomas Fowell Buxton, London, November 11, 1823, Papers of Zachary Macaulay, Part 1, reel 4.

76. Ibid.

77. "Account of Efforts, 1807–1824, to abolish Slavery," Ms. Essay CN 33, p. 113, Part 1, reel 1A, M/I 5657, Thomas Clarkson Papers.

78. Ibid.

Slavery was intended to persuade the British people and Parliament that the gradual emancipation proposed by the abolitionists was safe and practicable. After the Demerara slave revolt, Clarkson reinforced the defensive abolitionist position that the slavery upholders' allegations were groundless.

The recently formed Anti-Slavery Society also rejected the blame for causing slaves in Demerara to rebel. An article in the *Edinburgh Review* reflected, "The risks of Negro rebellion have always been greatly exaggerated, as we have frequently had occasion to show; but unquestionably such risks do exist, and are most fit to be considered when we are surveying measures of which the natural tendency is to promote discontent among the slaves, and to excite in them vague and undefined expectations of change."[79] It is difficult to imagine that the abolitionists did not appreciate the glaring contradiction in this statement. It clearly represented two incongruent attitudes. The abolitionists attempted to refute their opponents' allegations that agitating the slavery question would lead to revolts. At the same time, they wanted to demonstrate that they were aware of the need to take every precaution to ensure that their antislavery plans would guarantee peace in the colonies. It could not have been difficult for them to deduce that if the planters' predictions were without substance, the abolitionists were absolved from the need to exercise caution. The abolitionists sacrificed consistency to gain whatever advantage was to be had from speaking on both sides of the argument. Despite the weakness of the argument, the Anti-Slavery Society acknowledged that abolitionists were aware that measures of slavery reform had the potential to excite expectations in the slaves. This was only one step away from abolitionists' later deduction that if these expectations were not fulfilled, the slaves would rebel.

The Anti-Slavery Society had also taken up Buxton's 1823 argument that the abolitionists' proposed reforms could only improve rather than jeopardize the slave colonial societies of the British West Indies. "But how can any such effect [slave insurrection] be produced by measures of a plain and intelligible description, manifestly calculated to better their condition, without in the least weakening the authority of their masters?"[80] Of

79. *Edinburgh Review* 41, no. 81 (June 1824): 216.
80. Ibid.

course, the planters recognized that the very suggestion from home of measures for the regulation of their slaves was, in effect, a move that undermined their authority. Abolitionists overlooked this. They emphasized that should their admonitions for improvement be heeded, the relationship between the master and the slave could only improve. They stressed that "where it had been acted upon in its spirit, [the proposals of the 1823 Bathurst circular dispatch prompted by Buxton's 1823 speech] no disturbance had taken place."[81] The contrast in circumstances between Demerara and neighboring Berbice in 1823 seemed to confirm the abolitionist position. "The Governor of Berbice, on receiving Lord Bathurst's dispatch, very judiciously employed a missionary to explain its purport to the slaves, and to address to them the necessary precautions and qualifications. At Berbice all has remained tranquil. Such was not the course pursued in Demerara."[82] To deflect guilt, abolitionists insisted on the potentially positive effect of the measures they sponsored and blamed the Demerara revolt on the failure of the colonial authorities to comply with the instructions they received.

Buxton also had much to say on the servile warfare issue following the rebellion in Demerara. In one of his earlier statements, Buxton took the line that abolitionists' activities were not connected to the revolt. Writing from Cromer Hall to James Mackintosh on November 30, 1823, Buxton stated, "I am . . . I must confess, alarmed, not at the reproach which is heaped on me, nor at the danger said to be produced in the West Indies by my motion. I disregard the former and utterly disbelieve the latter."[83] In general, however, the tone of his arguments followed up on the positions he had taken when he had first addressed the issue of slave revolts in the Commons in May. After the Demerara uprising, Buxton was bolder in insisting that the real or imagined threat of servile wars in the colonies was a worthwhile risk of a campaign designed to produce incalculable good for the slaves. Buxton went so far as to position the slave at the core of his argument. He insisted that the slaves did not need to know that

81. Ibid.

82. Society for the Mitigation and Gradual Abolition of Slavery Throughout the British Dominions, "Negro Slavery No. 7, Insurrections of Slaves in the West Indies, Particularly in Demerara," in *Tracts of the Anti-Slavery Society* (London: J. Hatchard and Son, 1823), 56. (Hereafter this item is referred to as "Negro Slavery No. 7.")

83. Buxton (1852), 119.

men in Britain were fighting their cause to encourage them to rebel against slavery.

Buxton did not wash his hands of the Demerara slave rebels. He used the criticisms that the rebellion generated to defend the antislavery position. Buxton emphasized that the campaign he led was a great and noble humanitarian cause on behalf of powerless masses. Admittedly, it was an argument that conjured the image not of the rebel but of Wedgwood's cameo of the suppliant slave pleading for freedom. The abolitionists, however, went on to manipulate the dual image of the slave rebel as the victim/agent of the cause. On February 11, 1824, Buxton wrote that "it is worthwhile to spend one's strength on that which, if it succeeds, will change the condition, almost the nature of 700,000 human beings."[84] Buxton saw himself in the role of advocate "for more than half a million of human beings who cannot supplicate for themselves, and against whom there are many who can canvass and are canvassing stoutly."[85] Buxton reiterated this point by observing that "in the House there were hardly more than half-a-dozen staunch friends to the cause, while 200 members were considered to be more or less directly inimical to it."[86]

This was no exaggeration. From about 1807 to about 1832, the parliamentary strength of those who represented vested interests in the West Indian slave economy was relatively formidable. They constituted a core group of at least twenty-two members in the House of Commons. In the House of Lords, there were eight Jamaican planters, and the West Indian body totaled about eighteen. The antislavery supporters in the British House of Commons never numbered more than twelve. The proslavery faction in Parliament did not enjoy merely a numerical superiority. Henry Brougham commented that "their weight with the government is far more to be dreaded."[87] Barry Higman points out that "personal friendship existed between the Jamaican planter, Charles Ellis, and the prominent Tory politician, George Canning."[88] Ellis was not the only West Indian who influenced Canning. Kathleen Mary Butler writes:

84. Ibid., 124.
85. Ibid., 119.
86. Ibid., 127.
87. Cited in Barry Higman, "The West India 'Interest' in Parliament, 1807–1833," *Historical Studies* 13 (October 1967): 3, 8.
88. Ibid.

At the time of Buxton's motion for abolition, thirty-nine members of Parliament identified with the West India cause; eleven West India merchants, including John Gladstone and Joseph Marryat, represented London and the out ports, while the remaining twenty-eight members were the absentee owners of colonial estates ... Joseph Marryat owned estates in Jamaica, Trinidad, Grenada, St. Lucia and British Guiana and Gladstone had interests in seven properties in British Guiana and six in Trinidad ... as an active member of the Liverpool West Indian Association, Gladstone exerted considerable influence over George Canning, the Foreign Minister and Member of Parliament for Liverpool.[89]

In the eyes of the slavery agitators, the risk they were taking was necessary. Should they neglect to rally, the slaves would be left entirely to the merciless power of their masters. Buxton, consequently, saw his persistence as a pledge to his self-imposed humanitarian obligations to the slaves.

Despite the nobility of the position he took after the Demerara slave revolt, Buxton was alive as any other abolitionist to the infamy that was heaped upon the antislavery campaign in Britain in the 1820s. As soon as the abolitionists had taken the step to raise the question of gradual emancipation, a major slave revolt erupted in one of the colonies. Buxton, however, did not wilt under the pressure. The events in Demerara brought renewed attacks from the West India interest, and the ministers of the crown determined not to follow through with the May 1823 slave reform measures except in the crown colony of Trinidad. Buxton insisted, nevertheless, that rebellion should not block the march of freedom. In 1824 he declared: "I know that I call down upon myself the evident animosity of an exasperated and most powerful party. I know how reproaches have rung in my ears, since that pledge [to introduce the May 1823 slave reforms in all the British West Indian colonies] was given, and how they ring with ten-fold fury, now that I call for its fulfilment."[90] His courageous and impressive-sounding response was, "Let them ring. I will not purchase for myself a base indemnity with such a thing as this in my conscience."[91] On

89. Butler (1995), 8–9.
90. *Hansard's Parliamentary Debates,* new ser., 10 (March 16, 1824): 1115.
91. Ibid.

February 12, 1824, Buxton wrote a letter to a friend, "I much question whether there is a more unpopular individual than myself in the House just at this moment. For this I do not care."[92] Charles Buxton reported that in the aftermath of the Demerara slave rebellion, one of his father's friends asked him, "What shall I say when I hear people abusing you? He replied, You good folks think too much of your good name. Do right, and right will be done to you."[93] Thomas Fowell Buxton was determined that "if this fear [of slave rebellion] were well grounded, the English Government ought not to be terrified by it from examining into the infinitely greater evil in question."[94] He confirmed this opinion when he wrote: "I wish it to be distinctly understood that it is my firm and unalterable resolution to devote all my life and my efforts to advocating the cause of the slaves; and that I will persist in that course in spite of opposition, unpopularity, obloquy or falsehood."[95]

After the Demerara slave revolt of 1823, Buxton developed an argument that had only been hinted at by other abolitionists in the attempt to distance antislavery in Britain from slave revolts in the colonies. He argued that slavery was evil and naturally provoked the slaves to resist. Unique in its perspective at the time, it was an argument that aided in shifting the abolitionists' slave rebellion discourse away from the defensive strategy from which it emerged. It focused on the person of the slave. At length Buxton reflected: "He sees the mother of his children stripped naked before the gang of male Negroes and flogged unmercifully; he sees his children sent to market to be sold at the best price they will fetch; he sees in himself, not a man, but a thing—by West Indian law a chattel; an implement of husbandry, a machine to produce sugar, a beast of burden! And will any man tell me that the Negro, with all this staring him in the face, flashing in his eyes, when he rises in the morning and when he goes to bed at night—never dreams that there is injustice in such treatment till he sits himself down to the perusal of an English newspaper and there, to his astonishment, discovers that there are enthusiasts in England who from the bottom of their hearts deplore and abhor all Negro slavery!"[96]

92. Buxton (1852), 124.
93. Ibid., 125.
94. Ibid., 107.
95. *Hansard's Parliamentary Debates,* new ser., 13 (1832): 1285.
96. *Hansard's Parliamentary Debates,* new ser., 11 (March 16, 1824): 359.

Wilberforce, preparing to retire from Parliament at this time, exulted in the speech. He remarked, "Short and not sweet indeed, but excellent."[97] The speech carried more conviction than other attempts to prove that humanitarian activity was partially but not fundamentally responsible for causing slave revolts. Abolitionist investigation into the Demerara rising produced a convincing doctrine that the root cause of slave rebellion was slavery itself and that the greatest opponent of slavery was the slave. Slaves doomed the British West Indian pre-emancipation society, in its unmitigated form, to the perpetual threat of servile warfare.

The speech had the effect of reversing the direction of the accusing finger that the planters pointed at the abolitionists. Buxton condemned the obstructionist tactics that colonists employed against the religious and moral instructions of the slaves. He mocked the colonists' claims that slaves were in the habit of reading newspapers to follow events taking place in Britain on their behalf. He was acquainted with the extent to which planters opposed the education of slaves. Missionaries of the sectarian churches, who arrived in the colonies by the end of the eighteenth century to impart moral and religious instructions to the slaves, were routinely persecuted by the plantocracy. Sometimes they were denied licenses or these were revoked, their hours of contact with slaves were curtailed, and, especially following slave rebellions, their properties were razed and they were chased from the islands.[98] Above all, they were strictly forbidden to teach slaves to read. Rev. John Smith of the London Missionary Society, who worked among the slaves of the East Coast of Demerara, was forced to abandon his views on slave literacy to meet those of the plantation establishment. In their initial interview, Governor Murray frowned on Smith and sharply declared, "If ever you teach a Negro to read, and I hear of it, I will banish you from the colony immediately."[99] How then was it possible, the abolitionists wondered, for the slaves to gather subversive ammunition for their plans of rebellion from abolitionist literature? This question would ultimately prove to be the weakest link in an otherwise solid attempt to substantiate the claim that the British anti-

97. Wilberforce and Wilberforce (1838), 5:178.

98. Andrew Thomson, *Substance of the Speech Delivered at the Meeting of the Edinburgh Society for the Abolition of Slavery, on October 19, 1830* (Edinburgh: William Whyte and Co., 1830), 20–21. See also *Facts and Documents,* 5–18.

99. Wallbridge (1848), 22. See also *The London Missionary Society's Report,* 76.

slavery campaign was not primarily responsible for slave revolts. Planters were able to demonstrate that despite the general illiteracy that existed among slaves, they were able to gather information from local newspapers.[100]

The crucial point that Buxton made was that the slaves' rebellion was an undeniable manifestation of their intrinsic humanity. Buxton insistently implied that no race of the human species, not even black slaves stripped entirely of worth and dignity, would continuously and completely subject itself to acts of inhumanity. Slaves were not entirely objects of slavery. By rebelling, they actively responded to the conditions of their daily lives. Rebellion was unmistakably a response of the human spirit. In these reflections, Buxton, like Wilberforce before him, had exercised a measure of faith in the ability and willingness of slaves to shape their own destiny. Wilberforce's acknowledgment of this sentiment was clearly expressed in his 1807 *Letter to the Inhabitants of Yorkshire*. It was also a view that had been expressed by abolitionist Percival Stockdale in the immediate aftermath of the great St. Domingue slave rebellion of 1791. Wilberforce reasoned, "Negroes are men; that as men, they are subjected to human passions; that they can feel when they are injured; that they can conceive and meditate, and mature, can combine and concert, and at length proceed to execute with vigour what they have planned with policy."[101]

Abolitionists did not readily accept that the role of ideas, especially abolitionist ideas, made a mark on the resistance movement of the slaves. It was easier to believe that slave revolt was an emotional rather than an intellectual response to enslavement. By placing the slaves' emotions at the center of their rebellions, however, abolitionists were unable to deny that slaves exercised their ability to reason and to formulate and execute strategies against the system that they abhorred.

Essentially, the abolitionists' defensive arguments vacillated between outright rejection of proslavery charges and acceptance of limited re-

100. After the Barbados slave revolt, Pallmer, British M.P., had produced evidence to confirm that slaves were in the habit of reading, or paying others to read for them, information on the slavery debate carried in the local newspapers. See *Hansard's Parliamentary Debates*, new ser., 34 (June 19, 1816): 1171. This trend continued during the Demerara and Jamaican slave rebellions.

101. Wilberforce (1807), 252.

sponsibility for slave revolts. Both positions were taken to insist that their humanitarian campaign on behalf of the slaves was a noble undertaking. Their defensive arguments, however, soon caused the abolitionists to consider the slaves' role in their own rebellion. Open rebellion among the slaves in the midst of an era of abolitionists' attacks on slavery intensified proslavery accusations. In turn, these accusations led to the emergence of defensive abolitionist arguments. The continuous probing for a solid anti-slavery defense moved the abolitionist discourse on to its next stage. What began as a discourse to refute proslavery accusations of stirring slave rebellion soon produced an abolitionist articulation of the nature of slave rebellions.

3

THE OTHER SIDE OF SLAVE REVOLTS

The attempt to satisfactorily interpret the nineteenth-century slave rebellions in the British West Indies presents the historian with great difficulties. Generally uneducated, slave rebels were unable to leave records articulating their own perception of rebellion. The slave records that do exist, largely in the form of court-martial testimonies, are scarcely reliable. Elizabeth Johnson accurately captures the epistemological disadvantages of working with sources "obtained under conditions of duress. For the slaves involved testimonies were often extracted through torture and almost always with the understanding that survival depended upon the statements they made to the judges."[1] Planters dominated contemporaneous writings about slave revolts, and their skewed interpretations have led Hilary Beckles to charge that such proslavery writings were "negrophobic descriptions and commentaries . . . based on racist notions of angry and savage blacks in vengeful and mindless lust for blood and white women."[2] Presenting the slaves' personal struggle in a more positive light, Eugene Genovese postulates that slaves did not always react in a primitive manner to the hostile conditions of their enslavement when they revolted. The pattern of their recurrent resistance shifted over the years from a basic attempt to destroy their masters and escape enslavement to a conscious revolutionary struggle aimed at overthrowing the slavery system altogether.[3] Michael Craton, whose studies on slave resistance focus on the English colonies, argues that historians subscribing to Genovese's analysis have overstated the case. The essence of Craton's position is that by the nineteenth century the largely creolized British West Indian slave

1. Elizabeth Johnson, "The Historiography of Slave Rebellion: Cuba in a Hemispheric Perspective," *Journal of Caribbean History* 31, nos. 1 and 2 (1977): 103.

2. Hilary Beckles, "Caribbean Anti-Slavery: The Self-Liberation Ethos of Enslaved Blacks," in *Caribbean Slavery in the Atlantic World,* ed. Verene Shepherd and Hilary Beckles (Jamaica: Ian Randle Publishers, 2001), 871.

3. Genovese (1979), chap. 1.

populations sharply perceived strengths and weaknesses in the local colonial status quo. Thus they could make reasonable predictions about the most opportune times to take up arms against their masters and demand their freedom.[4]

Contemporaneous writings and current scholarship have presented a variety of interpretations of the nature of slave resistance. There still exists a failure to articulate satisfactorily the context within which the leaders of the British antislavery movement located slave rebellions. British abolitionists, however, did offer considerable commentary on the major nineteenth-century slave rebellions in the British West Indies. Abolitionists' characterization of slave revolts, while not quite as radical as Genovese's mature revolutionary interpretation, favorably depicted the protest actions of rebel slaves. Abolitionists read the admittedly faulty records and presented their version of the attributes that constituted a slave rebellion, a version that challenged the accounts of their opponents. This chapter examines the manner in which abolitionists depicted the rebellions of nineteenth-century slaves in the British West Indies.

THE ST. DOMINGUE BOGEY

When news of the 1816 Barbados slave revolt reached the British public and Parliament, it seemed that the planters could not but prevail in their goal of silencing the slavery reformers. The revolt appeared to justify predictions that discussion of the slavery question and attempts to reform colonial plantation society would inevitably end in disaster. To the planters, Barbados 1816 was the realization of their fears that the horror of the 1791 St. Domingue slave revolt had come to the British West Indies. St. Domingue had won notoriety among the British for being a place where vengeful and savage black slaves massacred their masters, razed their property, and spread crippling anxiety among the white population. Reports of events in the former French territory often depicted "garish images of rebellion . . . white captives hung from trees with hooks through their chains; men sawn in half; children impaled; women raped on the corpse of their husbands and fathers; hundreds of plantations ablaze."[5]

4. Craton (1982), 14.
5. David Geggus, *Slavery, War and Revolution: The British Occupation of St Domingue, 1793–1798* (Oxford: Clarendon, 1982), 88.

Historian W. F. Finalson records that *Allison's History of Europe* was regularly quoted in recreating the horror of St. Domingue.

> Twenty thousand Negroes broke into the city, and, with the torch in one hand and the sword in the other, spread slaughter and devastation around. The Europeans found themselves surrounded by the vengeance which had been accumulating for centuries in the African heart. Neither age nor sex was spared; the young were cut down in trying to defend their homes; the aged in the churches where they had fled to implore protection; virgins were immolated on the altar; weeping infants were hurled into the fires. Amid the shrieks of the sufferers, and the shouts of the victors, the finest city of the West Indies was reduced to ashes; its splendid churches, its stately palaces, were rapt in flames. Thirty thousand human beings perished in the massacre.[6]

Proslavery literature about St. Domingue outraged the European world, not just absentee plantation proprietors in Britain and their colleagues in the British West Indies. In the British Parliament, the agent for the colony of Grenada, Mr. Baille, underlined the atrocities that the white colonists suffered at the hands of the "Negroes." Mr. Baille reiterated that St. Domingue slaves had caused "the destruction of the most valuable colony in the world, the massacre of its inhabitants, the ravaging of the most beautiful part of the creation . . . the unnatural murder of fathers by the hand of their own children."[7] The devastation was indeed extensive, especially economically. St. Domingue at that time was the richest colonial possession of France and was more valuable to France's overseas trade than were all of the British islands to Britain. According to Bakpetu Thompson, "St. Domingue was the greatest supplier in the world of sugar, coffee, cocoa, cotton, spices and precious wood. Vessels of various nations visited and traded with the colony, the turnover amounting to two-thirds of France's overseas trade."[8] The greater portion of the colony's

6. W. F. Finalson, *The History of the Jamaican Case Being an Account Founded upon Official Documents of the Rebellion of the Negroes in Jamaica the Cause Which led to it and the Measures Taken for Its Suppression, the Agitation Excited on the Subject Its Causes and Its Character and the Debates in Parliament, and the Criminal Persecution, Arising out of It* (London: Chapman and Hall, 1869), viii, quoted from *Allison's History of Europe,* vol. 8, 77.

7. *Parliamentary History of England* (London: T. C. Hansard, n.d.), 29:1074.

8. Bakpetu Thompson, *The Making of the African Diaspora in the Americas, 1442–*

riches was virtually reduced to ashes in the flames kindled by slaves in rebellion. British colonial planters were confident that the St. Domingue revolt, with its record of economic as well as social and political devastation, had placed them in an indomitable position while wrecking the
morale of antislavery agitators. Reginald Coupland describes the essence
of the warning that British West Indian planters arrogantly directed to the
abolitionists in the wake of St. Domingue.

> A concrete example of the risk inherent in tampering with the estab-
> lished order of society in the West Indies was provided by the effects
> of the Revolution in the French islands and especially the French sec-
> tion of St. Domingue. In the course of 1791, that populous and fertile
> colony was plunged into anarchy and bloodshed. First the French
> Royalists fought the French Republicans: then the mulattos rose, de-
> manding equality with the whites; and finally the slaves, some 100,000
> strong, let loose the horrors of a servile war. About 2,000 whites were
> massacred. Over 1,000 plantations were destroyed . . . And the moral
> of St. Domingue was "Look what comes of undermining the old and
> natural subordination of blacks to whites with 'Jacobin ideas.'"[9]

The inconsistency in the figures for the death toll and material destruction recorded by varying sources does not corrupt the reliability of
the general impression that the devastation in St. Domingue (later renamed Haiti) was astounding. Jack Gratus observes that for West Indian
planters and merchants, "St. Domingue was the answer to every measure
of reform proposed by the abolitionists."[10] It was also the awful memory
that planters and merchants resurrected whenever slaves in the British
West Indies revolted against their masters in the first three decades of the
nineteenth century. Consequently, slavery supporters were confident that
in the wake of the 1816 Barbados revolt, it would only be a matter of time
before the British antislavery initiative withered. They certainly did not
expect that antislavery advocates could redeem the image of slaves in rebellion.

British abolitionists' commentary on the St. Domingue rebellion did

---

1900 (Harlow, Essex: Longman, 1987), 304; for the wealth of prerevolutionary St. Domingue, see also C. L. R. James, *The Black Jacobins: Toussaint L'Ouverture and the San
Domingo Revolution* (London: Allison and Busby Ltd., 1938), 55.

    9. Coupland (1933), 96.

    10. Gratus (1973), 91.

not stress the atrocities that white colonists suffered at the hands of the "Negroes." While abolitionists expressed alarm about the injurious impact of the overwhelming negative publicity about the revolt, they also used it to warn against the folly of Britain's continued involvement in the British West African slave trade. They blamed the eruption of the revolt on the extreme severity with which the white slave owners of St. Domingue treated their slaves.

Just prior to his address to the British Parliament in March 1792, William Wilberforce had written to fellow abolitionist Thomas Babington, sharing his concern that he had found people stricken by events in "St. Domingo." Wilberforce despaired that on account of the rising in the French territory, the number of antislavery opponents in Britain was growing.[11] Writing to Samuel Hoare, another abolitionist, Wilberforce was openly pessimistic in assessing the impact of St. Domingue on the British antislavery cause. He was "fully aware that the insurrection of St. Domingo would create some alarm amongst the friends of abolition."[12] Wilberforce did not add his voice to the defamation of the St. Domingue slave rebels of 1791, and he was able to rise to the challenge of meeting and opposing proslavery descriptions of the rising. Nevertheless, even Wilberforce could not resist becoming dubious over the prospects of the antislavery movement in the face of negative publicity.

Other abolitionists focused less on the problems that the rebellion had posed for the British antislave trade movement and more on the manner in which it served to strengthen the cause. On the heels of the rising, abolitionist Percival Stockdale wrote to veteran humanitarian Granville Sharp, justifying and defending the slave rebels of the French colony. Stockdale's reflections encompass a number of views that abolitionists were later to adopt. He insists that the decision of the French slaves to rise against their oppressors was sanctified by the laws of nature, of God, and of man. Stockdale goes on to justify the rebellion by declaring unapologetically that "when a man ceases to be free, he loses the power and the disposition to be virtuous." He argues that the slaves of St. Domingue took up arms against their masters because they were "most vigorously

---

11. Wilberforce and Wilberforce (1838), 1:343.

12. William Wilberforce, *The Correspondence of William Wilberforce,* vol. 1 (London, 1840), 89–90.

and inhumanely treated." Appalled by the manner in which "the Christian narrators of the event, in relating the particular acts of violence of the insurgence, have generally branded them with the term 'savage,'" Stockdale asks, had the insurgents of St. Domingue been Europeans violently resisting oppression and inhumanity, "should not we approve their conduct, or their violence (call it what you please). Should we not crown it with eulogism, if they exterminated their tyrants with fire and sword? Should they deliberately inflict the most exquisite torture on those tyrants, would they not be excusable in the moral judgement of those who properly value . . . personal, rational and religious liberty?"[13]

Thomas Clarkson, although as convinced as Wilberforce about the injury of the rebellion to the British abolitionist struggle, perceived that by rebelling the slaves of St. Domingue were vindicating the unalterable rights of man.[14] Opinions like this caused British abolitionists to be branded as Jacobin radicals, for the doctrine of the rights of man had emerged out of the French Revolution of 1789 and was perceived by many in Britain as extreme and dangerous. A document anonymously written and addressed to William Wilberforce in 1792 continued to justify and positively esteem the decision of the slaves in the French colony to rise. The abolitionist author empathized with the insurgents: "Put yourselves in their place . . . Say, in such a situation, what would you do? This circumstance, dreadful as it is, is a farther proof of a noble spirit, and an exalted mind, that cannot rest quietly in the chain of slavery—it is an evidence of a free born soul."[15] In the immediate aftermath of St. Domingue, Wilberforce was not so open in positively conceptualizing the rebels' actions. He fully agreed, however, as did several other abolitionists, that slavery itself catapulted the slaves into open rebellion. Wilberforce blamed the eruption of the St. Domingue revolt on the evils of the Atlantic slave trade.[16] He had the open support of fellow abolitionist Henry Brougham, who bluntly argued that "the two great causes of the Revolution in St.

13. Percival Stockdale, *A Letter from Percival Stockdale to Granville Sharp Esquire Suggested to the Author by the Present Insurrection of the Negroes in the Island of St. Domingo* (No pub., no date), 17–21. Available at Hull Public Library, England.

14. Turley (1991), 177.

15. Anon., *An Epistle to William Wilberforce Esq. Written During the Disturbances in the West Indies* (London: Darton and Harvey, 1792), ix.

16. *Parliamentary History of England* (n.d.), 29:1061.

Domingo have been the rapid importation of Negroes during the previous years and the extreme ill treatment of the whole flock of slaves in that ill-fated colony."[17]

British abolitionists extracted a clear message from the rebellion of slaves in St. Domingue that reinforced the strength of their campaign. Rebellion in the French West Indian slave possessions would bring similar disaster to the British West Indies if the servile regime remained unreformed. Brougham stated that "the planters have now to choose between the surrender of the Slave Trade and the sacrifice of their possessions . . . The events of the Negro War have led to a revolution, complete, and in all appearance permanent; connected with the Slave Trade more nearly than as a warning example; and calculated to prescribe, with more than the force of argument, the necessity of instantly abolishing that destructive commerce."[18] British abolitionists rejected allegations that humanitarian interference with the institution of slavery was responsible for the calamities and would produce the same effect in the British colonies. This defensive position was reenacted during the major slave risings in the British West Indies in the nineteenth century. Similarly, British abolitionists' conceptualization of the St. Domingue slave rebellion set the pace for their later commentary on the pre-emancipation West Indian slave revolts.

DEVOID OF TERROR

As discussed in chapter 2, William Wilberforce took a defensive and self-exculpatory position in the wake of the Barbados slave revolt of 1816. This position, however, did not cover the full range of the abolitionists' attempts to come to terms with what the slaves had done. The self-defensive argument was merely the brief prelude of a discourse that proved to cover diverse perspectives. In an anonymously published tract, *Remarks on the Insurrection in Barbados and the Bill for the Registration of Slaves,* an abolitionist was careful to point out that the rising of the slaves in Barbados bore no resemblance to proslavery commentaries on the St. Domingue revolt. The author admitted that "the insurrection in Barbados had indeed, been a great and deplorable calamity"[19] but di-

17. Henry Brougham, *A Concise Statement of the Question Regarding the Abolition of the Slave Trade* (London: J. Hatchard and T. N. Longman, 1804), 67.

18. Ibid., 76, 78.

19. *Remarks,* 6.

THE OTHER SIDE OF SLAVE REVOLTS

vested the revolt of the sharp and repulsive edges typical of planters' descriptions of such events. The writer asserted that the plot was not preconceived and was far from extensive, as it encompassed only the four southern parishes of St. George, Christ Church, St. Phillip, and St. John.[20] This observation was not made with the intention of undermining the significance of the rebellion but to distinguish between the nature of the slaves' actions in Barbados in 1816 and the resistance movements prior to the nineteenth century. During the slave-trade controversy, abolitionists believed that rebellion in the colonies would cease if fresh recruits from Africa were no longer imported. Wilberforce had argued then that "the annual importation into the West Indian colonies of a great number of human beings, from a thousand different parts of the continent with all their varieties of languages, and manners, and customs, many of them resenting their wrongs, and burning with revenge; others deeply feeling their loss of country and freedom, and the new hardship of their altered state; must have a natural tendency to keep the whole mass into which they are brought, in a state of ferment."[21]

When the predominantly Creole slave populations took up arms against their masters after the abolition of the slave trade, abolitionists' theory regarding the ethnicity of participants in slave rebellions was shattered. It was now clear that all slaves, regardless of their origin, contemplated active resistance. The author of *Remarks,* perhaps embarrassed or bewildered by the occurrence of revolts during the antislavery era, altered his position. The ethnicity of the rebels might be mixed, but the later rebellion did not inspire the same dread as had previous uprisings. The slaves of Barbados were so miserably armed that even if their intention was to inflict grievous bodily harm upon their masters, they were incapable of doing so. "What weapons the Negroes were armed with, we do not learn: had they been able to procure firearms and ammunition it would naturally have been mentioned."[22] Historians have pointed out that the slaves in Barbados were only equipped with sharp-edged instruments that necessitated close-range fighting.[23] They had broken into the residence of "a Mr. Bayne, who kept a dry goods and hardware [store],

20. Ibid.
21. Wilberforce (1807), 242.
22. *Remarks,* 6.
23. R. H. Schomburgk, *The History of Barbados* (London: Frank Cass and Co., 1971), 65.

and armed themselves with bills, axes, cutlasses and whatever edged instruments they could lay hold of."[24]

On April 16 on Bailley's plantation, where most of the action occurred, a lopsided confrontation took place between the rebels and the forces commanded by Colonel Codd. Codd controlled the garrison of St. Anne and commanded the local militia that crushed the rebellion. He had a fighting column of 400 white regulars, 200 men of the First Bourbon West India regiment, and 250 local militiamen. Against this formidable force, abolitionists wrote, were pitted the inexperienced and poorly prepared slave rebels whose strategies were unclear and devoid of central leadership. The author of Remarks underscored the pitiable maneuvers of the rebels, observing that they acted "so stupidly and irrationally as to employ themselves solely in burning the cane pieces in a particular spot . . . then to stand by their separate bonfires till their enemies arrived to destroy them."[25] Barbadian colonists had little to dread from their slaves. This abolitionist emphasis challenged the findings of the committee appointed by the Barbados House of Assembly to investigate the causes and the course of the 1816 slave revolt. One section of the committee's report stated, "the four largest and most valuable parishes were exposed to the ravages of the insurgents."[26] Members of the investigative committee strove to depict the slaves as wild and insensate villains. Like their ancestors, the 1816 slave rebels were blind in their destruction and violence. The author of Remarks, on the contrary, reserved doubts about applying the stereotypical image of slave rebels to the Barbados rising.

Wilberforce's address on the Barbados revolt in the British House of Commons was strikingly developed along the lines adopted by the author of Remarks. Wilberforce had gone so far in diluting the terror with which slave revolts were commonly associated that he was censored by proslavery M.P.s. Mr. Pallmer attacked Wilberforce, observing that his "speech . . . had lightly touched upon the ruined families, the desolated property and the lives lost in Barbados, and it had concluded with a jocularity

24. Codd to Leith, April 25, 1816, CO 28/85, ff. 12, Colonial Office Papers; Craton (1982), 395.

25. Remarks, 7.

26. The Report from A Select Committee to the House of Assembly, Appointed to inquire into the Origins, Causes and Progress of the Late Insurrection (Barbados: W. Walker, Mercury and Gazette Office, 1818), 3.

which he (Mr. Pallmer) thought was not very suited to the subject."[27] Mr. A. C. Grant was also upset about the way Wilberforce dismissed "those horrible events which have recently occurred in Barbados. Most assuredly, Sir, the learned member did speak in very light terms of the insurrection; he asked 'what, after all, was the extent of the evils, falsely attributed by us to the introduction of the Registry Bill last session, but a riot, quickly suppressed, in which two or three estates suffered.'"[28]

Certainly, the revolt did not last for more than three days, but the economic losses endured by planters were extensive. After setting on fire the trash heap on Bailley's plantation, which was the signal for the simultaneous outbreak of the revolt, "the trash heaps and cane fields on every estate in the upper part of the parish of St. Phillip were also set on fire. The fire spread during the whole night from field to field, from one estate to another."[29] The slave-ignited properties on several plantations in several parishes included Harrow, Bushby Park, Oughterson's the Thicket, Three Houses, and the Grove in St. Phillip, St. John, and St. George.[30] The committee investigating the revolt reported that damage to property caused by the slaves' arson amounted to £175,000, which was roughly equivalent to 25 percent of the year's sugarcane crop. Looting of property also accompanied the revolt, and shipping was restricted for some time.[31] It is almost certain that one factor influencing abolitionists' lenient depiction of the revolt, despite its record of economic devastation, was that it coincided with the campaigners' efforts on behalf of the slaves. Although they often refused to acknowledge their limited role in the revolts, it was not impossible that abolitionists reserved doubts about their subversive impact. Consequently, it was to their advantage to ignore or at least play down the economic ruin that slaves in rebellion unleashed on planters' property and to stress that planters' traditional accounts of the conduct of rebellious slaves were no longer relevant by the final years of slavery.

27. *Hansard's Parliamentary Debates,* new ser., 34 (June 19, 1816): 1168.
28. Ibid., 1222.
29. Schomburgk (1971), 395.
30. Ibid., 396–397.
31. Codd to Leith, April 25, 1816, CO 28/85, ff. 11–12, Colonial Office Papers; Beckles (1987), 89.

PRESSED BY AN INTOLERABLE WEIGHT

Wilberforce carefully probed among the scanty records available on the Barbados slave revolt of 1816 and emerged with a slave-centered depiction that has been scarcely recognized. Perhaps still attempting to disprove the planters' allegations, Wilberforce found a satisfactory explanation for the revolt by focusing on slaves' suffering. He confessed that the revolt represented "a conduct which, though it was to be lamented, and could not be justified, nevertheless admitted of explanation."[32] He could not condemn altogether the rebels and their admittedly counterproductive actions. Appealing to justice and humanity, hallmarks of the British anti-slavery movement, Wilberforce concluded, "that degraded race [was] pressed by a weight which they felt intolerable."[33] They were pushed into an act of desperation by "a class of people that did not so much consult the feelings or comforts of the slaves as in our other colonies."[34] Wilberforce reasoned, just as the slaves undoubtedly would, that in slavery lay the evil that prompted the irresistible stimulus to rebellion. He arrived at this sympathetic depiction after eliminating the mundane explanations that planters had repeatedly offered. Wilberforce reasoned, "They had no temptation to revolt from the peculiar nature of the country furnishing them with the means of concealment, nor could they have any sanguine hopes of success from the disproportion between themselves and the white inhabitants. There were no mountains, forests or great inequalities of surface in the island, and there was a considerable military force."[35] Wilberforce was keen on identifying the unique factor that set the Barbados slave revolt in a category of its own. The local conditions of the island hardly provided an answer. Regrettably, Wilberforce failed to declare simply that Barbados slaves revolted because they wanted to be free. He concluded, nevertheless, that "impatience under suffering, rather than hopes from revolt might be supposed to have stimulated them to the conduct they pursued."[36] Prefiguring Genovese's assessment of earlier slave revolts in the British West Indies, Wilberforce ended up believing that slaves in Barba-

32. *Hansard's Parliamentary Debates,* new ser., 34 (June 19, 1816): 1156.
33. Ibid., 1160.
34. Ibid.
35. Ibid.
36. Ibid.

dos were prompted by "desperation against extreme severity, hunger and the denial of privileges."[37]

Of course, the Barbadian planter class challenged Wilberforce's analysis. They rejected the suggestion that material deprivation stimulated the slaves' action. Their contradiction of this aspect of Wilberforce's interpretation seems a more accurate representation of the slaves' motivation. John Beckles, speaker of the House of the Assembly in Barbados, stated that just prior to the revolt, "the slaves had comfortable homes, were well fed and were well taken care of."[38] The committee investigating the causes and course of the revolt reinforced this view. It claimed that the 1816 harvest was abundant, especially in St. Phillip where the revolt began, and that a liberal allowance of corn and other provisions was proffered to the "Negroes."[39] Anthony Wiltshire has also been convinced that "the revolt . . . did not have its roots in bad treatment but involved a spirit of rising expectations unfulfilled."[40] Colonel Codd insisted in his report that when he inquired if ill treatment influenced the slaves, they consistently denied the suggestion.[41] It seems that on the eve of the Barbados rebellion, slaves were as comfortable as they could possibly be in slavery. That better treatment of slaves was no guarantee against rebellion, however, was a point that not even the abolitionists had yet grasped.[42] The slaves' aspirations had gone past the desire to acquire whatever material comforts their masters offered. Ironically, in at least one aspect, the planters' assessment of the revolt cast the rebels in a more revolutionary mold than that of the abolitionists. The planters admitted, blindly perhaps, that the revolt manifested not protest against bad treatment but the slaves' impatient desire to enjoy a freedom that seemed guaranteed.

Wilberforce had introduced to the House of Commons on June 19, 1816, a motion for the implementation of slave registration in the crown

---

37. Genovese (1979), 4.

38. Cited in Beckles (1987), 92.

39. Ibid.

40. Wiltshire (1983), 14.

41. Codd to Leith, April 25, 1816, CO 28/85, ff. 14, Colonial Office Papers.

42. Governor Sir James Leith seemed to have grasped this point, for he commented that "The planters of Barbados . . . had flattered themselves that the general good treatment of the slaves would have prevented their resorting to violence." Leith to Bathurst, April 30, 1816, CO 28/85, ff. 8, Colonial Office Papers.

and legislative colonies. He had resolved to avoid the question of slave rebellion in Barbados. He ended his address, however, by confessing that
"he had gone further than he had intended when he entered the House."[43]
In spite of Wilberforce's failure or reluctance to recognize the full extent
of the slaves' political aspirations in Barbados, his statements clearly
marked the revolt as the beginning of a new era in slave rising. Wilberforce went past merely defending abolitionists against the accusations of
slavery advocates and broadened the scope of the abolitionists' reflections
on slave revolts. It was not the last time that the abolitionists were to
speak extensively and favorably in interpreting the slaves' violent opposition.

RISING ANTISLAVERY FERVOR

By the time slaves in Demerara revolted in 1823, antislavery activities had
widened considerably.[44] Consequently, other abolitionists were in a far
better position than was Wilberforce, who was on his way out of the
movement, to analyze the position of slaves in rebellion. Thomas Clarkson, who worked indefatigably for the cause outside of Parliament, wrote
that by 1822, "the eyes of the friends of Africa began to be turned . . . to
slavery in the British colonies as the next evil to be subdued."[45] He confessed, however, that "they were obliged to go about their work at first,
as silently as they could . . . every member was pledged to secrecy."[46]
Eventually, "they found themselves strong enough to come forth and an-
nounce their measures as well as their undertaking to the public . . . on
the 31st of January 1823."[47] On that day, the London Society for the Mitigation and Gradual Abolition of Slavery, also called the Anti-Slavery Society or the Committee on Slavery, held its first meeting at the Kings Head
Tavern Poultry in London.[48] Soon, branch or corresponding societies were
established throughout England, Wales, and Scotland. On May 15, 1823,
the movement's new leader, Thomas Fowell Buxton, moved in the Com-

---

43. *Hansard's Parliamentary Debates,* new ser., 34 (June 19, 1816), 1160.

44. Northcott (1976), 65.

45. Manuscript essay, December 1824, CN 33, p. 110, Thomas Clarkson Papers.

46. Ibid., 111.

47. Ibid.

48. Committee on Slavery Minute Book, January 1823, p. 1, MSS. Brit. Emp. S. 20, E2/1,
Anti-Slavery Society Papers.

mons for the immediate emancipation of the children of slaves. Buxton also called for the implementation of reforms that would gradually prepare the older slaves for eventual freedom. Rising fervor was also manifested in the launching of the *Anti-Slavery Monthly Reporter* in 1823. This magazine became an important organ of abolitionist propaganda both to parliamentarians and to such as constituted the antislavery public. Zachary Macaulay began editing the *Reporter* in 1825. It was within this framework of a relatively radicalized British antislavery campaign that the slaves of Demerara rebelled on August 18, 1823.

THE DUTY TO REBEL

Just prior to the rising in Demerara, an article appeared in the February 1823 *Edinburgh Review* expressing an extremely radical view on slave rebellions. It stated that, in principle, slaves were justified in confronting their masters with arms demanding their freedom. "If one man or a class of men pretend to absolute dominion over the mass of their fellow creatures . . . it is quite manifest that the people are fully justified in rising up and, if it be needful, in utterly destroying them. But far more unrighteous is the horrible attempt at making property of man, holding them in the state of personal slavery or treating them as cattle or as inanimate objects, the absolute property of their owners. To terminate a state so repugnant to every principle, so abhorrent to all the feeling of our nature, is clearly and undeniably not merely a right, but an imperative duty."[49] Never before had a leading male abolitionist taken such a revolutionary position on slave resistance in the colonies. The closest that abolitionists came to such declarations was when they quoted a toast made by Dr. Johnson on a visit to Oxford, in which he proposed "success to the next revolt of Negroes in the West Indies."[50] When abolitionist James Mackintosh quoted Dr. Johnson in 1824, he was careful to stress that he was no champion of slave rebellion.[51]

Many of the contributions in the *Edinburgh Review* were anonymously submitted, but there is much evidence that Henry Brougham was the author of the incendiary article. Chester New, Brougham's biographer,

49. *Edinburgh Review* 28, no. 75 (February 1823): 169.
50. *Hansard's Parliamentary Debates,* new ser., 11 (June 1, 1824): 1046.
51. Ibid.

has noted that "the most prolific authors [of the *Edinburgh Review*] . . . Jeffrey, Brougham and Sydney Smith, often revealed their own authorship in letters written at the time."[52] Furthermore, New states that "the cause of the Negro slave was supported by articles in about half of the numbers of the *Edinburgh Review* . . . Nearly all were written by Brougham."[53] Correspondence between James Stephen Sr. and Brougham shows that the two were on the verge of ending their friendship as a result of Brougham's review of a paper written by Stephen. Brougham refused to acknowledge his authorship of the contentious article, but Stephen pressed him, "knowing as I do from yourself that the articles on the Slave Trade in the *Edinburgh Review* are generally, if not always, your own."[54] This information is significant because Brougham's anonymously published work on slavery expressed far more extreme views than those in which his authorship was clearly revealed. By June 1824, when Brougham examined the revolt of the slaves in Demerara, he expressed a view completely opposite to that in the February 1823 *Edinburgh Review*. Brougham asserted in the more formal forum of the House of Commons that "sudden, unprepared emancipation . . . effected by violent measures . . . would inflict the severest misery on those beings whose condition is already too wretched to require . . . any increase of calamity . . . emancipation must be the work of time, and, above all, must not be forcibly wrested from their masters."[55] Brougham's inconsistency suggests that he had not entirely resolved in his mind that it was wrong for slaves to rebel to obtain freedom. The discrepancy between his anonymous writings and his more public speeches indicates that Brougham harbored extreme attitudes about slave rebellion that he did not dare to reveal openly in defiance of the largely conservative principles of his abolitionist associates.

ONE REMARKABLE CIRCUMSTANCE

The general tone of Brougham's contextualization of the Demerara slave revolt of 1823 is contained in two marathon speeches he delivered in the

---

52. Chester New, *The Life of Henry Brougham to 1830* (Oxford: Clarendon, 1967), 419.

53. Ibid., 131.

54. Sir James Stephen to Henry Brougham, January 27, 1815 (26065), Henry Brougham Papers.

55. *Hansard's Parliamentary Debates*, new ser., 11 (June 1, 1824), 966.

House of Commons on June 1 and 11, 1824. A number of his other works repeated the main ideas expressed in these speeches, in which his stated objective was to examine the trial and persecution that John Smith, the London missionary to Demerara, endured after the rebellion. Brougham's investigation of Smith's trial opened a window through which the abolitionists perceived the slaves' rebellious experience. Like Wilberforce but with greater boldness, Brougham and others refused to lump the Demerara rebellion with those of the slaves in the pre-abolitionist era. In an article intending to review Smith's trial, the rising of the slaves was referred to as "the late, partial and inconsiderable commotion."[56] The author referred to the slaves' three-day resistance as a "movement" in which, according to the governor's bulletin, one white rifleman was slightly wounded and another was hit in the leg by the crossfire of his own party. The author asked rhetorically, "Now, can any man living believe in a deep laid plot for rising and massacring the whites after reading this result?"[57] The author of *Remarks* groped toward the same conclusion in commenting upon the Barbados slave revolt of 1816. In the House of Commons, Brougham was still skeptical of proslavery descriptions of "the transactions which are called the revolt of Demerara."[58] He rejected the accounts of the planters and accepted instead Reverend Smith's assertion that "the revolt has been unlike every other I have ever heard of or read of. In former revolts in this colony, in Jamaica, in Grenada and in Barbados, blood and massacre were the prominent features. In this a mildness and forbearance, worthy of the faith they professed (however wrong their conduct may have been) were the characteristics."[59] Brougham echoed Smith by declaring that the Demerara revolt was "a memorable peculiarity, to be found in no other passage of Negro warfare within the West Indian seas."[60] Brougham was convinced that Smith had authentically represented the slaves' conduct, adding, "the insurrection stands distinguished

56. *Edinburgh Review* 40, no. 79 (March 1824): 226.

57. Ibid., 246.

58. *Hansard's Parliamentary Debates*, new ser., 11 (June 1, 1824): 990.

59. *British Parliamentary Papers*, vol. 66: *Demerara Minutes of Evidence on the Trial of John Smith a Missionary 1824(158)*, vol. 23 (Shannon, Ireland: Irish University Press, 1969), 95. The entire document spans from pages 51–142.

60. Henry Brougham, *Works of Henry, Lord Brougham*, vol. 10, *Speeches on Social and Political Subjects* (London: Richard Griffin and Company, 1857), 159.

from every other movement of this description in the history of colonial society."[61]

In the planters' eyes slave revolts remained an irredeemable evil and the rebels who participated were murderous cutthroats. The abolitionists were not daunted by these hostile views. Brougham's reading of the event was reinforced by other campaigners. Clarkson, in his address to the gentlemen of Ipswich, was forthright in taking on the challenge of the pro-slavery interests and stated that the planters' alarms were intentionally exaggerated. He noted that the public had been misled by accounts of the insurrection provided by "the Planters only, and unhappily we have no opportunity of getting them from any other quarter . . . they come from persons . . . interested in making the occurrence a handle to prejudice the people of England against us, and to divert them for pursuing the great question of gradual abolition of slavery . . . the accounts have been greatly exaggerated."[62]

Clarkson believed that it was incumbent on the abolitionists to counter the planters' tactic of exaggerating the reports of the revolt by providing their own more reasonable interpretations. He insisted that there was no need to be horrified of the slaves. He recently had heard speaking in Brighton one Mr. Brooks, whom Clarkson introduced to his Ipswich audience as "an eminent minister on a plantation in neighbouring Berbice [who] did not feel the need to flee the territory for in his view all had been quiet at Berbice, and as to the Demerara Insurrection, it had been more magnified than it ought to have been."[63] The question might arise as to why Mr. Brooks was in England three months after the revolt if indeed he was not apprehensive of the state of affairs in the neighboring colony. The possible answers, not provided by Clarkson, are numerous. Nevertheless, Clarkson shared Brougham's conviction that the slaves in Demerara, a ter-

61. Ibid.; *The Missionary Smith—Substance of the Debate in the House of Commons on Tuesday the 1st and Friday the 11th of June 1824 on a Motion of Henry Brougham, Esq. Respecting the Trial and Condemnation to Death by a Court Martial of the Rev. John Smith, Late Missionary in the Colony of Demerara With a Preface Containing Some New Facts Illustrative of the Subject* (London: J. Hatchard and Son, 1824), 38. Hereafter this cite is referred to as *The Missionary Smith*.

62. Address to the gentlemen at Ipswich, December 5, 1823, Thomas Clarkson Papers.

63. Ibid.

ritory where rebellion was no novelty, had embarked on a new and less violent phase of active resistance to slavery.

A COMBINATION OF EUROPEAN WORKMEN

On separate occasions, Brougham, Mackintosh, and the Anti-Slavery Society as a body raised the dignity of the Demerara slave revolt by perceiving within it the features of a European labor protest movement. The society detected that one marked dimension of the so-called rebellion was the slaves' bid to alter their social and economic position within the plantation system. "In Demerara, a slight commotion was occasioned among the Negroes . . . and far more resembling a combination of European workmen to strike for wages, for time or other indulgence than a rebellion of African slaves."[64] Abolitionists' examinations of and commentaries upon the nature of the Demerara revolt dismissed the paranoia that planter accounts brought to it and established a level of esteem for the slaves' resistance. Brougham boosted the respectability that the Demerara revolt was commanding through abolitionists' discourse when he underlined that the slaves were "satisfied with combining not to work . . . to ascertain the precise nature of the boon reported to have arrived from England."[65]

James Mackintosh continued in this line of argument, interpreting the terms used by slaves in their court-martial testimonies to refer to their resistance as a process in labor bargaining. In Mackintosh's explanation the slaves devised "a plan for obliging or 'driving,' as they called it, their managers to join in an application to the governor on the subject of the new law . . . The expedient of a general 'strike' or refusal to work appears to have been the project spoken of most by the slaves."[66] The abolitionists performed a major paradigm relocation in their conceptualization of a slave revolt. They lifted it out of the world of terror and deposited it into a typical British nineteenth-century confrontation between labor and management. The basis for this dimension of abolitionists' analysis was

64. *Edinburgh Review* 41, no. 81 (October 1824): 209.

65. *Hansard's Parliamentary Debates,* new ser., 11 (June 1, 1824): 994.

66. Ibid., 1060. This evidence was based on information provided by the *London Missionary Society's Report* reflecting the testimonies of the slaves Bristol and Seaton, and the Reverend Smith quoting the slave Quamina, 24, 43, and 83.

partly facilitated by the testimony of Colonel Leahy, who was instrumental in the speedy suppression of the revolt. Leahy acknowledged that he learned of the slaves' aspirations to specific improvements in their working and living conditions during a discussion with them just previous to the mopping-up operations that the militia carried out against the slaves. "Some wanted three days and Sunday for church . . . some wanted two days . . . At first there was a demand for freedom . . . then, three days . . . than any thing else."[67] Leahy even testified that he had made a list of the insurgents' demands but had subsequently destroyed it, believing that the document was useless.[68] For abolitionists, the dialogue between slaves and colonial authorities justified their comparison of the conduct of the rebels in Demerara and that of workers at home.

Nineteenth-century Britain was so steeped in the throes of industrial unrest that it was no surprise that abolitionists drew parallels between slave rebellion in the colonies and labor protest activities in the metropolis. From about 1812 to about 1830, just about the time when the major slave revolts erupted in the English colonies, laborers throughout Britain assembled illegally, posted placards, demanded higher wages, wrote threatening letters signed by a Captain Swing, and called for the abolition of the tithe.[69] For agricultural workers, the threshing machine was singled out for attack. Like the cane field in the colonies, the threshing machine was "the symbol of injustice and the prime target of their fury."[70] Many in Britain agreed that the "the great political catalyst of the period was economic distress."[71] Radicals like William Cobbett and the mysterious Swing were blamed for the riots, but many knew that the predisposing factors were "wars, national debt, increased population, corn laws, maladministration of the poor laws [which] had reduced the great mass of the people, and especially the agricultural labourers, to the verge of starvation and despair."[72] Many identified with the plight of the laborers and sympathized with their protest actions. Some abolitionists supported the measures taken by the authorities to curb what they regarded as the ex-

67. *British Parliamentary Papers*, vol. 66, 101–102.
68. *The London Missionary Society's Report*, 106.
69. Hobsbawm and Rude (1969), 198.
70. Ibid.
71. Evans (1989), 15.
72. Molesworth (1877), 53.

cesses of the working class. In the incident that became known as the "Peterloo Massacre," for example, "Wilberforce, predictably, supported the
measures [of the government]."[73]

On that occasion, a crowd of about 50,000 to 60,000 men, women,
and children had gathered on St. Peter's Field on the outskirts of Manchester to listen to Henry Hunt and other orators who were branded by
the government as dangerous radicals. Before the meeting began, the magistrates ordered the yeomanry to make their way through the throng to
arrest Hunt. The mounted force was entangled in and hustled by the
crowd, and eleven people were killed or died as a result of their wounds.
Several hundreds were injured by sword cuts or horses' hoofs or were
crushed in the panic to rush to safety. The government subsequently
thanked the magistrates, declared the meeting illegal, and committed
Hunt and some of his colleagues to trial for conspiracy to alter the law
of mass meetings by force and threat.[74] Some abolitionists, like Henry
Brougham, opposed such repressive and high-handed government measures. In 1819, Brougham raised his voice to censure the government and
Manchester's local magistrates for the Peterloo Massacre. He condemned
the prison sentences imposed on Henry Orator Hunt, John Knight, Samuel Bamford, and other organizers of the meeting at St. Peter's Field.[75] On
August 31, 1819, Brougham wrote to Earl Grey, "The magistrates there
and all over Lancashire, I have long known for the worst in England, the
most bigoted, violent and active. I am quite indignant at this Manchester
business, but I fear, with you, that we can do nothing till the parliament
meets."[76]

In August 1812 Brougham had actively supported some working-class
radicals charged for mobilizing workers. In his capacity as a lawyer,
Brougham defended thirty-eight handloom weavers, who had been arrested by Joseph Nadin, deputy constable of Manchester. The weavers had
attempted to form a trade union. Their leader, John Knight, was charged
with administering to weavers oaths that pledged them to destroy steam
looms. The rest of the men were accused of attending a seditious meeting.

73. Cormack (1983), 105.
74. Coupland (1923), 418–419.
75. www.spartacus.schoolnet.co.uk/PR Brougham htm (accessed August 10, 2001).
76. Ibid.

As a result of Brougham's brilliant defense, all thirty-eight were acquitted.[77]

In responding to workers' protest actions at home, Buxton's approach was more moderate than Brougham's, but he too was convinced that there was justice in the workers' actions. "I voted with ministers because I cannot bring myself to subject the Manchester magistrates to a parliamentary inquiry; but nothing has shaken my convictions that the magistrates, ministers and all, have done exceedingly wrong."[78] Buxton compromised his conviction to avoid humiliating authorities at home. Nevertheless, he joined the Anti-Slavery Society because he believed that laborers, whether in Britain or in her colonies, ought to enjoy the right of combining to protest appalling conditions. Thus, in an antislavery tract commenting on the rebellion in Demerara, the abolitionists saw a ready comparison between the plight of slaves in rebellion and

> the miners of Cornwall, . . . the ironworkers of Wales, . . . the keelmen of the Tyne, . . . the weavers of Lancashire, . . . the unhappy affair at Manchester, . . . large bodies of Spitalfields crowded last year to Westminster filling Palace-Yard and all the avenues and passages of the House of Parliament with their numbers, beseeching and imploring the members of the Legislatures to protect them from the unjust purposes of their masters . . . Or take a stronger case, that of the agricultural labourers, who in open day have been proceeding in bodies to the destruction of threshing machines, and to other acts of destruction of lawless violence; or that of the Luddites or, that of the Blanketeers. And let us ask whether it would have been endured that even these misguided, and many of them most criminal, individuals should have been dealt with as the poor, ignorant, oppressed, cart-whipped slaves of Demerara have been dealt with?[79]

Abolitionists maintained that slaves were only acting like any English laborer facing harsh conditions when they resisted their servile existence.

77. Ibid.
78. Buxton (1852), 79.
79. "Negro Slavery No. 7," 60–61.

The slaves rose to confront the managers of the system and bargain for much-needed reform in the servile regime.

JUST GROUND FOR ALARM

Despite the comparisons that abolitionists could and did make between slaves in Demerara and workers in Britain, many aspects of their commentary set the revolt apart from any other kind of industrial impasse. Brougham and Mackintosh argued that the rising in Demerara was due in part to the deliberate failure of the colonial authority to provide politically curious slaves with accurate and straightforward information. Not coincidentally, the missionary John Smith had come to that very conclusion. In the final entry of his private journal, Smith wrote on August 8, 1823, that the governor and the Court of Policy of Demerara had acted imprudently in withholding from the slaves information concerning the orders of the British government.[80] Slaves were not forever prepared to await patiently a formal report of the measures that they knew had arrived from England concerning their well being. Brougham explained that the procrastination of Demerara officials provided the slaves with just ground for alarm and rebellion. At length he reasoned,

> those instructions arrived in Demerara on the 7th of July last, and great alarm and feverish anxiety appear to have been excited by them amongst the white part of the population. That the existence of this alarm . . . at the arrival at some new and beneficial regulations were marked and understood by the domestic slaves, there cannot be a doubt. By them the intelligence was speedily communicated to the field Negroes. All this time there was no official communication of the Instructions from the Colonial Government. A meeting had been made public in consequence of its assembling. A second was held in the prevalence of the general alarm, rendered more intense by the inquisitive anxiety of the slave population . . . most certainly, the . . . authorities of Demerara overlooked that course of proceeding best calculated to allay at least the inquisitive anxiety of the slaves; namely; promulgating in the colony what it really was that had been directed

80. Quoted in Jakobsson (1972), 314; Northcott (1976), 55. John Smith had identified this cause among the four principal causes of the rebellion. See also the *The London Missionary Society Report,* 86, 188.

in the Instructions of the King's ministers . . . Week after week was suffered to elapse and up to the period when the lamentable occurrence took place . . . no . . . authoritative communication, whether of what had arrived in England, or of what was the intention of the authorities at Demerara was made to the slaves. This state of suspense occupied an interval of seven weeks.[81]

Perhaps the officials in Demerara, aware of events in Barbados, determined by their relative silence not to repeat the mistake of publicizing slave legislation to slaves. The abolitionists indicated that such action was ineffectual. Slaves were attuned to and curious about discussions on the slavery question taking place in the colonies and across the Atlantic, and they had managed to discover what the colonists attempted to conceal. Abolitionists realized that an intelligentsia was to be found among the domestic slaves. Although they were relatively more comfortable than their brethren in the field, "elite" slaves were least contented with slavery. James Mackintosh observed about the Demerara revolt, "The moving cause of this insurrection . . . is the distress of the great body of insurgents; but the ringleaders are generally, and almost necessarily, individuals who, being more highly endowed, or more happily situated, are raised above the distress which is suffered by those of whom they take command."[82]

"Privileged" slaves used their positions to undermine the system, giving the field slaves an often garbled interpretation of the state of the pro- and antislavery debate. Mackintosh was not surprised that domestic and other "elite" slaves in Demerara were at the forefront of the revolt. They "had heard from seamen arrived from England, by servants in the governor's house and by the angry conversations of their masters that some project for improving their condition had been favourably received in this country. They naturally entertained sanguine and exaggerated hopes of the extent of the reformation."[83]

81. Henry Brougham, *The Speeches of Henry, Lord Brougham, Upon Questions Relating to Public Rights, Duties and Interests With Historical Introduction and A Critical Dissertation Upon the Eloquence of the Ancients*, vol. 2 of 4 (Edinburgh: Adam and Charles Black, 1838), 56–57. It is apparent that Brougham had carefully read the extract that Governor Murray dispatched to Colonial Secretary of State Earl Bathurst on the meeting of the Court of Policy of August 11, 1823. See Murray to Bathurst, Demerara, August 11, 1823, CO 111/39, ff. 73, Colonial Office Papers.

82. *The Missionary Smith*, 82.

83. *Hansard's Parliamentary Debates*, new ser., 11 (June 1, 1824): 1055, and *The Lon-*

Brougham and Mackintosh made the important point that the slaves were not altogether stupid even though they may have misunderstood the specific details of the regulations that colonial secretary Lord Bathurst had sent to Demerara. The abolitionists were convinced that the slaves had proven that they would use their general impressions of the debate on slavery in an attempt to loosen the chains of their bondage. The abolitionists believed that for the sake of maintaining peace and stability, the restless slaves ought to have been clearly informed earlier of Lord Bathurst's circular. The slaves of Demerara had just grounds for alarm and resolved to take decisive action on an issue that their masters and other colonial authorities were reluctant to confront.

SLAVERY ITSELF AND SLAVERY ALONE

Wilberforce had attempted to demonstrate that the 1816 Barbados revolt was an attack upon the brutal system of slavery itself. Other abolitionists commenting upon the Demerara slave revolt were more precise and direct. Brougham stated that the slaves were "exasperated by ancient as well as by more recent wrongs (for a sale of sixty or more of them had been announced), and they were about to be violently separated and dispersed."[84] An objection to the British colonial system of slavery often raised was that of the sale and separation of slave families. This practice more than any other reflected the extent to which slave owners regarded their laborers not as fellow humans but as chattel. One abolitionist complained, "the slave has no legal property in his own body . . . he has no property in anything else . . . He is . . . a chattel. He may be sold or bequeathed at the pleasure of his master. He may be put up to auction by process of law, for the benefit of the creditors or legatees of his master . . . he may be, in a moment, torn for ever from his home, his associates, his children. He is, in addition to this, legally a subject of mortgages, demises, leases, settlements in tail, in remainder and in reversion."[85]

---

don Missionary Society's Report, 86. Smith stated here that "the Negro Jack was informed of it [Bathurst's circular] by one of the Governor's servants, who, it seems, heard his master speak to some gentlemen concerning the instructions." See also Northcott (1976), 53.

84. *Hansard's Parliamentary Debates,* new ser., 11 (June 1, 1824): 1160. In *The London Missionary Society's Report* (p. 85), John Smith had mentioned "a number of our congregation being advertised for sale by auction, some on the same day of the revolt." See also Northcott (1976), 76.

85. *Edinburgh Review* 41, no. 82 (January 1825): 467; *Anti-Slavery Monthly Reporter*

Abolitionists believed that the inhumanity of slavery as reflected by this treatment was a major aggravation against which slaves in Demerara rose in rebellion. Thomas Fowell Buxton's reflections on the subject maximized its emotive appeal. He personalized the experience of separating slave families. Buxton narrated the experience of a slave whom he called "respectable Billy," a slave of Clonbrock plantation in Demerara. Billy lived with a woman as his wife for nineteen years. Together, they had thirteen surviving children. The family was separated when the owner divided his plantation property between his two sons; one received the wife and children, and the other, the husband. Billy was barred from seeing his wife and children although their estates were contiguous. The new gang of slaves to which the husband now belonged was to be sold by August 26, 1823.[86] Buxton ended his tale on a note of dramatic pathos: "He was— and is it to be wondered at?—one of the insurgents, and was, when the last accounts left Demerara, hanging in Georgetown!"[87]

Buxton's account of Billy's experience justified Billy's rebellious action and reinforced the abolitionists' sympathetic depiction of slave revolts. It also marked an increase over time of the abolitionists' insistence that the slaves had rights, the violation of which tended to justify their rebellion. Consequently, the Anti-Slavery Society stated, "Everything dear to them was felt to be at issue, and knowing the men to whose decision their fate and that of their children was left, their alarms and apprehension must be pardoned. We must place ourselves in their situation, if we would duly estimate its difficulties and temptations."[88] Thomas Clarkson summed up abolitionists' sentiment on the rebellious actions of Demerara slaves by concluding, "It is a fact that slavery itself and slavery alone . . . produced this insurrection."[89]

1, no. 18 (December 30, 1826): 251; Sir James Stephen, *The Slavery of the British West India Colonies Delineated, As It Exists Both in Law and Practice, and Compared with the Slavery of Other Colonies, Ancient and Modern*, vol. 1 (Aberdeen: A. Constable and Co., 1824), 62, 435.

86. *Hansard's Parliamentary Debates*, new ser., 10 (March 16, 1824): 1132–1133.

87. Ibid., 1133.

88. Society for the Mitigation and Gradual Abolition of Slavery Throughout the British Dominions, "Negro Slavery No. 8, Insurrections in the West Indies; St. Lucia, Trinidad, Dominica, Jamaica and Demerara," in *Tracts of the Anti-Slavery Society* (London: J. Hatchard and Son, 1823), 56. Hereafter this cite is referred to as "Negro Slavery No. 8."

89. Address to the gentlemen of Ipswich, December 5, 1823, Thomas Clarkson Papers.

A HOLY WAR

Antislavery agitators believed that the influence of Christianity elevated the Demerara revolt of 1823 above former rebellions in the West Indies. Abolitionists tended to be contradictory, however, in attempting to prove this point. Henry Brougham was convinced that Christianity guided the slaves along a relatively nonviolent course. John Smith's unfinished letter to the secretary of the London Missionary Society, Rev. George Burder, was one piece of evidence the abolitionists depended upon in coming to this conclusion. Smith had written, "The Negroes on this coast . . . have seized the firearms belonging to the several plantations and retired; . . . they put some of their managers into the stocks, to prevent their escaping to give an alarm, but . . . they offered no personal violence to any one; neither did they set fire to a single building; nor rob any house . . . except of arms and ammunition."[90] Brougham concurred that the explanation for this nonviolent and nondestructive course of action was Christianity. He stressed that "the gospel of peace was upon their lips in the midst of rebellion and restrained their hands when no other force was present to resist them . . . 'We will take no life,' said they, 'for our pastors have taught us not to take that which we cannot give.'"[91]

In attributing to Christianity so significant an aspect of the new phase of the slaves' resistance, the abolitionists were not being true to their overall assessment of the relationship between Christianity and slavery. They had made dogged efforts to dispel proslavery accusations that Smith's presence among the slaves contributed to the revolt. Brougham insisted that John Smith, far from living up to the reputation of instigator, used his influence over his Bethel congregation to dissuade rather than encourage slave resistance. Chester New discusses the several arguments upon which Brougham based his statement. At trial, Smith's prosecutors accused him of being aware that the slave Quamina was a rebel and of having conversed with him before and during the revolt.[92] Brougham dismissed the accusation, citing Smith's response that he had conversed with

90. Unfinished Letter of Mr. Smith to Reverend Burder, Secretary of L. M. S. from Plantation Le Resouvenir, Demerary, August 21, 1823, *The London Missionary Society's Report*, appendix 15, p. 184.

91. Brougham (1857), 159–160.

92. New (1967), 293.

and counseled Quamina that he must have nothing to do with any revolt against authority or any resort to violence.[93] Smith's accusers charged that he knew of the revolt six weeks previous to its eruption, but Brougham reiterated Smith's observation that the evidence at the trial proved that it was planned only a day or two before it broke out.[94] Smith was further implicated in planning the revolt by the testimony of the slave Paris. Brougham read a letter that was submitted in evidence by Reverend Austin of the Established Church undermining the credibility of Paris's testimony. Reverend Austin had received "the last confession of Paris, who stated that Mr. Smith was innocent and he [Paris] prayed that God would forgive him the lies that Mr. ——— had prevailed upon him to tell."[95]

James Mackintosh supported Brougham in making this point by observing that "the witnesses who gave that evidence . . . were accomplices in the revolt, who had no chance of life but what acceptable testimony might afford."[96] Smith had also been charged with the offense of failing to seize Quamina. Brougham quoted Smith's answer that missionaries were incapable of restraining the slaves' deep love of liberty. "Look . . . on these poor limbs, feeble with disease, and say how was it possible for me to seize a powerful robust man like Quamina, inflamed with the desire of liberty, as that slave must have been if he were a revolter."[97] The abolitionists sought to prove that Smith did not share his personal revulsion toward slavery with the members of his slave congregation, many of whom were implicated in the revolt. Even the documents submitted to the London Missionary Society by Mrs. Smith and Smith's legal adviser Mr. Arrindell sought to establish beyond doubt that Christianity did not influence the chief participants in the rebellion. Mrs. Smith's letter to secretary George Burder was written precisely for this purpose.

From all we can learn from the evidence on Mr. Smith's trial, it appears that the plot was laid by two Negroes named Jack and Paris. Jack was

93. Ibid.
94. Ibid.
95. Ibid.
96. *Hansard's Parliamentary Debates,* new ser., 11 (June 1, 1824): 1058.
97. Brougham (1838), 70. See also *The Missionary Smith,* 33–35, for Brougham's treatment of the charges brought against Smith.

the son of Quamina (one of the deacons in question) and he was the person to whom the governor's servant made the communication concerning the instructions from England. Jack was a desolate, gay young man, very irregular in his attendance at chapel. Religion, it is to be feared, he had none. Paris was boat captain of Bachelor Adventure and, had been disposed to attend the chapel but it was out of his power to do so nineteen Sundays out of twenty. His work was to take plantains to town, to sell on Sunday. I do not suppose he attended chapel more than once a year.[98]

The Smiths doggedly maintained that Christianity exerted no influence in the lives of the slaves who led the rebellion. Furthermore, abolitionists insisted that Smith's ministry taught implicit obedience and submission; it did not sow seeds of discontent and rebellion. How, then, could the abolitionists justify their claim that Smith's influence shaped the relatively peaceful nature of the revolt? The Smiths and the abolitionists attempted simultaneously to credit the missionary for the nonviolent nature of the rising while insisting that parson Smith played no role in setting it off.

It seems more probable that the slaves of Demerara had interpreted Christianity in their own way. They did not passively accept the doctrine that they heard from the altar. They actively transposed and subjected religion to the realization of their main political aspiration. The gospel of peace that John Smith and other missionaries conveyed went through various transformations before slaves received it into their heads and into their hearts. Although it was tinged with Christian elements, the revolt had less to do with the ministers' influence and more with the slaves' own anxious desire for freedom. Brougham himself quoted from Smith's personal journal to show how slaves used Christianity to defy their masters. "Lucinda is a member of the church, and much affected with the gospel. She is an old woman, and though her manager tells her not to come to church, she tells him she will come, even if he cuts her throat for it."[99] Brougham's use of this extract to demonstrate the independent choices that slaves were making in the name of Christianity does not reconcile

98. Letter of Mrs. Smith, December 4, 1823, from Demerary, *The London Missionary Society's Report*, Appendix 7, p. 185.

99. "West India Missions—Insurrection in Demerara," *Edinburgh Review* 40, no. 79 (March 1824): 252.

with his conviction that their pastors were chiefly responsible for the largely nonviolent nature of the slaves' rebellion.

Thomas Clarkson had come to a more reasonable assessment of the secondary significance of Christianity in the slaves' rebellion.

> I know that it has been stated that this insurrection was set on foot and promoted by the missionaries . . . I disbelieve the fact, tho' I have it not in my power to deny it. But let us suppose that it was so . . . Let us suppose that in that unlucky moment, not only his compassion but also his indignation had been roused and that he had incautiously given vent to his feelings and burst out into expressions which had inflamed the minds of the slaves and which had led to this insurrection— Still I maintain that this insurrection had its origins in slavery. There are original causes and sub causes or occasions—The missionary in this case would have been the occasion of the insurrection . . . had the slaves been in happy circumstances, a few words dropped by a missionary could never have led them astray.[100]

Clarkson had a greater appreciation than Brougham of the sense in which the revolt of the slaves was more internally rather than externally triggered.

Further reflections on the effect of religious instructions on slaves suggest that indeed the abolitionists believed at times that slaves were responding autonomously to Christianity. An article in the January 1825 *Edinburgh Review* helps demonstrate this point. The author spoke on behalf of the antislavery body and explained, "We have already given it as our opinion that . . . if the great body of the Negroes . . . become Christians . . . we are sure that their political state would very speedily be changed. At every step which the Negro makes in the knowledge and discrimination of right and wrong . . . he will learn to reprobate more and more the system under which he lives. He will not indeed be so prone to engage in rash and foolish tumults; but he will be as willing as he now is to struggle for liberty and far more capable of struggling with effect."[101]

---

100. Address to gentlemen at Ipswich, December 5, 1823, Thomas Clarkson Papers.

101. *Edinburgh Review* 41, no. 82 (January 1825): 472–473. See also Society for the Mitigation and Gradual Abolition of Slavery, *Analysis of the Report of a Committee of the House of Commons on the Extinction of Slavery With Notes by the Editor* (London: J. Hatchard and Son, 1833), 119, for a similar view expressed after the Jamaican slave revolt of 1831–1832. Hereafter this cite is referred to as *Analysis of the Report.*

Abolitionists at times appreciated the subtle and profound ways in which religion helped shaped the revolt of the slaves. Anxious, however, to exonerate the missionaries, whom slavery supporters perceived as abolitionists' advocates, they attributed only what they perceived as the positive aspects of the revolts to the sectarians. In so doing, however, antislavery advocates ended up admitting that slaves of their own accord would use Christianity in a bid to overthrow slavery, not in a savagely ruthless manner but in a manner befitting the status of Christian slaves.

FREEDOM STRUGGLE

Henry Brougham declared that the Demerara revolt of 1823 was a natural manifestation of the slaves' desire for liberty. This declaration defied the planters' assertion that rebellions were nothing but savage attempts to overturn slavery. Brougham's simple statement of counterattack was that the slaves were "inflamed with the desire for liberty."[102] He argued that it was "natural that the slaves would believe that the hidden circular was freedom."[103] Brougham's view removed the slaves from the periphery of a chaotic experience and brought their main aspiration into sharp focus. He declared that the slaves' desire for freedom permeated the very core of the rebellion. He imagined that in their conversations, the slaves asked themselves, "Has not our freedom come? Freedom! Freedom," Brougham wrote, "was the sound unceasingly heard, and which continuously raised the vision on which their fancy loved to repose."[104] Brougham was echoing Governor Murray's firsthand account of a conversation he held with the insurgent slaves. Murray may not have realized how his testimony assisted the abolitionists in positively conceptualizing the slaves' overt resistance. Nevertheless, in the parley he held with the slaves on Monday, August 18, Murray wrote that he sought "to ascertain their visions which they stated to be unconditional emancipation."[105] Murray strengthened Brougham's perception that the revolt was a freedom struggle by explaining that the slaves could have but did not injure any member of his party. During the governor's discussion with the insurgents, the number of slaves present grew from about forty to two to

102. *Hansard's Parliamentary Debates*, new ser., 11 (June 1, 1824): 991.
103. Ibid., 965.
104. Brougham (1838), 56.
105. Murray to Bathurst, Demerara, August 24, 1823, CO 111/39, ff. 77, Colonial Office Papers.

three hundred. The slaves at the back insisted on firing on him and the militia dragoons who had accompanied him. The slaves at the front with whom he had talked prevailed in opposing this suggestion.[106] Based on this important information, abolitionists paid one of the most positive tributes to nineteenth-century slave rebels in the British West Indies: The Demerara slave revolt was a freedom struggle. It was a tribute that was repeated with greater conviction by Thomas Fowell Buxton when he reviewed events in the Jamaican slave revolt of 1831–1832.

THREE HUNDRED THOUSAND NEGROES

Historian Mary Turner has observed that, considering the political scene that was about to unfold in Britain, 1831–1832 was an opportune time for slaves in Jamaica to rise.[107] The struggle over the British Reform Bill was approaching its consummation, and many of the returning M.P.s in the House of Commons had pledged their support for the abolition of slavery. Barry Higman notes that this effectively halved the representatives of the West Indians.[108] By May 1830, the antislavery campaigners had abandoned gradualism and increasingly pressed the government for total abolition. Significantly too, the Jamaican slaves rose against their masters at a time when the abolitionists had already laid much of the groundwork in presenting their views on slave rebellions.

Sir James Stephen and another abolitionist, one Mr. Garrat, continued boldly to challenge the planters' interpretation of revolts by speaking of "the insurrection in Jamaica, or the disorders so called."[109] They emphasized that, as in Demerara in 1823, Jamaican slaves were attempting to bargain with the owners of labor. The slaves' resistance consisted essentially of "striking work at a holiday season longer than the Drivers permitted."[110] The Baptist missionary William Knibb had testified that when he examined Samuel Sharpe, the leader of the rebellion, it became clear that the slaves were seeking better working conditions. Sharpe had insisted

---

106. Ibid., ff. 78.

107. Turner (1982), 31–41.

108. Higman (1976), 231.

109. Letter of Sir James Stephen and Garrat to the Anti-Slavery Society, April 11, 1832, Committee on Slavery Minute Book, p. 132, MSS. Brit. Emp. S. 20, E2/3, Anti-Slavery Society Papers.

110. Ibid.

that the king of Britain had granted the slaves their freedom and that they had worked for nothing long enough. They were resolved not to work after Christmas unless they received wages. Sharpe also confessed to Knibb that the slaves had little intention of rebellion.[111]

The abolitionists accepted this account. In their assessment of the House of Commons committee report on slavery, which focused considerably on the rebellion in Jamaica, the Anti-Slavery Society stated, "As far as he [Knibb] could learn, it was not their intention at first to destroy property or to injure the whites, but to insist on having wages at the rate of 2s. 6d. currency or 20d. a day, the present rate of wages."[112] The abolitionists further endorsed Knibb's conviction that the slaves' primary objective was to alter their position in the economic system. At length, anti-slavery activists quoted Knibb, "Meetings of the drivers of different estates were held at a place called Retrieve, where Samuel Sharpe appeared to be the leading man. On Christmas morning Sharpe spoke to Hilton, at the chapel at Montego Bay, to be sure, if the Minister asked him about freedom, or not working after Christmas, to tell him he knew he was free, and that he would not work again for anybody anymore unless he was paid for it."[113] Buxton emphasized that the revolt was devoid of any deliberate intention to massacre planters and destroy their property. Buxton's insistence that the Jamaican slave rebellion was a mass strike action to improve the conditions of the laboring population was substantiated by Governor Belmore's correspondence to the Colonial Office. When Governor Belmore wrote to colonial secretary Viscount Goderich about the outbreak of the rebellion, he repeatedly referred to the fact that the slaves insisted on their refusal to work after New Year's Day without wages. Belmore even reported that in Morant Bay, while slaves refused to

111. Ibid., 133. As in the case of Demerara, the abolitionists depended on the evidence provided by missionaries in coming to their conclusions about the Jamaican slave rebellion. See Baptist Missionary Society, *Colonial Slavery—Defence of the Baptist Missionaries from the Charge of Inciting the Late Rebellion in Jamaica; in a Discussion between the Reverend William Knibb and Mr. P. Borthwick at the Assembly Rooms on Saturday 15 December 1832* (London: Tourist Office, Paternoster Row, 1832), 4 (hereafter this cite is referred to as *Colonial Slavery*), and *Analysis of the Report,* 121, for abolitionists' analysis of the testimony of the Rev. William Knibb given before the 1832 House of Commons committee on slavery.

112. *Analysis of the Report,* 107.

113. Ibid., 115.

work, they had committed no depredations on the property of their masters.[114] He was struck by the self-control that the slaves exercised when they had an opportunity to revenge their countless years of suffering.

Buxton described the scene of the servile war in Jamaica. "Three hundred thousand Negroes in gloomy silence stood against them . . . then the first whispers of that whirlwind seemed beginning, which was to sweep off the white population. I thought indeed that the sword of eternal justice was unsheathed, but it was pleased to deal with us not in vengeance but in mercy and to say to the howling winds and swelling bellows, peace be still and there was a great calm."[115] Buxton's description seems more imaginary than real. The slaves, in spite of their overwhelming numbers, did not stand a chance of defeating the white forces in the colonies. In the *Cornwall Courier,* for example, the planters boasted that "the result of the rebellion has been to open the eyes of the community to the utter incapacity of our laboring class as combatants, and has completely dispelled the idle panic which pervaded the island, on account of their vast numerical strength. This bubble has burst."[116] For Buxton, however, it was crucial that slaves seemed to have deliberately decided to curb the extent of the violence that they would practice. Considering the more bloody rebellions staged in Jamaica in the pre-abolitionist era, Buxton had a point. The slaves in Jamaica were not seeking to exact bloody revenge against their masters but to assert the rights of free men. Buxton thus insisted on speaking not of the rebellion but of the "riot which had lately occurred at Jamaica . . . it might have been more—it might have been an insurrection, although, if so, I could show who were the insurgents, and that it was the planters by whom it had been caused."[117]

Buxton widened the antislavery position on slave revolts. If proslavery forces insisted on describing the slaves' protest actions in wild and licentious terms, then he must conclude that it was the planters' conduct in these events that had not changed over the years, not the slaves'. To the Jamaican plantocracy whose material suffering in the rebellion was evi-

114. Belmore to Goderich, January 6, 1832, CO 137/181, ff. 3, 5, 7, 8, Colonial Office Papers.

115. Notes and Drafts for Speeches 1829–1839, vol. 10, ff. 63–64, MSS. Brit. Emp. S. 444, Thomas Fowell Buxton Papers.

116. *Cornwall Courier,* February 22, 1832.

117. *Hansard's Parliamentary Debates,* 3d ser., 11 (March 23, 1832): 841.

dent, this accusation was outrageous. Property owners in slave plantation societies had taken it for granted that all would appreciate that they were the obvious victims of slave revolts. The report of Hamilton Brown on the estate of Mrs. John L. Tweedie, for example, centered on the economic distress experienced in Trelawney as a result of the revolt.[118] Another correspondent on the Tweedie estates reported that the rebellion was "unsuccessful for the rebels but economically devastating for the planters."[119] Willoughby Cotton, who superintended the suppression of the revolt, provided an early assessment of the economic devastation. "The Eastern half of Hanover, and the whole of the Northern part of St. James are in open revolt, and almost the whole of the estates destroyed, and the Negroes gone boldly away."[120] In Belmore's first dispatch to Goderich at the Colonial Office, the governor highlighted that the rebellion left in its wake "scenes of devastation and ruin."[121]

This gloomy picture of planter economic distress was minutely investigated and registered. The following is an extract of a report of the Jamaican Assembly sent to Lord Howick at the Colonial Office.

> The injury sustained by the late Rebellion, by slaves wilfully setting fire to buildings, by grass and cane-fields destroyed, robbery and plunder of every description, damage done to the present and succeeding crops, the loss of the labour of slaves, besides those killed in suppressing such rebellion, and executed after trial as incendiaries, rebels and murderers has been ascertained ... to amount to ... £1,154,589 s2 d1. To which is added the sum of £161,569 s19 d9 being the expense incurred in suppressing the late rebellion; and a further expense not yet ascertained ... being the pay and rations of a portion to the Maroons, as well as to the detachment of the Island Militia.[122]

118. File 4/45, January 5, 1832, No. 49, Tweedie Estate Records.

119. Ibid., February 11, 1832, No. 50.

120. *London Gazette Extraordinary,* a special issue of the *Times,* February 23, 1832.

121. Belmore to Goderich, January 6, 1832, CO 137/181, ff. 2, 5–7, Colonial Office Papers.

122. *British Parliamentary Papers, Papers Relating to the Slave Trade 1831–1834, Slave Trade 80. Jamaica: A Report from the House of Assembly on the injury sustained during the recent Rebellion, 1831–1832 (561),* vol. 47 (Shannon, Ireland: Irish University Press, 1966), 189–234. Sent to Lord Howick, Colonial Department, Downing Street, 27th June 1832.

It was a description not quite unlike those of the ravages in French St. Domingue in 1791. As did Wilberforce and Brougham when they examined the Barbados and Demerara slave revolts, respectively, Buxton ignored this self-proclaimed suffering. He insisted that "the planters were the cause of . . . the insurrection and rebellion that ensued. He [Buxton] wished his words to be taken down."[123] It was an assertion that reflected the growth of abolitionists' confidence in addressing the issue of slave revolts in the struggle against slavery. It was also an attempt to redirect the course in which sympathy flowed whenever servile warfare erupted in the slave plantation colonies.

CHRISTIAN RETRIBUTION

Buxton's comments on the Jamaican slave revolt provided another dimension to how abolitionists perceived the crisis between slavery and Christianity as made evident through slave rebellions. After the revolt, Jamaican planters insisted that sectarian missionaries were "men who have been the cause of destroying the fairest portion of Jamaica, and who had to answer for the blood that has been shed in consequence . . . we abhor the whole race of Methodists and Baptists."[124] The proslavery discourse of the interaction between Christianity and slavery insisted on the role of the sectarian missionaries as catalysts of rebellion. The abolitionists, however, did not objectify slave rebels in assessing their relationship with missionaries. Buxton agreed that the Jamaican slave revolt was partly a protest against planters' intolerance of Christianity. However, he shaped this argument by paying attention not merely to the persecution of the missionaries but to the religious persecution endured by slaves themselves. Buxton stressed that the examples he would produce to demonstrate the tensions between slavery and Christianity would not consist of the often repeated experiences of John Smith and William Knibb.[125]

The experiences of the slaves, he believed, most clearly demonstrated the crisis. He narrated the circumstances that surrounded the punishments of Henry Williams and Swiney for praying, and George Atkins for attending a prayer meeting. These slaves were flogged, sentenced to periods

123. *Hansard's Parliamentary Debates*, 3d ser., 11 (March 23, 1832): 842.
124. *Jamaican Courant*, January 24, 1832.
125. *Hansard's Parliamentary Debates*, 3d ser., 11 (March 23, 1832): 842.

of hard labor in Rodney-Hole Workhouse, and confined.[126] Buxton insisted, as Brougham had done, that when slaves in Jamaica rose, they were staging a holy war against an unholy regime. Christian slaves took their own action against the aggravation of their masters. Within this context, Buxton was persuaded that the slaves were justified in their conduct. "Suppose the riot had occurred on the occasion [of the flogging of Henry Williams] . . . who could have lamented it? If the miscreant who had committed the atrocity had been put to death, who could have lamented it?"[127] Buxton had begun to echo the radical view expressed anonymously in the *Edinburgh Review* that it was the duty of the slaves to rebel against the injustices of a cruel regime.

STRUGGLE FOR FREEDOM

To come to terms with the slaves' rebellious conduct, the abolitionists had carefully examined the official dispatches that passed between the governor of Jamaica and colonial secretary Viscount Goderich. Some of these dispatches referred to the parish meetings held in Jamaica in the summer of 1831 protesting the new 1830 slave code that was forwarded both to the crown and legislative colonies. These parish meetings took place three months prior to the rising of the slaves, and a number of slaves were present during the discussions.[128] Buxton suggested a cause-and-effect rela-

126. Ibid., 840–842; Stanley Brian, *The History of the Baptist Missionary Society, 1792–1992* (Edinburgh: T&T Clark, 1992), 74–75. See also Turner (1982), 139–140; Jakobsson (1972), 433–488 for the Swiney case. The cases of Henry Williams and Samuel Swiney were presented to the House of Commons in the following parliamentary papers: *Jamaica: Return to an Address of the Honorable the House of Commons dated 15th December 1830;—for Copies of all Communications Relative to the Reported Maltreatment of a Slave Named Henry Williams, in Jamaica* addressed to Lord Howick, Colonial Department, Downing Street, December 23, 1830, and *Jamaica: Slave Punishment Returns to an Address to His Majesty, dated 23 March 1832; for, No. 1 Copies of All Communications from Jamaica Relating to the Trial of George Ancle, a Negro Slave, and of Samuel Swiney, a Negro Slave, for Certain Alleged Offences Relating to Religious Worship.* These papers are contained in a bound volume entitled *Slavery Parliamentary Papers &c,* Angus Library, Baptist Missionary Society Archive, Regent's Park College, Oxford.

127. *Hansard's Parliamentary Debates,* 3d ser., 11 (March 23, 1832): 841.

128. *British Parliamentary Papers, Report from the Select Committee on the Extinction of Slavery Throughout the British Dominions with the Minutes of Evidence, Appendix and Index,* August 11, 1832 (Shannon, Ireland: Irish University Press, 1966), 243; John Howard

tionship between the timing of the parish meetings and the revolt. He was developing a point initially raised by Wilberforce that slaves would seize and act upon any idea remotely linked to their well-being. Buxton noted that the *Port Royal Gazette* for August 13, 1831, reported the intention of the white inhabitants of St. Ann's Parish to secede from Britain.[129] In the *Jamaican Courant* of August 16, 1831, Buxton noted a more decisive resolution. The parishioners of St. Ann's had declared that "the Government which arbitrarily or capriciously invades the right of private property, releases the oppressed sufferer from obedience and allegiance."[130] Buxton believed that such an open show of contumacy on the part of the planter class toward imperial resolutions on slavery could not but fuel the slaves' restlessness. The Jamaican parish meetings in the summer of 1831 were the immediate impetus in the war for freedom that the island slaves staged just after the Christmas holidays.

Buxton's final words on the action in 1831–1832 infused the Jamaican rebellion with the spiritual and political dimensions with which the slaves themselves perceived it. William Annand, the overseer of Ginger Hill Plantation in the Parish of St. Elizabeth, had sworn on oath that when he was taken prisoner by a group of slaves, they stated their intention to "fight for their freedom."[131] The overseer went on to state that "they said that I knew as well as themselves that Jamaica was now free and that half of the estates from Ginger Hill to Montego Bay were burnt down the night before [December 27, 1831] . . . they were obliged to assist their brethren in the work of the Lord, that this was not the work of man alone, but they had assistance from God."[132] Buxton shared the view that the Jamaican slave revolt was a protest action upon which the stamp of approval of Almighty God was fixed. He was unwilling, therefore, to summon the English people to suppress a war opposing such an authority. The slave rebellion in Jamaica represented the noble aspirations of a people to secure lives as free men. Buxton declared in the House of Commons, "War was

Hinton, *Memoir of William Knibb, Missionary in Jamaica* (London: Houlston and Stoneman, 1847), 112–113; *Analysis of the Report,* 51.

129. *Hansard's Parliamentary Debates,* 3d ser., 11 (March 23, 1832): 842.

130. Ibid.

131. Deposition on oath of William Annand, Overseer of Ginger Hill Plantation in the Parish of St. Elizabeth, January 2, 1832, CO 137/181, ff. 106, Colonial Office Papers.

132. Ibid.

to be lamented anywhere and under any circumstances but a war against a people struggling for their freedom and their rights, would be the falsest position in which it was possible for England to be placed. The people of England would not support this loss of resources to crush the inalienable rights of mankind . . . in such a warfare, it was not possible to ask, nor could we dare to expect, the countenance of heaven. The Almighty had no attribute that would side with them in such a struggle."[133]

With this positive interpretation of the Jamaican slave revolt, abolitionists dismissed the terror with which proslavery voices were wont to speak of slaves in rebellion. It also encompassed the tendency of the abolitionists to overlook the material losses about which planters complained when slaves revolted. Abolitionists' depiction of revolts identified the several ways in which slaves acted autonomously in responding to their enslavement. British abolitionists offered the answer to Eugene Genovese's later "deceptively simple question . . . What was a slave revolt?"[134] It was a multiple protest action; it was a holy war, a war against the injustices of slavery, and a labor protest movement. But it was more than these. Thomas Fowell Buxton, British antislavery leader by 1823, climaxed the discussion on the issue by agreeing with the one compelling answer. A slave revolt was the slaves' own struggle for freedom. Faced with the challenge of finding a way to not let slave revolts hinder their campaign against slavery, the abolitionists presented to Parliament and a restricted public the hidden side of slave revolts—a side that was decidedly more sympathetic and, on all counts, diametrically opposite to that depicted by the planters. Nineteenth-century slave rebels in the British West Indies had succeeded in directing British abolitionists to a transformed perception about their open opposition to enslavement. From as early as 1816, following the revolt in Barbados, slaves swung abolitionists' reflections on slave revolts away from a defensive strategy to a concentrated analysis of the nature of the revolts themselves.

133. *Hansard's Parliamentary Debates,* 3d ser., 13 (May 24, 1832): 48.
134. Genovese (1983): 2.

4

LOADED WITH DEADLY EVIDENCE

British abolitionists challenged the common and negative perception of slave revolts that was shaped by slavery advocates and presented instead a more sympathetic depiction of the slaves' revolt. They did not merely intend to dismiss planter descriptions of slave revolts or to examine the slave rebels' role in shaping the plantation colonies of the New World. The abolitionists were marshalling the evidence for useful antislavery material. They best achieved this goal when they examined the manner in which colonists crushed the rebellions. This chapter traces how abolitionists presented the defeated slave rebel as both victim and agent, and used this dual image as a propaganda tool for the antislavery cause.

On January 31, 1823, British abolitionists publicly announced their intention to work more vigorously for the mitigation and gradual extinction of colonial slavery. They were no longer hopeful that improvement in the slaves' daily lives would follow the abolition of the slave trade as a matter of course, and they sought a more practical method to achieve their objectives. They perceived that the most effective way to bring about the mitigation and gradual abolition of slavery was to embark on a program of exposure of the evils of the system. On February 19, 1823, a little more than two weeks after the formal launching of the London Committee on Slavery, the leading abolitionists resolved, "that this Committee are of opinion that an exposition of the laws of slavery as it exists in the British West India Islands would essentially promote the object of enlightening the public mind as to the true condition of the slaves."[1]

Society members believed that a good starting point for highlighting the evils of the system was the publication and circulation of James

---

Title is from Coupland (1933), 67–68, in reference to the field work undertaken by Thomas Clarkson on behalf of the Anti-Slavery Society.

1. February 19, 1823, p. 8, MSS. Brit. Emp. S. 20 E2/1, Anti-Slavery Society Papers; see also the *Anti-Slavery Monthly Reporter* 1, no. 6 (November 30, 1825): 53, which stated that the colonists themselves were the witnesses who proved that slavery was evil.

Stephen Sr.'s *The Slavery of the British West India Colonies Delineated.*[2] Stephen wrote to the society on February 28, 1823, accepting the challenge and informing the members that his work did not focus only on the laws of the colonies but also on the practice of slavery itself.[3] In producing the work, he had intended to awaken the public to the suffering of the wrongs of the slaves.[4] *Slavery Delineated* paved the way for the immediate post-1823 exposure tactics of the abolitionists. This tract was well supported by a series of antislavery pamphlets under the common title *Negro Slavery.* The stated objective of *Negro Slavery* was to "furnish to the public a plain, authentic and unvarnished picture of Negro Slavery . . . as it exists at the present moment."[5] The publication of many other antislavery treatises was to follow. Stephen's son George noted that "in 1825 and 1826 the subject of slavery was often brought before Parliament in one form or another. The Mauritius slave trade . . . the administration of the slave laws, the proceedings of the colonial assemblies, the slave holding interest of colonial officers, were so many texts on which Buxton, Whitmore, William Smith, Brougham, and Lord Suffield preached most orthodox and powerful sermons."[6]

Although abolitionists did not set out intentionally to publicize slave rebellions, their treatment of the manner in which slaves were victimized in the suppression of revolts soon became a central feature of their program of exposure. Charles Buxton, the son of abolitionist leader Sir Thomas Fowell Buxton, observed that after 1824, "the next three years were spent in discussion of Smith's death and the treatment of the rebel slaves."[7] The abolitionists were able to put enough distance between the act of rebellion itself, which they denounced, and the suffering of rebel slaves, which they manipulated, to be able to reinforce the British antislavery cause.

2. Ibid.

3. Ibid., p. 16.

4. Ibid.

5. Society for the Mitigation and Gradual Abolition of Slavery Throughout the British Dominions, *Negro Slavery, or A View of the More Prominent Features of That State of Society as It Exists in the United States of America and in the Colonies of the West Indies Especially in Jamaica* (London: J. Hatchard and Son, 1823), 1.

6. Stephen (1971), 97.

7. Buxton (1852), 211.

Notwithstanding abolitionists' conservatism, their sympathetic treatment of rebels was not at all surprising. British antislavery campaigners were humanitarians who had established a tradition of identifying, exposing, and condemning acts of man's inhumanity to man. This scrutiny was not limited to West Indian slavery but included various humanitarian causes at home and abroad. Colonial slavery, however, had distinguished itself as an institution abounding in atrocities, and the worst punishments were reserved for slaves found guilty of rebellion. Thus, it was only consistent that much of abolitionists' discourse addressed the cruelties colonists inflicted on slaves in the name of suppressing rebellions.

It was not merely for the sake of sentimental rhetoric that abolitionists spoke out against the excessive punishment of rebel slaves. Had this been the case, then the conjecture that slaves were nothing but passive victims in the British struggle against slavery would seem unquestionable. Such a perception, by extension, would reinforce the narrow and simplistic interpretation that casts the humanitarians as the great benefactors largely responsible for the emancipation of the slaves. Additionally, the perspective that the cruelty of West Indian colonists was itself a crucial argument for ending slavery would be strengthened. The discourse British abolitionists fashioned on crushed slave revolts does not, however, allow these interpretations to stand on their own as definitive representations of the antislavery campaign. Antislavery's sentimental depiction of suppressed slave revolts acted as a corollary to their tactical propaganda program, conservative though it was. Through their victimization, British abolitionists converted slave rebels into agents of the campaign against slavery.

THE SENTIMENTAL TRADITION

The most popular leader of the British antislavery movement, William Wilberforce had committed almost all of his life's work to the abolition of the British Atlantic slave trade. He was not, however, a man of one project. He had assigned to himself an all-compassing and consuming mission. "God has set before me as my object the reformation of [my country's] manners."[8] This assignment, he believed, involved infusing "amongst his numerous friends a determination to resist the growing vices

8. Wilberforce and Wilberforce (1838), 5:50.

of the times . . . to prevent crime . . . to resist that general spirit of licentiousness, which is the parent of every species of vice."[9] Wilberforce supported schemes for the relief or improvement of the lives of prisoners and of the poor at home and in Ireland. He devoted to "acts of munificence and charity, from a fourth to a third of his annual income."[10] In an interview regarding his opinions about the role of the statesman in society, Wilberforce responded, "It appears to me that public men in this country should consider it one of the duties imposed on them by Providence, to receive and inquire into the case of distressed persons, who from finding them interesting for suffering individuals, or classes of mankind, are naturally led to apply to them for the redress of their own grievances, or the supply of their wants."[11] Wilberforce converted this principle into action by supporting a "multitude of daily charities."[12] Everyday he filled a tray with letters responding to one cause of humanity or the other. Lord Clarendon recalled how, on one occasion, Wilberforce was preparing an important motion to put before the House of Commons and was interrupted by a poor man who was in danger of being imprisoned for a small debt. Instead of sending him away at this busy moment, Wilberforce spent some time inquiring into the details of the distressing case and eventually paid the man's debt. Lord Clarendon commented that Wilberforce had never learned to "stop his ears at the cry of the poor."[13]

Critics of Wilberforce, such as his contemporary William Cobbett and the historians Eric Williams and Jack Gratus, seem to be persuaded that he was a hypocrite who did good works to parade his generosity. Gordon Lewis makes the valid point, however, that "no one can read the record of the men who led the battle for abolition . . . and . . . emancipation . . . without a profound respect for the sense of stricken conscience that converted a disparate conglomeration of fine poetic-literary indignation into a highly efficient movement of at once parliamentary manoeuvre and national propagandist agitation."[14] Wilberforce commenced the movement that resulted in slave emancipation, but he never openly advocated com-

9. Ibid.
10. *Edinburgh Review* 67, no. 135 (July 1838): 162.
11. Wilberforce and Wilberforce (1838), 5:232.
12. Ibid.
13. Ibid., 5:232–233.
14. Lewis (1978), 36.

plete and immediate emancipation nor was he very keen on adopting a public national program of agitation against slavery. Lewis, however, is perhaps right in believing that Wilberforce's humanitarian conscience, which led him to agitate on behalf of the downtrodden around the world, proceeded from a genuine conversion to Christianity. This spiritual awakening took place soon after Wilberforce's entry into active parliamentary politics.[15] The skepticism nevertheless persists concerning the motives underlying his overall leadership of and involvement in the British movement against slavery. Given the impressive record of his support of charitable causes on the national and international scene, however, it was almost inevitable that Wilberforce and his circle of agitators would have drawn from the slaves' experience of crushed rebellions to formulate their antislavery ideology.

Still, Wilberforce was extremely conservative in the options he advocated to make the rebels' experience count in dismantling the slave system. He favored the tactic of exerting antislavery pressure from within parliament and was reluctant to broaden the base of support by appealing to the wider populace. Sir George Stephen, ardent antislavery member of the Agency Committee established in the summer of 1831, attempted to explain Wilberforce's conservatism. "He felt, perhaps unconsciously, too much deferential regard for rank and power, irrespective, not of the morality, but of the sterling worth of their possessors."[16] Stephen's comment provides a useful insight into the complexity of the principles upon which not only Wilberforce but also the majority of the antislavery leaders operated. Yet, Stephen's commentary must be read guardedly since one of the major aims of his book was to justify the centrality of the Agency Committee at the expense of the more traditional abolitionists. While it is true that the leading abolitionists reserved a deep regard for the respectable classes of society, they were not opposed to using slave rebellions to advance their cause. It was a mixed stance that risked the introduction of significantly incongruent elements into the movement. Yet it was a risk that British abolitionists, consciously or unconsciously, were to take time and again.

The man who succeeded Wilberforce in the leadership of the antislav-

15. Ibid., 37.
16. Stephen (1971), 79.

ery movement was just as involved as his predecessor in agitating on behalf of the poor or distressed. Thomas Fowell Buxton became a member
of Parliament for Weymouth in 1818. Soon after the beginning of his political career, he joined two select committees to champion "the battle for
reforming the prisons and the penal code."[17] In February 1818 he published a work entitled *An Enquiry Whether Crime may be Produced or
Prevented by our present system of Prison Discipline.* This work exposed
to the British public the abuses suffered by prison inmates. So considerable was its effect that "it was translated into French and distributed on
the continent. It even reached Turkey and . . . India."[18] At home the work
helped to induce the British government to ameliorate the wretched conditions of prisoners, and in India a similar effect was achieved. Buxton's
exertions in this and other fields were paramount in convincing Wilberforce that Buxton was the most appropriate candidate to succeed him in
representing the slaves in Parliament. After Buxton delivered a speech depicting the materially depraved conditions in which the aged and the
weavers subsisted in Spitalfields, Wilberforce wrote to Buxton, confessing: "I have both heard and read of your successful effort on Tuesday last
on behalf of the hungry and naked . . . I anticipate success of the effort
which I trust you will one day make in other instances, in an assembly in
which I trust we will be fellow labourers, both in the motives by which
we are actuated, and in the objects to which our exertions will be directed."[19]

Making representations on behalf of men by isolating and featuring
the severity of their conditions was not a novel approach. It was a method
central to British abolitionist policy. Buxton was one of the main spokesmen to convert the story of defeated rebels in Jamaica into valuable anti-
slavery material even though he was uncomfortable, to say the least, using the elements of popular radical behavior to maximize the strength of
his cause.

Thomas Clarkson was most responsible for collecting the empirical
data to support the abolitionist argument. Gordon Lewis calls him "a

17. Coupland (1933), 138.
18. Ibid., 65.
19. Letter to T. F. Buxton from Wilberforce addressed from Kensington Gore, November 18, 1816, in Buxton (1852), 52.

born detective . . . a Benthamite utilitarian in his passion for facts."[20] Clarkson had written about Britain's involvement in slavery in his 1785 Cambridge University prize-winning Latin essay "Is it Right to Make Men Slaves Against Their Wills?" Research on the subject sent him beyond the quest for academic reputation to a consideration of the extent to which Europe was injuring Africa. He resolved to act upon what he had written, becoming a member of the Society for the Abolition of the Slave Trade. Formed in 1787, its main object was to collect incriminating evidence that would lead to the dismantling of the system. To conduct research for his essay, and to fulfil the objective of the slave-trade committee appointed by Parliament to investigate this branch of British commerce, Clarkson toured Liverpool, London, Lancaster, and Bristol. He boarded slave ships and measured the quarters provided for slaves. He found out how much profit was made by traders. He obtained specimens of the shackles, thumb-screws, and mouth openers—instruments of human torture that were used in the trade. He read all he could about the trade, talked to London businessmen involved in it, and even created local antislavery groups throughout the country. After indefatigable labor, "he completed his inquiries and returned to London loaded with deadly evidence."[21] Clarkson's industry and propaganda were more directed toward the abolition of the slave trade than slavery. Even after 1807 and the passage of an act to end the trade, he continued to work for the cause. Between 1822 and 1824, Clarkson was the Anti-Slavery Society agent lecturing and helping to organize branch societies throughout the United Kingdom.

Clarkson also believed in the effectiveness of bringing the slavery question before the British legislature. In 1824, he insisted that the treatment of the "Negroes" must be removed from the hands of the planters. "To whom then are we to turn our eyes for help on this occasion? I answer, to the British Parliament, which has already heard and redressed in part the wrongs of Africa."[22] Clarkson, however, did not put his entire confidence in the policy of applying pressure within the House. In a very real sense, he had provided the abolitionists with a practical demonstration of how best to combine antislavery rhetoric and tactic to achieve their objectives.

20. Lewis (1978), 40; Klingberg (1926), 77.
21. Coupland (1933), 67–68.
22. Clarkson (1824), 6.

Clarkson was a man of the people, unshackled by class partiality, who strove to engage men of all walks of life in the fight for the great cause.

In attacking the institution of slavery itself, however, Clarkson's example was only partially followed. The new leaders were more inclined to adopt Wilberforce's conservative style of appealing directly to the highest authority. George Stephen observed that "it was the Anti-slavery policy at this time, and for several years afterwards, to address the million through the House for it was the only way of getting into the newspapers."[23] Stephen went on to state that many abolitionist leaders "forbade all the obtrusive weight of pressure from without."[24] The leaders believed that their movement was of such a character that it "required the influence and talents of acknowledged men in Parliament."[25] Yet abolitionists did not completely refrain from enlisting the support of extraparliamentary bodies. After 1823 a new vigor in the campaign witnessed the increase of petitions, annual mass meetings, corresponding societies, and distribution of tracts and antislavery pamphlets. Antislavery views flooded the *Morning Chronicle* and the *Edinburgh Review*.[26] Antislavery propaganda was not always read and, when read, did not always provoke the intended response. Nevertheless, it was out in the open.

Another drawback in the national propagandist policy was that the groups and individuals whose support the abolitionists targeted and accepted were notably limited. Patricia Hollis notes that abolitionist leaders did not wish to appear to intimidate Parliament by presenting support from a mob of unruly people out of doors.[27] They felt it was more appropriate to receive testimony from ladies and sectarian ministers and their congregations.[28] Even the emergence of ladies' antislavery societies by the 1820s was unacceptable to Wilberforce. Around 1824, he instructed leaders of the movement not to speak at women's antislavery societies.[29] The male leaders also made some attempts to suppress informa-

23. Stephen (1971), 97.
24. Ibid., 112.
25. Ibid., 112–113.
26. Ibid., 117.
27. Hollis (1980), 295.
28. Ibid.
29. www.spartacus.schoolnet.co.uk.reanti-slavery.htm (accessed March 14, 2002); and Wilberforce and Wilberforce (1838), 5:264–265.

tion about the existence of Elizabeth Heyrick's antislavery pamphlet entitled *Immediate not Gradual Abolition of Slavery*.[30] Hollis observes that "anti-slavery leaders in any case were no radicals."[31] They were responsive to the fact that British opinion, especially parliamentary opinion, was characterized and swayed by "inherent caution and fair-mindedness . . . love of compromise and dislike of violent courses."[32] Hence "the backing for abolition . . . remained throughout respectable, rational and articulate, even when plebeian."[33] The gender issue in the leadership and policies of British antislavery is quite interesting. The male leaders were apparently opposed to the perceived radical views of abolitionist Elizabeth Heyrick. Yet, without acknowledging how she shaped their slave rebellion discourse, many of the views that the males expressed about the pre-emancipation revolts strongly resembled the opinions she expressed in *Immediate*.[34]

In spite of the limitations of their program, the abolitionists were great propagandists, in part because the language they employed to fight their battle appealed to the sentimental humanitarianism of the middle classes. God-fearing men and women in nineteenth-century Britain who supported charitable organizations and who agitated against cruelties of all kind tended to respond to abolitionists' outrage over the inhumane treatment of slaves.[35] It was within this admittedly narrow range of popular support of a predominantly conservative campaign that slave rebels etched their space in the abolitionists' attack on British West Indian slavery.

CALL FOR PAPERS

Following the first major rising of slaves in Barbados in 1816, common themes began to emerge from abolitionists' descriptions of failed revolts. Although lack of official documents restricted what they could say, they

30. Ibid.; Midgley (1992), 93, 114, 115. Note that Midgley comments that "Heyrick's pamphlets, while officially ignored by the leadership of the Anti-Slavery Society, were . . . privately given serious attention."

31. Hollis (1980), 295.

32. Coupland (1933), 114.

33. James Walvin, *England, Slaves and Freedom, 1776–1835* (London: Macmillan, 1986), 153.

34. Heyrick (1824), 39, 43–45.

35. Midgley (1992), 95.

were quick in articulating their responses. Abolitionists insisted that Barbadian colonists were not merely interested in putting down the rebellion. They seemed intent on making their slaves victims of bloody and hysterical carnage. Within the British House of Commons, Thomas Fowell Buxton referred to the events in Barbados as scenes of "blood not of whites but of blacks in abundance."[36] The London Anti-Slavery Society reinforced this impression, reporting, "All we know is that the alleged insurgents made no attack; they were the party attacked. No white man appears to have been killed or even wounded by the Blacks, while from one to two thousand are said to have been hunted down, and put to death, without resistance."[37]

Abolitionists' writings immediately attacked the excessive vindictiveness of the planters' initial moves to crush the revolt and emphasized the pitiable position of the slaves. They were building upon the observation of Colonel Codd, commander of the garrison at St. Anns, who had expressed the opinion that "under the irritation of the moment and exasperated at the atrocity of the insurgents, some of the militia of the parishes in insurrection were induced to use their arms too indiscriminately in pursuit of the fugitives."[38] The abolitionists were keen to stress that the very first blow that the planters struck was thoughtlessly swift and fatal. From the outset, guilt lay with the colonists, not with the slaves. Another abolitionist expressing this view was the author of the anonymously published *Remarks on the Insurrection in Barbados and the Bill for the Registration of Slaves.* The author reinforced the doctrine that the planter class resorted to actions that surpassed the exigencies of the occasion. "The repression of the revolt was responsible for the extent of the mischief."[39] The author took another step in converting the suffering of the slaves into useful antislavery materials. He advised that "the repetition of such horrors may be prevented by the timely interposition of parlia-

36. *Hansard's Parliamentary Debates,* new ser., 10 (June 19, 1816): 1142.

37. Society for the Mitigation and Gradual Abolition of Slavery Throughout the British Dominions, *A Review of Some Of The Arguments Which Are Commonly Advanced Against Parliamentary Interference in Behalf of the Negro Slaves, With a Statement of Opinions Which Have Been Expressed on That Subject by Many of Our Most Distinguished Statesmen* (London: J. Hatchard and Son, 1824), 12. Hereafter this cite is referred to as *Review.*

38. Codd to Leith, April 25, 1816, CO 28/85, f. 13, Colonial Office Papers.

39. *Remarks,* 6.

ment."[40] The 1816 Barbados revolt foreshadowed abolitionists' demands for improvement in the slavery system and for the intervention of the British Parliament in colonial affairs, which the campaigners embraced more fully after 1823.

The suppression of revolt in Barbados propelled the abolitionists to request official documents detailing the treatment of slaves in the colonies. Although the abolitionists made bold assertions about the revolt, they had no solid basis for their conclusions. They drew attention to the fact that the events were shrouded in mystery. The London Anti-Slavery Society remonstrated, "Into this bloody transaction, Parliament has made no inquiry whatever! Why have not the West Indians called for such an inquiry?"[41] The abolitionists' initial interest in accessing supporting documents on the treatment of slaves in the vicious aftermath of slave rebellion was not primarily due to concern for the punished rebels. It was stimulated by the desire to defend themselves against planter accusation. The campaigners were anxious to prove that, contrary to the assertions of the planters, their debates on the slavery question were not responsible for fomenting rebellion. Thus, they found an opportunity to exonerate themselves and, at the same time, to justify their agitation of the slavery question. "Until the whole of this mysterious affair is placed in the light of day, it will be impossible for them [the West Indians] to use it as an argument against discussion . . . not a syllable has been officially published, either in England or in Barbados, which can throw light on these dark and sanguinary occurrences."[42]

In demanding that colonial authorities in Barbados dispatch detailed information on the treatment slaves endured in rebellion or in other circumstances, abolitionists were attempting to break new ground in colonial administration. By 1816, "official returns of slave treatment could only be obtained from the crown colonies . . . unencumbered by 'Assemblies.'"[43] It was a proverbial truth that "from 1807 to 1820, the market place of a West Indian colony was a sealed book to the British public."[44]

40. Ibid., 8.
41. Ibid., 12.
42. Ibid.
43. Stephen (1971), 89.
44. Ibid., 41.

The selfish impetus that prompted abolitionists to demand colonial documents soon gave way to more altruistic motives. Abolitionists cited the
brutal suppression of the rebellion in Barbados to peer more closely into
slavery as it existed in the legislative colonies. A committee appointed by
the Barbados House of Assembly eventually published an official report
of the rebellion in 1818.

DEATH IN THE BATTLEFIELD AND PROPAGANDA IN BRITAIN

Of the three major slave rebellions that erupted in the British West Indies
in the nineteenth century, the 1823 Demerara revolt received the most
abolitionist attention. In their commentary on this revolt the abolitionists
most sharply portrayed the victimization of rebel slaves. It was through
this episode, too, that they grasped the opportunity to call on the British
Parliament to implement measures of slave amelioration, and on sections
of the British public to rally to the cause of the slaves. The suppression of
rebellion in Demerara was alluring to the abolitionists because its victims
most irresistibly presented their shed blood as a sacrifice crying out for redress. That slave revolts ended in the slaughter of blacks not whites was
most visibly presented in abolitionists' account of the rebels' confrontation with colonial militia forces. "While they were thus conferring with
Colonel Leahy, or just as their conference ceased, the troops are said to
have begun firing upon them . . . As the slaves were crowded together, and
were not expecting an attack, the carnage was considerable. In a few minutes, one hundred and fifty of them . . . lay dead or wounded on the spot;
the rest, as soon as they recovered from their surprise, fled with precipitation, and without offering any resistance whatever. The carnage appears
for a time to have been pursued. The Indians were called in and used as
blood hounds, and to bring them in alive or dead."[45]

This wanton, indiscriminate, and apparently deliberate massacre appeared to the abolitionists as a repetition on a larger scale of events in Barbados. In the initial confrontation, planters seemed to make no attempt
to bring the slaves to justice. Vengeance consumed their attention. Campaigners protested such unhesitating brutality. The Anti-Slavery Society
insisted, "It becomes the Parliament of this country to make diligent in-
quisition respecting the blood which has been thus profusely shed, and to

45. "Negro Slavery No. 7," 59.

judge fairly between the oppressor and the oppressed."[46] The killing of so many slaves irrefutably showed that Demerara planters were not benevolent masters. The points on which abolitionists raised their objections were becoming all too familiar, and these objections soon became tenets of antislavery thought.

Abolitionists did not simply create a picture of defeated rebels; they demanded that action be taken to redress the suffering of the slaves. Correctly identifying the perpetrators of crime in the colonies was only an initial, though important step in this direction. The abolitionists used the suppression of the Demerara slave revolt to become more emphatic in demanding that documents concerning the treatment of slaves be produced for their perusal and for the perusal of ministers of Parliament. In time, these documents were passed on to corresponding societies around the country and to nonconformists and other friends in the form of antislavery tracts and pamphlets. The abolitionists demanded,

> Let the documents necessary to elucidate this transaction be produced—the entire documents—the records of the Fiscal's office, the dispatches of the Governor, the reports of the inferior officers, both civil and military; the examinations and depositions of witnesses, the previous interrogatories addressed to the accused, with their answers, the whole detail of the proceedings on their trial, their defence, their sentence, and their punishment. And let the evidence of witnesses and the declarations of prisoners be communicated to us, not in the language into which they have been translated, but in that which they were given; not in the balanced phrases which would be unintelligible to the Slaves . . . but in the mongrel dialect of Dutch and English, which forms the colloquial language of the Slaves of Demerara. We shall then . . . ascertain whether our wretched fellow-subjects . . . have met with their fair share of even-handed, temperate, British justice.[47]

Indeed, using the colonists' detailed accounts of defeated rebellions to undermine the slave system was one of the abolitionists' expressed objectives. In 1822 James Cropper had written to Thomas Clarkson, "Let us show what the slavery of the British colonies is and then our opponents

46. Ibid.
47. Ibid., 61–62.

will be speechless."[48] Significantly, it was the intention of the abolitionists to dumbfound their opponents not only by their own evidence but also by the literal testimonies of the slaves. It was an ambitious objective, with which the colonists only partially complied. Colonial dispatches were sent regularly from colonies with and without legislative assemblies by 1820. The verbatim testimonies of the slaves, however, were not forthcoming, and even the translated testimonies of the slaves were corrupted.[49] To the credit of the abolitionists, they demanded and did hear, though in transmuted tones, the voice of the slaves in the official documents posted to the Colonial Office at Downing Street. At the same time, it is interesting to note how the slave revolts led abolitionists to adopt doctrines that emerged in the revolutionary age of nineteenth-century Europe. The abolitionists did not neglect to mention that the slaves, fellow citizens of Britain, were denied but were entitled to "their fair share of even-handed, temperate, British justice."

Steps were also taken in Britain to disseminate antislavery views on colonial practice, which included the treatment of slaves in the suppression of rebellions. The pamphlet *Review of Some of the Arguments,* which contained the opinions of the London Anti-Slavery Society on the suppression of the 1816 Barbados slave revolt, had been circulated among both houses of Parliament.[50] The first formal information about the Demerara slave rebellion reached the London Committee on Slavery on October 24, 1823. In December of that year Thomas Clarkson was "requested to proceed on his new tour as soon as convenient . . . in behalf of the Society . . . to visit the Principal Places in all the fourteen counties . . . rather than to confine himself to the complete organization of nine as it seems important that petitions should be procured without delay from those places which will have the greatest weight of influence with Parliament."[51]

48. Cited in James Walvin, "The Rise of British Popular Sentiment for Abolition, 1781–1832," in *Anti-Slavery, Religion, and Reform: Essays in Memory of Roger Anstey,* ed. Christine Bolt and Seymour Drescher (Folkestone, England: W. Dawson, 1980), 154.

49. See Article 10, *Edinburgh Review* 40, 79 (March 1824): 258, and *The Missionary Smith,* 19, on Brougham's view that Demerara authorities twisted the evidence to conceal their own guilt in the revolt. Doctoring the testimonies of slaves was the main reason why the London Missionary Society was determined to produce its own version of Smith's trial.

50. Committee on Slavery Minute Book, April 30, 1823, p. 24, MSS. Brit. Emp. S. 20 E2/1, Anti-Slavery Society Papers.

51. Ibid., 75.

In addition to touring the country, Clarkson wrote the pamphlet *Thoughts on the Necessity of Improving the Condition of Slaves* after the Demerara slave revolt. Clarkson noted that "the London Committee printed and circulated many citations of it among the committees in the country."[52] Subsequent to the circulation of *Thoughts,* Wilberforce congratulated Clarkson "in the success of your endeavours to call the public voice into action."[53] That public was small and very restricted. Slave rebellions nevertheless led the abolitionists to adjust their plans so as to maximize the potential effects of petitioning the legislature and circulating antislavery opinions.

The reprehensible conduct of slaveholders on the battlefield of insurrection was also evident in the Jamaican slave revolt of 1831–1832. The British general Sir Willoughby Cotton had circulated in January 1832 a proclamation offering clemency to all slaves who were not leaders among the rebels. These slaves were expected to return to their estates and submit to the authority of the established forces of law and order in the colony. This offer was disgraced by "officers of the militia bent upon revenge . . . who fired upon the returning culprits . . . Cheated by the proffer of mercy, the poor wretches fled to the woods again, where Maroons were sent to hunt them down, stimulated by the bribe of a price for each pair of human ears brought in."[54] Antislavery agitators were incensed by the unmitigated vengeance to which the planter class in the various colonies had resorted. On April 11, 1832, the leading abolitionists met at the Anti-Slavery Society's London office at 18 Aldermanbury and discussed the recent events in Jamaica.[55] In its minutes the society recorded its disapproval of "the terrible means resorted to for its [the Jamaican slave rebellion] suppression."[56] The commentary reiterated the statements made after the suppression of the Demerara revolt. On account of the "large effusion of innocent blood"[57] shed in the colony, James Stephen

52. CN33 MS Essay, p. 114, Thomas Clarkson Papers.

53. Ibid.

54. George Findlay, *The History of the Wesleyan Methodist Missionary Society* (London: Epsworth, 1921), 89.

55. Committee on Slavery Minute Book, April 11, 1832, pp. 132–135, MSS. Brit. Emp. S. 20 E2/3, Anti-Slavery Society Papers.

56. Ibid.

57. Ibid.

and a Mr. Garrat referred to the rebels as the "sure victims of insurrection."[58] The abolitionists had obviously read the various accounts dispatched from Jamaica to the Colonial Office, thanks to the demands that
followed the 1816 Barbados slave revolt. Stephen and Garrat were horrified that in the attempt to nip the rebellion in the bud, slaves had "fallen
by the muskets, the swords . . . of the British soldiery."[59] Abolitionist observations were confirmed by many accounts in the colony. The missionary, the Reverend George Waddell, had commented that "the Negroes began to cower under the storm they had raised, terrified by consequences
never anticipated."[60] In analyzing Rev. William Knibb's testimony on the
Jamaican slave revolt, the abolitionists expressed their outrage that some
slaves were shot by the random firing of the militia.[61] Slave rebels were
caught completely off guard by the reaction of their injured masters. They
were deceived by their masters into thinking that in seeking to address
their wrongs through the enlightened approach of demonstration, they
would be spared the planters' wrath. They did not believe that the king's
troops would fire on them.[62]

The slaves were pitiable in their defeat. The crucial lesson of their failure helped stir the abolitionists into propaganda action. After discussing
the events of the Jamaican slave revolt, the London Anti-Slavery Society
resolved to hold a public meeting in Exeter Hall on Saturday, May 12,
1832.[63] In a subsequent meeting, it was reported that "Great Britain and

58. Ibid.

59. Ibid.

60. Rev. Hope Masterston Waddell, *Twenty-Nine Years in the West Indies and Central
Africa: A Review of Missionary Work and Adventure, 1829–1858*, 2d ed. (London: Frank
Cass and Co., 1970), 63.

61. *Analysis of the Report*, 108.

62. *British Parliamentary Papers, Papers Relating to the Slave Trade 1831–1834, Slave
Trade 80. Papers Relating to Slave Insurrection, Jamaica. Copy of the Report of a Com-
mittee of the House of Assembly of Jamaica, Appointed to Inquire into the Cause of, and
Injury sustained by, the recent Rebellion in that Colony; together with the Examinations on
Oath, Confessions and other Documents annexed to the Report* (Shannon, Ireland: Irish
University Press, 1969), 215. Sir Willoughby Cotton, commander in charge of the armed
forces suppressing the revolt, testified that he heard that a report had been circulated among
the slaves that the navy and the military would not act against them.

63. Committee on Slavery Minute Book, May 9, 1832, p. 143, MSS. Brit. Emp. S. 20
E2/3, Anti-Slavery Society Papers.

Ireland raised upwards of 6,000 petitions to Parliament pronouncing that slavery was wholly repugnant to the spirit of Christianity, to the claims of humanity and justice and to the principles of the British Constitution."[64] The success of this propaganda campaign after the Jamaican slave revolt was certainly not completely due to the extent to which rebellion won support for the campaign or stirred the abolitionists into greater action. Parliamentary reform, the demand for the end of the monopoly that the West Indians enjoyed in Britain, persecution of sectarian missionaries and the general evils of the servile regime, among other factors, played their part. The discussions of the society's Committee on Slavery following the revolt, however, confirm that the experiences of defeated rebels were also taken into significant consideration.

THE LETTER OF THE LAW

Although the planters' vindictive behavior during the nineteenth-century slave revolts in Barbados, Demerara. and Jamaica outraged humanitarian sensitivity, it was consistent with the insular codes of the various island legislatures. Stephen had observed in his *Treatment and Conversion of African Slaves* that animals enjoyed greater protection under colonial laws than did slaves. It was well known that an apparent contempt in all legal matters was reserved for the slaves. Stephen explained,

> Nay, a horse, a cow, or a sheep, is much better protected with us by the law, than a poor slave. For these, if found in a trespass, are not to be injured, but secured for their owners; while a half-starved Negro, may, for breaking a single cane, which probably he himself has planted, be hacked to pieces with a cutlass; even though, perhaps, he be incapable of resistance, or of running away from the watchman, who finds him in the fact. Nay, we find men among us, who dare boast of their giving orders to their watchmen, not to bring home any slave that they find breaking of canes, but, as they call it, to hide them, that is to kill, and bury them.[65]

In spite of the gross vulgarity of this state of affairs, the worst was still in store "for the wretches who had committed the diabolical crime of in-

64. Ibid., 147.

65. James Ramsay, *An Essay on the Treatment and Conversion of African Slaves in the British Colonies* (London: James Phillips, 1786), 63; see also Stephen (1824), 58.

surrection."[66] Stephen recorded that rebellious slaves were "roasted alive, hung up in irons to perish of thirst, shut up in a cage and starved to death."[67] He also commented that rebellion was a crime "of such a nature, that you always annex to it the most excruciating pain."[68]

Planters in Barbados demonstrated that here at least, they adhered to the strict letter of the law. The preamble to the Barbados law of 1661, *An Act for the Better Ordering and Governing of Negroes,* had declared that slaves were "heathenish, brutish and a dangerous kind of people."[69] Consequently, colonial lawmakers deemed it appropriate that "criminal slaves should be branded, whipped, mutilated, suffer amputation of limbs and capital punishment for public crimes like rebellion."[70] Thus, following the discovery of the 1675 Barbados slave plot to revolt, of the seventeen slaves who were found guilty and executed, six were burned alive and eleven were beheaded and their bodies were dragged through the streets of Speightstown. The horror of the last act was intended to deter other slaves from contemplating rebellion. One of the conspirators, however, urged to reveal the full nature of the plot, scornfully refused. He resigned himself to the cruel fate that he knew awaited him and boldly declared, "If you roast me today, you can't roast me tomorrow."[71]

Captured nineteenth-century slave rebels, like their predecessors, felt the full blast of the merciless power of colonial law. Slaves in rebellion lost their lives not only when the whites panicked in the chaos of an uprising but also when colonial authorities had time to consider and execute punishments. Court-martial sessions were held in the colonies in the aftermath of slave revolts, and the Anti-Slavery Society made it clear that they regarded the sentences as part of the irrefutable proof that slavery was evil and was in need of reform. The society stated that in using the colonists' recorded evidence to condemn British West Indian slavery, "we allude . . .

66. Stephen (1824), 7.

67. Ibid., 8.

68. Stephen (1786), 162.

69. Cited in Beckles (1987), 21

70. Ibid.; Society for the Mitigation and Gradual Abolition of Slavery Throughout the British Dominions, "Barbados—New Slave Law," in *The Slave Colonies of Great Britain; or A Picture of Negro Slavery Drawn by the Colonists Themselves; Being An Abstract of the Various Papers Recently Laid Before Parliament on That Subject,* corrected 2d ed. (London: J. Hatchard and Son, 1826), 15.

71. Beckles (1987), 38.

to their criminal slave courts—to the nature and imperfections of the judicial returns—from the Fiscal of Demerara—to the trials of the insurgents in that colony in 1823 . . . in which every species of judicial irregularity appears to find a place."[72]

Several abolitionists condemned the courts martial that put to death alleged slave rebels in Demerara. In the House of Commons Henry Brougham strongly objected to the fact that "they [the slaves] are cut off in hundreds by the hand of justice."[73] This was how Quamina, the alleged leader of the revolt, met his end. Quamina was a deacon at the Bethel Chapel, the Methodist slave congregation over which Rev. John Smith presided. He was one of those slaves who, after fleeing the initial carnage unleashed by colonial forces in the mopping-up operations, had been hunted in the bushes. An Indian called Cattaw killed him. Such was the master's desire to exact revenge that after Quamina was shot and his dead body recovered, "he was dragged to the front of Success Estate, and there, between two cabbage trees still standing, he was gibbeted as a rebel, the corpse bound together with chains, and allowed to swing in the breeze for many months after, to the terror and disgust of every passer-by."[74]

Quamina's corpse was subjected to this brutal treatment despite that the court had no conclusive evidence that he was indeed involved in the rebellion. According to the testimony of Dr. Michael McTurk of Plantation Felicity and Burgher General in Demerara, Quamina may have had a cutlass or a stick with him at the time of his death, but it was not certain that he was armed.[75] Quamina was not the only slave whom the planters subjected to deliberate and calculated disgrace for the role he was accused of playing in the 1823 slave rising. Almost all slaves who appeared to be prominent rebels were subjected to hasty trials and executions. "Ringleaders were rounded up, tried by court-martial and hanged the very day they were sentenced."[76] Among the slaves thus swiftly condemned to

72. *Anti-Slavery Monthly Reporter* 1, no. 6 (November 30, 1825), 53; see also Society for the Mitigation and Gradual Abolition of Slavery Throughout the British Dominions (1826), 29–33.

73. Brougham (1857), 158.

74. Wallbridge (1848), 83.

75. *London Missionary Society's Report,* 36

76. R. F. Webber, *Centenary History and Handbook of British Guiana* (British Guiana: Argosy Co., 1931), 50.

death were "two prisoners, Louis of Plaisance and Natty of Enterprise, [who] were tried on the first day, found guilty, sentenced and brought in procession to the Parade Ground about five in the afternoon, where after engaging in prayer they ascended the gallows with much firmness and were hanged under the discharge of cannon. The following day, five more were executed, and so it went on for several days."[77]

British abolitionists read the reports documenting the operations of the courts martial and the executions that they authorized. They questioned the nature of the legal system in which slaves were summarily executed. Henry Brougham remonstrated, "How many victims were sacrificed we know not with precision. Such of them as underwent a trial before being put to death were judged by this court martial . . . I fear we must admit that far more blood was thus spilt than a wise and just policy required."[78] Dr. Stephen Lushington reiterated the sense in which Brougham believed that slaves in rebellion were cheated of the justice to which they were entitled as citizens of Britain. "Many have perished by sentence of the court . . . by September, forty-seven had been executed."[79] Lushington was struck by the possibility that innocent slaves might have been hastened to their end by the faulty system that operated in the aftermath of slave rebellion. He disapprovingly and sarcastically noted, "a sentence which their humane tribunal passed on several of the unfortunate beings at their bar and which, to the everlasting disgrace of the British name, was, in some instances actually carried into execution."[80] In the colonies slave resistance unleashed brutal repression. In Britain, however, it was widening the ground upon which abolitionists opposed the servile regime.

Brougham's attack of the malpractice in Demerara also stressed the unnecessary prolongation of martial law in the colony. Governor Murray had stated in a dispatch to Colonial Secretary of State Lord Bathurst that "I shall not hesitate to seize the first justifiable period for restoring to the colony [Demerara] its regular course of law . . . but the alarm of the white inhabitants is too great and too general to lead one to hope for an early return of confidence; they at present place none but in their arms and a

77. James Rodway (1893), 11:240.
78. *Hansard's Parliamentary Debates,* new ser., 11 (June 1, 1824), 994.
79. Ibid., 1062.
80. Ibid., 1212.

rigorous militia service must be permanently resorted to."[81] Brougham, however, refused to accept that Governor Murray exercised reasonable judgment in the length of time that he maintained martial law in Demerara. Brougham was aggrieved that the massacre continued for "five calendar months, although there is the most unquestioned proof, that the revolt had subsided, and indeed that all appearance of it had vanished."[82] James Mackintosh supported Brougham on this issue. He remarked, "I know not how many Negroes perished on the gibbet . . . These dreadful cruelties, miscalled punishments, did indeed occur after the 17th of August."[83] The Anti-Slavery Society as a body had taken notice of the fact that by January 14, 1824, the Demerara tragedy had not yet closed. A Mrs. Elliot, a friend of Mrs. John Smith and also a missionary's wife, had written that in the week prior to January 14, a slave had been executed for his alleged role in the revolt.[84] To the abolitionists the perpetuation of the executions looked like violence for violence's sake. The mass action of slaves in rebellion and the punishments they suffered in the aftermath caused abolitionists to carefully scrutinize and be critical of the legal system that governed the life of the slave in the West Indian colonies of Britain.

Henry Brougham's legal acumen enabled him to capture the whole range of abuses of the legal system that took place in the aftermath of Demerara 1823. He condemned the individuals who conducted the court martial. He questioned the admissibility of the testimony of slaves against a white man, a practice which on other occasions, though permitted in the former Dutch colony, was not readily accepted by English colonists. He also condemned the charges brought against Smith, the inappropriateness of the line of questioning, and, in general, the anomalous nature of the entire proceedings.[85] Although Brougham sought redress for the

81. Murray to Bathurst, August 24, 1823, Demerara, CO 111/39, ff. 84, Colonial Office Papers.

82. *Hansard's Parliamentary Debates*, new ser., 11 (June 1, 1824), 968; *The Missionary Smith*, 8. Brougham had pointed out that according to the August 26 dispatch of General Murray to Earl Bathurst and subsequent dispatches of August 30 and 31, "no further disturbance had taken place; nor was there from that time any insurrectionary movement whatever."

83. *Hansard's Parliamentary Debates*, new ser., 11 (June 1, 1824), 1062.

84. "Negro Slavery No. 8," 76.

85. *Hansard's Parliamentary Debates*, new ser., 11 (June 1, 1824): 961–999; *The Missionary Smith*, 39–40.

persecution of Smith, it was apparent that he disapproved of the suffering of the slaves in the aftermath of rebellion. In one of two marathon
speeches in June 1824, he said, "It would appear, indeed, that in these
colonies, it was sufficient evidence of a man's being a revolter that he was
first shot and afterwards gibbeted."[86] He argued that it was nothing
short of scandalous that slaves lost their lives on the testimony of a "prisoner, trembling upon his trial, and crouching beneath their remorseless
power."[87] The Anti-Slavery Society supported Brougham by summing up
that "Martial law, blood, slaughter, pursuit, summary and sweeping execution are promptly resorted to by the local authorities of Demerara. Day
after day and week after week, witness the steady undeviating march of
their retributive vengeance. Scores, nay hundreds, of victims are required
to satisfy its demands. For the Negroes to have demanded what it was
which the benevolence of his sovereign really designed for him, must be
expiated by a river of blood."[88]

Abolitionists justified their campaign in Britain by pitting the colonists'
abuse of power against the rights of the slaves to inquire peacefully about
their status. Consequently, in the House of Commons Brougham called
for a cessation of the practice of courts martial in the colonies. He reminded members of the House of Commons how the system had

> become so unbearable that there arose from it the celebrated *Petitions
> of Rights* . . . left to this country by that illustrious lawyer, Lord Coke
> . . . The petition declares, that all such proceedings shall henceforward
> be put down: it declares that "no man shall be fore-judged by life and
> limb against the form of the Great Charter;" that "no man ought to
> be adjudged by death but by the laws established in this realm, either
> by the custom of the realm, or by acts of parliament;" and that "the
> commissions for proceeding by martial law should be revoked and an-
> nulled, lest, by color of them, any of his Majesty's subjects be destroyed
> or put to death, contrary to the laws and franchise of the land." Since
> that time, no such thing as martial law has been recognized in this
> country; and courts founded on proclamations of martial law have
> been wholly unknown . . . Afterwards came the annual Mutiny Acts,

86. Henry (1857), 140.
87. *Hansard's Parliamentary Debates,* new ser., 11 (June 1, 1824): 986.
88. "Negro Slavery No. 7," 60.

and Courts Martial, which were held only under those acts . . . These courts were restricted to the trial of soldiers for military offences; and the extent of their powers was pointed out and limited by law.[89]

The colonists could have argued that proclamation of martial law rendered every man to be treated as a soldier and therefore susceptible to be tried by the court. Brougham's conclusion was that once the revolt had been quelled, martial law should have ceased. The court martial in Demerara had overstepped its jurisdiction. The abolitionists used this abuse of power as an opportunity to call upon Parliament to exercise its duty to reconcile the colonial legal system with that which operated in Britain. The proposal to end courts martial in the colonies also showed that slave rebellion was a basis upon which abolitionists sought to reform the structure of the slave plantation societies of the English Caribbean. Brougham's June 1824 speeches ended with a motion praying most earnestly that "His Majesty adopt measures . . . for securing such a just and humane administration of law in that colony as may protect the voluntary instructors of the Negroes, as well as the Negroes themselves, and the rest of His Majesty's subjects from oppression."[90]

Brougham and others used the deaths of slaves following the Demerara rebellion to pressure Parliament and the public to rethink and take corrective action on the regime of slavery. Brougham energized the suffering of the slaves by urging "Parliament to rescue the West Indians from the horrors of such a policy; to deliver those misguided men from their own hands; I call upon you to interpose while it is yet time to save the West Indies . . . their masters, whose short-sighted violence is, indeed, hurtful to their slaves, but to themselves is fraught with fearful and speedy destruction if you do not at once make your voice heard and your authority felt, where both have been so long despised."[91]

The Anti-Slavery Society was convinced that the mode of the trials "will afford no small matter of deep reflection to the people."[92] The abo-

---

89. *Hansard's Parliamentary Debates*, new ser., 11 (June 1, 1824): 969.

90. Ibid., 1206.

91. Brougham (1857), 165. Brougham also warned that by their brutal suppression of the Demerara slave revolt, the colonists "place in jeopardy the life of every white man in the Antilles." *The Missionary Smith*, 39.

92. "Negro Slavery No. 7," 59.

litionists therefore expected that the details of the evils of the suppression of revolts would lead to action on the part of the highest authority in the land. Looking back on events in Demerara as late as 1830, the society admonished, "Let these things be fully weighed, and neither the Government nor the Parliament can hesitate as to the imperative necessity of radically reforming a system which produces such abominations as have been detailed;—such perversions of the very forms of law to purposes of cruelty and oppression . . . These things must come to an end, and that speedily."[93] The society went so far as to assert that if their assessment of events in Demerara was accurate then "Parliament and the Public will feel that if they hesitate to apply an effectual remedy to such evils as have been placed before them, they will be justly chargeable with all the atrocities which have been or may henceforth be committed and with all the blood which has been or may still be shed, in the maintenance of this abominable system."[94]

The abolitionists were equally censorious of the abuse of martial law in the suppression of the Jamaican slave rebellion. Again they relied almost explicitly on the evidence provided by a slave missionary, the Baptist William Knibb. The Anti-Slavery Society noted that "in the report of a speech of Mr Knibb, he had spoken of the innocent blood that had been shed during the insurrection. He said he referred to the number who, during martial law, had suffered innocently!"[95] Knibb concluded that the sentences that court-martial officials in Jamaica passed on alleged slave rebels were not just punishments but painful and alarming excesses of a corrupt system of law. The society echoed Knibb, writing, "The executions were conducted with considerable levity; four or six being sometimes executed in a day at Montego Bay . . . The bodies of those shot and hung at Montego Bay were buried in a trench; those put to death in the country were left to be devoured by vultures. The feeling produced by all this is very painful and alarming, as many have lost not only fathers and brothers, but wives also."[96]

In the eyes of abolitionists slaves accused of and punished for staging rebellions were martyrs of a corrupt interpretation of British law and order. The antislavery activists emphasized that Jamaican colonists, like

93. *Anti-Slavery Monthly Reporter* 1, no. 6 (November 30, 1830): 53–54.
94. Ibid., 61.
95. *Analysis of the Report*, 120.
96. Ibid., 112.

their colleagues in Demerara, had overstepped the legal bar. Knibb had explained, "They could not have had sanction, as persons were shot at distant places on the same day. There were about 300 shot, many by drum-head courts. Some were tried, and shot or hung in half an hour, Sir Willoughby Cotton being then absent. He [Knibb] had himself seen men hung at Montego Bay when Sir Willoughby Cotton was so far distant that he could not have been referred to. The trials and execution went on the most rapidly in St. James's while the general was in Westmoreland."[97] There is no discrepancy between the abolitionists' assessment of slave casualties during and after the suppression of slave revolts and the final recorded figures. James Walvin approximates that the death toll among the slave population totaled "400 in Barbados, 250 in Demerara and 500 in Jamaica."[98] The figures that Michael Craton has found do not differ greatly. He calculates that in Jamaica, 200 slaves were killed while fighting and the judiciary executed 340.[99] Craton also provides a comprehensive breakdown of deaths in Demerara. He tallies that 100 or 150 rebels were killed or wounded by the Black West India Regiment, and twenty-three leading rebels were shot or fled south into the trackless mountains where they were hunted and some were shot. Of the seventy-two who were tried in the five months between August 25, 1823, and January 19, 1824, thirty-three were actually executed.[100]

The victimization that slaves endured in defeated rebellions fed an antislavery discourse that denounced the evils of the servile regime. It also bolstered abolitionists' tactics of pressuring the British government to assume responsibility to correct an evil that was taking place under its colonial direction. These views were expressed as early as 1823, when the campaigners were still committed to the gradual abolition of slavery, and reiterated after the 1831–1832 Jamaican slave revolt when immediate slave emancipation had just become their objective.

A MORE HORRIBLE TALE

Abolitionists were not satisfied that the deaths slaves endured in the field and at the merciless hand of colonial executioners were sufficient examples of the evidence that revolts piled up against slavery. Henry Brougham

97. Ibid.
98. Walvin (1977), 12.
99. Craton (1982), 314.
100. Ibid., 288.

stated that in Demerara "a more horrid tale of blood yet remains to be told."[101] Brougham had consulted the *Port Royal Gazette,* an organ of planter propaganda in Demerara, to formulate conclusions on the revolt and to supply him with further detailed evidence of the afflictions of the slaves. He noted that on January 16, 1824, "seven more of the rebel Negroes have been flogged according to their respective sentences . . . Louis of Porters Hope, . . . 1000 lashes, . . . Field of Clonbrock, . . . 1000 lashes, . . . Mercury of Enmore, 700 lashes, . . . Austin of Cone, . . . 600 lashes, . . . Jessamin of Success, . . . 300 lashes, John Campbell of Otto, . . . 200 lashes, . . . August of Success, . . . 300 lashes."[102] Brougham believed that the flogging of slaves was "a fate hardly preferable to execution."[103] He was appalled that they actually received the whole or almost the whole of these cruel sentences. He also read in the *Port Royal Gazette* of July 24, 1824: "This morning, the brigade were under arms, at an early hour, to witness the flogging of three convicted insurgents, who had been some time under sentence—Cobino, Sammy and Cudjo; the first to receive 1000 lashes and be worked in chains for life, the second, the same number of lashes, and to be worked in chains for seven years, and the third the same as the first. Cobino received the whole amount of the number of lashes awarded; Sammy only 900 and Cudjo only 800. There are several more who still remain for punishment."[104]

Sir James Mackintosh was similarly disturbed that the floggings continued "five months after the rising when hot blood might have cooled."[105] Mackintosh was more contemptuous, however, of the fact that the colonists regarded the flogging of slave rebels as an act of mercy. He described this manifestation of the planters' effrontery as nothing more than an "insolent, atrocious, detestable pretext of mercy."[106] The Anti-Slavery Society also supported Brougham's condemnation of the floggings, stating that "immediately after quiet was restored, many of the survivors were torn in pieces by infliction of the scourge, more merciless than anything upon record in modern times, and in Christian countries."[107]

101. *Hansard's Parliamentary Debates,* new ser., 11 (June 1, 1824): 995.

102. Article 10, *Edinburgh Review* 40, no. 79 (March 1824): 246–247.

103. Ibid., 246.

104. Ibid., 247, Brougham quoting from *Port Royal Gazette* of July 24, 1824.

105. Coupland (1933), 128.

106. *Hansard's Parliamentary Debates,* new ser., 11 (June 1, 1824): 1062.

107. *Edinburgh Review* 41, no. 82 (January 1825): 209.

The driving system in which the planter regarded the use of the whip as a badge of authority and an inducement of labor had been a bone of contention between the pro- and antislavery M.P.s. This was partly why Buxton had brought the notorious Huggins case, though not related to open and violent acts of slave resistance, to the attention of the House of Commons in 1824. Buxton confessed that a case like this "is painful to me to state, and it will doubtless be as painful to the House to hear these sad details."[108] Nevertheless, he ran through

> the celebrated case of Mr Huggins, who himself a magistrate, in the presence of other magistrates, in the public market place of Nevis, in the year 1810, inflicted on one Negro 115 lashes; on another 65; on another 47; on another 165; on another 242; on another 212; on another 181; on another 59; on another 187; on a Negro woman 110; on another woman 58; on another woman 97; on another woman 212; on another woman 291; on another woman 83; on another woman 49; on another woman 68; on another woman 89; and on another woman 56—for which treatment the following whimsical reason was assigned by his son—"he conceived that moderate measures, steadily pursued, were more likely to produce obedience."[109]

Huggin's case, which took place in 1811, was a precursor of the floggings that alleged slave rebels of Demerara endured in 1823–1824. Antislavery campaigners distinctly objected to this mode of punishing and driving the slaves to work. "Punishments are usually inflicted on the naked body with the cart whip, an instrument of dreadful severity, which cruelly lacerates the flesh of the sufferer. Even the unhappy females are equally liable with the men to have their persons thus shamelessly exposed and barbarously tortured by the caprice of their master or overseer."[110]

On account of these dreadful cruelties, the author of an *Edinburgh Review* article felt compelled to quote two extracts from the journal of John Smith that eventually passed into the mainstream of antislavery ideology. On March 22, 1819, Smith had written, "I have thought much of the treatment of the Negroes, and likewise of the state of their minds. It appears

108. *Hansard's Parliamentary Debates,* new ser., 11 (June 1, 1824): 1118.
109. Ibid.
110. Anti-Slavery Society, *A Brief View of the Nature and Effects of Negro Slavery as it Exists in the Colonies of Great Britain* (London: J. Hatchard and Son, 1823).

to me very probable, that, ere long, they will resent the injuries done to them."[111] This idea probably appealed to the author because the abolitionists too were closely examining the treatment and conduct of the slaves. They were beginning to accept that rebellion was a response of the slaves to the brutality of their servile existence. After 1823, several abolitionists began to whisper that if slavery were not abolished by the British Imperial Parliament, the slaves would abolish it in the colonies. The second extract of Smith's journal embodied another antislavery ideology that began to take shape after the Demerara revolt. Smith, in a conversation with a plantation manager, had agreed that "the project of Mr. Canning will never be carried into effect . . . The rigors of Negro slavery . . . can never be mitigated: the system must be abolished."[112] The flogging slaves endured in Demerara provided abolitionists with the opportunity to launch another attack against the use of the cart whip in the colonies.

Abolitionists also noted the flogging of slaves in the aftermath of the Jamaican revolt by again retailing the evidence produced by the missionary William Knibb, who reported that at Falmouth, thirty-six slaves were flogged and that "some were flogged to death, dying of the infliction on the next day. One of Mr. Burchell's members, sentenced to 500 lashes, died of flogging."[113] The floggings, the executions, and the massacre that slaves experienced in the cruel suppression of revolts encouraged British antislavery campaigners to focus more sharply on and to speak out against the penal codes of the British West Indian slave system.

PLEADING THE NEGROES' CAUSE

Several historians argue that the suffering that was truly valuable to the antislavery campaign was that not of the slaves but of persecuted missionaries. Chester New, for example, asserts that because of the Demerara slave rebellion "the movement [would have been] seriously retarded . . . had it not been for the case of missionary Smith."[114] Reginald Coupland is similarly of the opinion that the trial of Smith "may well have been the decisive factor in starting the last irresistible current of anti-slavery

---

111. Article 10, *Edinburgh Review* 40, no. 79 (March 1824): 253. This extract appears in the *London Missionary Society's Report*, 6.

112. Ibid., and the *London Missionary Society's Report*, 8.

113. *Analysis of the Report*, 112.

114. New (1961), 290.

opinion."[115] According to Michael Craton, "The news [of Smith's death] provoked an uproar among the British emancipationists who, typically, regarded Smith's ordeal as far outweighing the death of 250 slaves."[116] Frank Klingberg asserts that "hopes of emancipation seemed shattered, until Brougham by his masterly handling of the case of the missionary, Smith, revived the cause and dealt British slavery a blow from which it never recovered."[117]

Undoubtedly, British abolitionists treated planter reaction to sectarian missionaries in the aftermath of slave rebellion as part of the practice of slavery that demanded exposure and condemnation. After rebellions, sectarian missionaries working among colonial slave congregations were arrested, imprisoned, tarred and feathered, driven into exile, and their properties were subjected to arson attacks.[118] The abolitionists openly expressed the view that these experiences were fortuitous to their movement. Most popular among such incidents was the case of John Smith of the London Missionary Society. He was charged with complicity in the Demerara slave rebellion of 1823.[119] The court martial that tried him brought in a guilty verdict but recommended him to mercy. Smith died in jail before he could be released on the full exoneration that was granted him from Britain.[120]

In very optimistic terms, abolitionists commented on the great advan-

115. Coupland (1933), 131.
116. Craton (1982), 289.
117. Klingberg (1926), 220.
118. *Colonial Slavery*, 5. See also *Facts and Documents*, 5–16; Baptist Missionaries, *A Narrative of Recent Events Connected with the Baptist Mission in This Island Comprising Also a Sketch of the Mission from Its Commencement in 1814 to the End of 1831* (Jamaica: Edward Jordan and Robert Osborn, 1833), 35, 38–51; *Analysis of the Report*, 108–110; Society for the Mitigation and Gradual Abolition of Slavery Throughout the British Dominions, letter of Henry Bleby to J. Barry dated Montego Bay April 24, 1832, in *Abstract of the Report of the Lord's Committees on the Condition and Treatment of the Colonial Slaves, and of the Evidence Taken by Them on That Subject; With Notes by the Editor* (London: J. Hatchard and Son, 1833), 87 (hereafter this item is referred to as *Abstract of the Report*); Hinton (1847), 126, 128–129, 135; Jakobsson (1972), 472; Stanley (1992), 76.
119. See *British Parliamentary Papers, Demerara Minutes of Evidence on the Trial of John Smith a Missionary 1824*, 83, for the four charges brought against Smith.
120. Cited in Jakobsson (1972), 349 [Bathurst to King George IV, February 13, 1824, copy, CO 111/42, Colonial Office Papers]. On the recommendation of Lord Bathurst, Foreign Secretary of State for the Colonies, the king remitted Smith's death sentence.

tage to the cause of Smith's tragic fate. Thomas Fowell Buxton declared, "We have a capital case as to the Demerara insurrection. Smith is innocent."[121] In the *Edinburgh Review,* the Anti-Slavery Society echoed Buxton, stating, "The great debate in Parliament upon the missionary question produced an invaluable acquisition to this great cause."[122] The society openly hailed Smith as "the martyr and victim of our cause."[123] In his *Recollections,* George Stephen remembered Smith as "a martyr to the missionary zeal for the cause."[124] Stephen asserted that "Demerara murdered Smith but at the same time, it contributed largely to the extinction of slavery."[125] Joseph Sturge's memoirs recorded that "the furious persecution of the missionaries, displayed by the destruction of their chapels, their own wanton imprisonment, or expulsion from the islands and culminating at last in what was, in effect, the judicial murder of Smith, 'the Demerara martyr,' helped, by degrees, to prepare the country for that cry of total and immediate emancipation which a few earnest spirits were already beginning to raise."[126]

The abolitionists were not so positive and direct in stating the value to the cause of victimized slaves. Perhaps this reticence reflected their caution not to appear too radical as they defended the position of slaves who had dared to use force to challenge the system. Abolitionists, however, did not tend to elevate the significance of persecuted missionaries over defeated slave rebels. Although they did not use the term *martyr* to refer to the slaves, the evidence demonstrates that they upheld both parties, slaves and missionaries, as agents of the antislavery cause. At times abolitionists even admitted that in relation to the slaves, the missionaries were secondary. In the *Edinburgh Review* it was explained,

> If it should be surmised that I speak with peculiar complacency of the Wesleyan missionaries and with a tendency to lead to a preference of them, the imputation . . . is groundless. I plead the cause of the Negroes, and not that of the Wesleyans . . . in the course of the researches

121. Buxton (1852), 124.
122. *Edinburgh Review* 41, no. 81 (March 1824): 227.
123. Ibid.
124. Stephen (1971), 99.
125. Ibid., 96.
126. Richard (1864), 77.

and the communications which I have had to enter into for the attainment of the end I had a view, . . . the Wesleyan Missionary Society . . . affords at present by far the most powerful means of introducing Christianity among the slave population; and . . . its action has been materially thwarted and counteracted by suspicion, mistrust and occasionally by injurious and unfounded accusation.[127]

Abolitionists appreciated the proper perspective in which the missionaries had assumed roles in the scenario of British West Indian slavery. In the *Edinburgh Review* the abolitionists made it clear that they understood that "these proceedings [trial and persecution of Smith] are all intimately connected with the great question of Negro improvement."[128] Wilberforce in particular made it clear that while Smith's case "involves the question of the rights and happiness of a British subject, and, still more, the administration of justice in the West Indian colonies . . . there is another point of view in which the question is to be regarded, in which it will assume far more importance and excite a still deeper interest."[129]

In Wilberforce's estimation the greater context of Smith's trial and persecution was colonial obstruction to slave amelioration, which included obstacles to the moral and religious instruction of the slaves.[130] In a tract examining the rebellion in Demerara, the Anti-Slavery Society observed, "The case of Mr. Smith must be reserved for another opportunity. That of the slaves is sufficient to engage our present attention."[131] The abolitionists did at times separate the experiences of persecuted missionaries from those of crushed rebels. It was more typical, however, to speak of "the blood of martyred missionaries and murdered Negroes"[132] or "oppressed missionaries and their persecuted followers."[133] Charles Buxton, writing about his father, adequately demonstrated the point. Without making distinctions between slave and missionary, "the colonial legislatures . . . had punished the rebel Negroes with a severity that shocked

127. *Edinburgh Review* 41, no. 81 (March 1824): 238.
128. Ibid.
129. *The Missionary Smith*, 205.
130. Ibid.
131. "Negro Slavery No. 7," 60.
132. "Negro Slavery No. 8," 76.
133. Stephen (1971), 131.

every feeling of humanity; they had condemned Smith to the gallows and thus turned the Independents against them; they forced Shrewsbury to fly for his life, and the Wesleyans were aroused, . . . the Baptist chapels were razed to the ground, and the Baptists became their enemies."[134]

In 1830, the Anti-Slavery Society condemned the "persecution which Christian missionaries and their Negro converts have had to endure, and are still enduring in that island [Jamaica]."[135] By September 7, 1832, British abolitionists made their position clear by insisting that events in Jamaica, "whether viewed as religious persecution on the part of the masters or as insurrection on the part of the slaves" necessitated a speedy settlement of the slavery question.[136] This perspective underscores that when abolitionists set out to examine the trial and persecution of a missionary, they were primarily drawn into a large-scale examination and denunciation of the system of slavery itself. They found it almost impossible to differentiate between the suffering of missionaries and that of slaves. The two parties had firsthand experience of planter degradation of which the abolitionists disapproved. Abolitionists did not overlook that the persecution of the missionaries was intimately bound up with the service they provided to the slaves.

The abolitionists played no small part in stimulating public support at home for missionaries like John Smith in Demerara, William Shrewsbury in Barbados, and William Knibb, Burchell Whitehorne, Abbot, and Henry Bleby in Jamaica. The religious public was included in the handpicked elite among whom the London antislavery leaders circulated their views. "Respectability" was the criteria for selection. James Stephen provided this cue when he encouraged the group of London abolitionists with the report that "a Society, respectable as yours and others of the same character have been formed and are forming in different parts of the kingdom for the purpose of mitigating and gradually terminating that odious oppression . . . among their number men like yourself whose characters are a pledge for resolute perseverance."[137]

134. Ibid., 209.

135. *Anti-Slavery Monthly Reporter* 3, no. 61 (June 1830): 251.

136. Committee on Slavery Minute Book, September 7, 1832, p. 163, MSS. Brit. Emp. S. 20 E2/3, Anti-Slavery Society Papers.

137. Committee on Slavery Minute Book, April 16, 1823, p. 16, MSS. Brit. Emp. S. 20 E2/1, Anti-Slavery Society Papers.

On June 17, 1823, in keeping with the campaign of exposure to the respectable, pamphlets were sent to members of the Bible and Missionary Societies and the African Institution.[138] Again, it was resolved on September 9, 1823, to send copies of the substance of Buxton's May 1823 House of Commons speech to the "President and Vice President of the Society, the Board of Directors of the African Institution as are not members of the Anti-Slavery Society, all speakers in the debate who are not members of the Society, all members of Cabinet, R. Wilmot Horton at the Colonial Office, each of the periodical works and to each of the newspaper . . . and 500 Circulars and 50 debates . . . to the Church Missionary Society for distribution and the same number to the Methodist Society."[139]

These attempts to create a religious antislavery public were taken prior to the formal announcement among abolitionist circles of the eruption of slave rebellion in Demerara. Thus, when news that planters in the colonies threatened the lives and the rights of their white Christian brethren and destroyed their property, the support of the missionaries was a forgone conclusion. After the rebellion, abolitionists were so confident of this that their approach to the dissenters was forthright. It was resolved on June 19, 1824 that "Mr Macaulay be requested to confer with the Secretary of the Missionary Society upon the publication of the late speeches in Parliament relative to the Missionary Smith."[140]

A letter written by Joseph Sturge to the secretary of the Anti-Slavery Society in 1828 reveals that targeting the church was not only a means to incorporate respectable support for the cause. It was also a pragmatic approach to meet the financial demands of disseminating information on the state of British West Indian slavery. Sturge suggested, "Perhaps the quickest way of getting a large number of petitions would be through the different religious congregations."[141] Abolitionists before Sturge had already appreciated that the church presented a ready meeting place for many individuals. Circulating materials among the congregations was relatively

138. Committee on Slavery Minute Book, June 17, 1823, p. 39, MSS. Brit. Emp. S. 20 E2/1, Anti-Slavery Society Papers.

139. Ibid., 56

140. Ibid., 123.

141. Joseph Sturge to Thomas Pringle, March 20, 1828, Correspondence of Thomas Pringle, Secretary of the Committee on Slavery, March 13, 1827–December 1834, MSS. Brit. Emp. S. 18, C1/61, Anti-Slavery Society Papers.

inexpensive. This was an important consideration to the Anti-Slavery Society, whose funds were almost always dangerously low. On July 8, 1823, the treasurer of the society's subcommittee on finance reported that while its balance stood at £1.1.1, "the outstanding bills against the Society . . . do not amount to less than between £700 and £800."[142] The society's poor financial state may well have been due to its unwillingness to extend its network of public support. It certainly provides some explanation why the nonconformist ministers and their congregations were included in the narrow range of groups and individuals to whom the abolitionists turned to create a public voice for their cause while other classes of society were avoided.

Finally, as is suggested from their limited publicity program, it is important to emphasize that abolitionists were not solely responsible for the remarkable number of petitions on behalf of Smith that poured into the House of Commons in the spring of 1824. London Missionary Society petitioners from all over the kingdom sent about two hundred petitions. The abolitionists, of course, endorsed the gesture and on April 13, 1824, Sir James Mackintosh presented the London Missionary Society petitions to Parliament.[143] The directors of the London Missionary Society wanted to arouse as much public interest as possible in the case. Thus, they launched an extensive campaign. It was a perfect replica of the abolitionist propaganda tactics. The directors sent letters all over the country to members and supporters of the London Missionary Society. They encouraged members of the House of Commons to be present at the debate about the trial of Smith. They sent a copy of the court-martial proceedings to every member of the House of Commons and to one hundred members of the House of Lords.[144] The London Missionary Society and not British abolitionists were primarily responsible for the dissemination of information that led to the surfeit of petitions. Additionally, the petitioners had made it clear that their objectives had nothing to do with the slavery question itself. They wanted a reversal of the sentence that had been pronounced on

142. Committee on Slavery Minute Book, July 8, 1823, p. 43, MSS. Brit. Emp. S. 20 E2/1, Anti-Slavery Society Papers.

143. William Alers Hankey, Treasurer of the London Missionary Society, to Wilmot Horton, Secretary of State for the Colonies, CO 111/47, March 6, 1824, ff. 180–189, Colonial Office Papers; Jakobsson (1972), 353–354.

144. Jakobsson (1972), 355.

Smith and future protection for missionaries in the slave colonies.[145] Smith's popularity in Britain, then, although used by the abolitionists to win support for the cause, was truly developed and exploited by the sectarians themselves to achieve a much narrower objective than the gradual and eventual emancipation of the slaves.[146]

Despite the abolitionists and church leaders' efforts to enlist sectarian support for the struggle against slavery, however, the attention provided by the dissenters was not constant. George Stephen commented in his *Anti-Slavery Recollections* that "the dissenters rendered good service, for they were greatly excited by the case of Missionary Smith, but it was not at this time, even with them, a topic of constant interest; a casual allusion to it was all that their preachers could spare from more serious subjects. It is perhaps scarcely going too far to say that at the beginning of 1830, not one in ten thousand of the whole population had any but the most vague and general idea of the nature of the colonial controversy, or even of the state of slavery itself . . . An anti-slavery public was yet to be created."[147] Apparently, the older heads directing the antislavery campaign were satisfied with the limited inroads they had made in canvassing the sectarians. George Stephen was not. He considered himself to be a young British abolitionist and identified with the members of the vigorous Agency Committee who wanted to do more to rouse greater public participation in the movement.

The historian Madge Dresser, who has conducted considerable research on the slavery question in the English city of Bristol, supports

145. The directors of the London Missionary Society were grateful that the ministers of his majesty's government "thought it proper to remit the punishment of death but they appear to your petitioners to have given an approval of the findings of the Court, by directing that Mr Smith should be dismissed from the colony and should enter into recognizances never to return." Petition of Directors of London Missionary Society to Secretary of State for the colonies Wilmot Horton, March 24, 1824, CO 111/47, ff. 187, Colonial Office Papers; *Hansard's Parliamentary Debates*, new ser., 11 (April 13, 1824): 401.

146. The petitioners requested that "your Honourable House will institute such Enquiries or direct or adopt such measures as may best tend to obtain the revision of the Sentence passed on Mr Smith and also will adopt such measures as shall ensure needful protection to Christian missionaries in every part of the British Empire throughout the world, and will afford such further relief as shall seem meet to the Humanity, Wisdom and Justice of Your Honourable House." CO 111/47, ff. 187, Colonial Office Papers.

147. Stephen (1971), 117.

Stephen's conclusions. Dresser weighs the strength of dissenter support for the movement against other coverage of the slavery question in Britain. The arrest of the Bristol Baptist missionary William Knibb in Jamaica in 1831 was of particular concern to members of that sect.[148] The *Baptist Magazine* expressed its fury that the Colonial Church Union, formed by Jamaican planters after the rebellion, burned nine Baptist and six Methodist chapels, tarred and feathered at least one missionary, and imprisoned not only Knibb but also his fellow minister the Rev. Thomas Burchell.[149] Like the suffering of the slaves, however, publicity on the persecution of the missionaries was almost completely confined to antislavery tracts and House of Commons remonstrance made by abolitionists.

Dresser goes on to state that the cry of the dissenters in the *Baptist Magazine* was drowned by more popular journals in Bristol. The editor of "the *Felix Farley Bristol Journal* though unforthcoming about the cruel treatment of slaves, and the harassment of missionaries, . . . ensured that his paper detailed descriptions of slave violence . . . the bloodthirsty and savage cruelties of the slaves knew no bounds, and whilst white men were horribly murdered, their unfortunate females were reserved in their caves and fastness often witnessing the maligning of their fathers, husbands and brothers, for the more brutal purposes not to be described."[150] Dresser demonstrates that the public in Bristol responded to the Jamaican revolt much as they had to news of the great St. Domingue slave rebellion of 1791. Before 1830, apart perhaps from Smith's case, the fact that white missionaries faced persecution alongside defeated slave rebels made little impact in altering this public response. What really caused the suffering of missionaries to hit home was when Knibb and others returned to England toward the end of 1831 and joined the antislavery circuits established by the Agency Committee. This continued till slavery was declared abolished in 1833.[151]

148. Madge Dresser, *Slavery Obscured: The Social History of the Slave Trade in an English Provincial Port* (London: Continuum, 2001), 218.

149. Ibid.; *Facts and Documents*, 5–13.

150. Dresser (2001), 219.

151. Missionaries Knibb and Phillipo were intent on using their persecution in Jamaica to advance the cause of the slaves. However, when the Baptist Missionary Society Committee met on May 25, 1832, to discuss the infringement of their missionaries' civil and religious liberties in Jamaica, nothing was said of slavery itself. See Stanley (1992), 77–78. The

Antislavery agitators did not elevate persecuted missionaries above slaves who were victimized in the suppression of revolts. They developed a discourse that attempted to capture slavery as it existed in the colonies and did not ignore the experience of slaves facing the vicious aftermath of slave revolts. In fact, this discourse gauged in turn the roles of planters, missionaries, and slaves. What is regrettable is that before 1830 and before the activation of the more radical Agency Committee, the abolitionists failed to disseminate this countervailing discourse among a broader public.

DEFEATED HEROES

As a result of the bloodshed among slave rebels in British plantation colonies, an extensive and significant aspect of antislavery discourse was written. In converting the rebels' experience to useful antislavery material, however, the abolitionists necessarily left in the shadow the courage slaves demonstrated in confronting cruel but powerful masters. Abolitionists' narration of the suppression of revolts appeared to rob the slaves of the respect and dignity they deserved. It was admittedly a discourse in which slaves were identified on the basis of their impotence and their suf-

---

Baptist Missionary Society admonished Knibb and Phillipo not to speak about the rebellion in Jamaica at the annual general meeting of the BMS on June 21, 1832, at Spa Fields Chapel. Phillipo confined his address to a general appeal for renewed effort to sustain the Jamaican mission. The more radical Knibb ignored the admonition and insisted that the question of slavery and Christianity could no longer be separated and that the former ought to be abolished to enable slaves to worship God. See also Hinton (1847), 145–148. The Baptist Missionary Society was cautious. On June 25, 1832, it agreed to meet with Buxton, but the object in view was still defined in terms of religious liberty in Jamaica. In August 1832 the *Missionary Herald* raised the subject of abolition for the first time. The article was a sanguine warning that better times were approaching for slaves and masters but that emancipation was fraught with difficulties and that time was necessary before it could be safely accomplished. See Stanley (1992), 79–80. Finally, the conservatism of the *Missionary Herald* was overtaken by August 15, 1832, in an interdenominational meeting held in Exeter Hall to adopt measures to safeguard religious liberty in Jamaica. John Dyer moved to call on the legislature and government to implement the complete and immediate extinction of slavery throughout the British dominions. In the closing months of 1832, Knibb, Burchell, and Phillipo toured England and Scotland, mobilizing humanitarian opinion in favor of immediate abolition. See Hinton (1847), 136–137, 151–152; William Fitzer Burchell, *Memoir of Thomas Burchell* (London: B. L. Green, 1849), 255; Edward Bean Underhill, *Life of James Mursell Phillipo* (London, 1881), 103–104; Stanley (1992), 76; Jakobsson (1972), 471.

fering. The humanitarians focused upon the pain, degradation, and cruelty the slaves endured. In order to elevate the slaves they had first to be
pictured in the most miserable terms. In their absolute suffering they at-
tained a purity that was beyond reproach. It was a purity earned by being outside of power and the victims of power. While the scales tipped on
the side of their degradation, however, it must neither be forgotten nor ignored that suffering slaves brought the subject of slavery to the attention
of the British Parliament and, to a limited extent, to the British people.

The abolitionists recognized that "the slaves in the colonies, who are
not permitted to speak for themselves—who have no tongues, [use] their
bleeding wounds to plead their cause."[152] The anonymous author of an
article in the *Edinburgh Review* advised the British West Indian plantocracy of the true strength that lay behind the apparent weakness of the defeated rebels. "You may renew all the atrocities of Barbados and Demerara, you may inflict all the most hateful punishments authorized by the
insular codes. You may massacre by the thousand, and hang by the score,
you may even once more roast your captives in slow fires and starve them
in iron cages or flay them alive with the cart whip. You will only hasten
the day of your retribution. Therefore we say, let them go forth from the
house of bondage. For woe unto you, if you wait for the plagues and the
signs, the wonders and the war, the mighty and the outstretched hand."[153]
British abolitionists had realized that the suffering slaves endured in the
aftermath of rebellion would not, as the planters had assumed, produce
such terror that slaves would no longer dare to oppose by force their enslavement. After the Jamaican slave rebellion the Anti-Slavery Society reiterated the verdict that had been reached after Demerara by commenting
that "the severity exercised is much more likely to excite a deep-rooted
feeling of revenge, and to accelerate a recurrence to violence, than to produce terror."[154]

This warning was directed not only to stubborn colonists, who refused
to cooperate with reform attempts, but also to the British government and
Parliament. In 1825, the Anti-Slavery Society warned that "if the government and the parliament and the people of England should be so lost to

152. *Anti-Slavery Monthly Reporter* 1, no. 9 (February 28, 1826): 83.
153. *Edinburgh Review* 41, no. 82 (January 1825): 487.
154. *Analysis of the Report*, 112.

a sense of their obligations, as to suffer them [the evils of slavery] to continue, they must find their close in one of those convulsions which will involve White and Black, master and slave, the oppressor and the oppressed,
in one common and undistinguishing and overwhelming calamity. Such
must, sooner or later, be the effect of going on to delegate, to the colonial
assemblies, the solemn duty, which parliament alone can discharge."[155]
This was one of the abolitionists' early whisperings that injured slaves
as well as cruel masters and persecuted missionaries were tearing down
the system. In their abject victimization during the suppression of revolts,
the abolitionists portrayed slave rebels as agents of the antislavery cause.
The rebels led the abolitionists to focus their attacks on the most significant dimension of the plantation society—the draconian penal codes of
the various island legislatures. Slaves in rebellion facilitated the opportunity for abolitionists to highlight and condemn the legalized corruption
that colonists practiced through the court-martial judicial system. As the
discourse expanded, it became more instrumental. Chapter 5 explores
how slave rebels continued to energize the movement through the damage
they were inflicting on the British West Indian slave plantation economy.

155. *Anti-Slavery Monthly Reporter* 1, no. 1 (November 30, 1825): 54.

5

APOCALYPTIC WARNING

This chapter explores the most dynamic lesson that British abolitionists extracted from the nineteenth-century slave rebellions in the British West Indies. It examines how abolitionists used rebellions to warn of the dangers they posed to the British Empire and to individuals with economic stakes in the colonies. While the basic message of warning remained the same, it was used to justify different objectives at different periods of the antislavery movement in Britain. The discussion moves from 1823, when the abolitionists embarked on a campaign for gradual emancipation, to 1834, when they were skeptical whether the adopted emancipation plan would secure peace and safety in the colonies.

British abolitionists repeatedly referred to Samuel Johnson's inflammatory toast. One version stated that in the hearing of a black servant Dr. Johnson raised his glass and declared, "A speedy insurrection of slaves in Jamaica and success to them!"[1] As often as they chose to quote the doctor, however, antislavery advocates were hardly at liberty even to seem to champion the self-liberating attempts of the slaves. To do so not only was dangerous to the continued survival of the colonies but also would cause the abolitionists to appear hypocritical. They had made known their intolerance of all violent means of addressing the problem since the time of the slave-trade debates. They had advised that emancipation must not come by the slaves but that the masters themselves should be its willing authors. They had stated then that only an enemy or enemies of the slaves would resort to violence to secure immediate and premature emancipation.[2] It was easy for their opponents to construe as malicious any abolitionist effort to turn to advantage the issue of servile war. It did not seem to matter that this was exactly what the slaving interest did in their attempt to forestall the antislavery initiative.

1. *Edinburgh Review* 39, no. 77 (October 1823): 119.
2. Ibid., 126; Wilberforce and Wilberforce (1838), 5:240.

British abolitionists, in spite of intense opposition, found it pragmatic to employ the slave violence argument. Harboring no sense of self-condemnation, they reasoned that operating as if the problem did not exist would only exacerbate the danger. It was their duty to warn the slaving interests and the British government of the dangers inherent in slavery while fervently expressing the hope that both or either of these parties would take measures to prevent the abolitionists' dreadful foreboding from materializing.

Almost as soon as the abolitionists embarked on the mission of attacking the system of slavery itself as it existed in the British West Indian colonies, they began referring to the dangers of servile war. By 1823, Thomas Fowell Buxton, the new leader of the antislavery movement, and his predecessor William Wilberforce voiced the issue. These were only early reflections, however, and were put forward at a time when rebellion but was not a pressing issue on abolitionists' minds. It had been seven years since the Barbados revolt, and the rising in Demerara would not occur for a few months. However, in the aftermath of the Demerara rebellion, several abolitionists took up with greater fervency the question of the dangers of slavery.

None was more outstanding in his concentrated treatment of the subject in this period than Wilberforce. His coverage of the theme of rebellion in British abolitionism was seminal and furnished a clear general overview of the topic. In the mid-1820s, the slave rebellion argument in antislavery ideology was taken up in more detail by Thomas Clarkson and by the Anti-Slavery Society. Most of this discussion was published in the *Edinburgh Review* and in the *Anti-Slavery Monthly Reporter,* later called the *Anti-Slavery Reporter.* Throughout the 1820s, however, the abolitionists were committed only to amelioration or the mitigation and gradual abolition of slavery. Consequently, while they did shape and present the dynamic vision inherent in the slave rebellion argument, the abolitionists suffocated its strength by requesting mere pastoral measures of slave reform. It was not until the 1830s that the abolitionists were finally persuaded of the failure of amelioration. They grew more convinced that the only solution to the slavery problem was complete and immediate emancipation. When slaves in Jamaica rose against their masters in 1831–1832 in what was the largest rebellion of the century in the British West Indies, they strengthened the abolitionist commitment to immediate emancipation. Thus, the abolitionists used the danger of slave rebellion to give greater force to their movement than they had in the 1820s.

In the British attack against the system of slavery, the use of the threat of revolt can conveniently be divided into three phases; the limited treatment it received in 1823 when the abolitionists announced for the first time their objective of gradual emancipation; Wilberforce's comprehensive summary of the subject, reinforced by abolitionists' reviews in the *Edinburgh Review* and in the *Anti-Slavery Monthly Reporter* in the aftermath of Demerara; and the intensified force of its application after the revolt in Jamaica.

ON THE EVE OF DEMERARA

Thomas Fowell Buxton was under immense pressure when he took the first step to introduce the subject of gradual abolition of slavery in the House of Commons in 1823. The lengthy preamble of his speech was an indication that he sought to find a strong justification for this move. Buxton finally declared that he was resting his motion against slavery on the principles of humanity, justice, and Christianity. He also referred to the threat of slave revolt to persuade Parliament to adopt his motion for gradual abolition. Buxton stated that British West Indian slaves were geographically hemmed in by examples of neighboring states of free blacks. No one could deny outright that danger lurked in this scenario. The English colonies were strategic targets for the horror of servile war. Free blacks modeled the possibility of freedom to those still in bondage "What does the Negro, working under the lash on the mountains of Jamaica, see? He sees another island, on which every labourer is free; in which eight hundred thousand blacks; men, women, and children, exercise all the rights, and enjoy all the blessings—and they are innumerable and incalculable—which freedom gives. . . . It would be singular enough if, the only emperor who did not feel a desire to meddle with the affairs of his neighbours should be the emperor of Hayti. I touch lightly upon this subject. Let government—let the West Indians—justly appreciate the danger with which they may be menaced from that quarter."[3]

Warning of the threat of slave rebellion by pointing to the proximity of states of liberated "Negroes" was regularly repeated by other aboli-

3. *Hansard's Parliamentary Debates,* new ser., 9 (May 15, 1823): 264.

tionists and soon became a distinct theme of the antislavery discourse. Buxton asserted that it was unwise for the West Indians to oppose the antislavery initiative on the grounds of interference of property because slaves would continue to destroy their plantation works and other structures if mismanagement continued unabated. It was another point that the abolitionists repeatedly made until slavery was abolished in 1833. Buxton insisted, "I am fully persuaded that security is to be found—and is only to be found—in justice towards that oppressed people. If we wish to preserve the West Indies—if we wish to avoid a dreadful convulsion—it must be by restoring to the injured race, those rights which we have too long withheld."[4] Buxton's comment on the dangers inherent in slavery, brief as it was at this time, went a long way in cementing the links between abolitionist activities in Britain and rebel slaves in the colonies. It was also significant that the signature of the man leading the new direction of the antislavery cause was stamped on this position.

Wilberforce supported Buxton's 1823 motion for slave amelioration in and out of the House by making reference to the recurrent crisis of slave war. In Parliament he used the issue to further deflect blame for rebellions away from the abolitionists' agitation.[5] He warned planters and the British government that the tendency of slaves to rebel made slave reform a necessity. "Whatever may be the dangers to be apprehended from such discussions, there are yet no dangers so great, or so formidable, as those which must arise from a continuation of the present West Indian system."[6] Wilberforce was clearly intent on converting this message of warning into practical politics. He stated further that "[we] must enter into investigation of the evils . . . with a recollection of the infinite danger which must attend a continuance of the present system of slavery."[7] Outside of Parliament, Wilberforce addressed again the problem that English colonists could expect to confront when their slaves compared their unfavorable condition with that of free black neighbors. He wrote that if the planters in the English colonies were blind to the dangers accumulating around them, the slaves were not. The slaves were restless and curious. Like the maroons in the cockpit country of Jamaica, these neighboring ex-slave

4. Ibid., 263.
5. See chap. 2.
6. *Hansard's Parliamentary Debates,* new ser., 9 (May 15, 1823): 288.
7. Ibid.

communities stood out as beacons of hope to those still ensnared by the chains of slavery. Wilberforce asked, "Within a community of near 800,000 free blacks, many of them accustomed to the use of arms, within sight of the greatest of our West Indian islands; . . . with the example afforded in many of the United States, and in almost all the new republics of South America where Negro slavery had been recently abolished—is this the time, are these the circumstances in which it can be wise and safe, if it were honest and humane, to keep down in their present state of heathenish and almost brutish degradation, the 800,000 Negroes in our West Indian colonies? Here, indeed, is danger, if we observe the signs of the times."[8]

The abolitionists took note of the fact that British West Indian slavery, especially by the nineteenth century, was not operating in a vacuum. They contended that the slaves would find motivation from outside the system if the impetus for change was not coming from within. Abolitionists' observations contradict the belief that slaves in rebellion in the British West Indies in the nineteenth century were unresponsive to the political upheavals beyond their immediate world. Abolitionists lodged their slave rebellion discourse within an international context of rising revolutionary spirit in the Western Hemisphere. The colonists in the British West Indies were out of step with the march of progress, and their poor timing was ill fated.

IN THE WAKE OF DEMERARA

William Wilberforce was responsible for presenting the most comprehensive single exposition of the slave revolt argument in the debates on British West Indian slavery in the 1820s. He did this not when he was leading the British antislavery movement but almost immediately after turning over that position to Thomas Fowell Buxton. In fact, by 1824, Wilberforce was already preparing to leave Parliament and public life in general. Despite the relaxation of his efforts in the struggle, after the Demerara slave revolt, Wilberforce expounded at length on the slave violence issue. He highlighted the major perspectives from which the threat of slave violence

8. William Wilberforce, *An Appeal to Religion, Justice and Humanity of the Inhabitants of the British Empire, in Behalf of the Negro Slaves in the West Indies* (London: J. Hatchard and Son, 1823), 72–73; see also Wilberforce (1807), 329.

could be made to serve the antislavery cause. His deliberations were not to be surpassed by any other abolitionist before or after, even when he himself examined the subject in his *An Appeal to Religion, Justice and Humanity of the Inhabitants of the British Empire in Behalf of the Negro Slaves in the West Indies* (1823). His earlier reflections on servile war lacked the conviction that marked the later discourse. Wilberforce's 1824 speech on the dangers of slavery was the most complete delineation of a single treatment of the subject by a single abolitionist.

The speech was given during the House of Commons debate of March 16, when colonial secretary George Canning informed the House that the government intended to restrict its enforcement of the 1823 amelioration proposals to the crown colony of Trinidad. Canning explained that the reaction of slaves and masters, culminating in the Demerara revolt of 1823, was responsible for the decision to limit the application of the measure.[9] Buxton, not Wilberforce, was the first abolitionist to protest against this backward step. Buxton had come prepared for the announcement and had written to his wife before the session, noting, "I expect to see Canning tomorrow; he seems very cold to me, and the report is he will join the West Indians. If he does, we shall go to war with him in earnest."[10]

Buxton was indeed livid. He chided Canning, "A pledge was obtained. You were, therefore, in some sort, to be considered holder of that pledge . . . And then, fearful of a little unpopularity . . . you sat still, you held your peace, and were satisfied to see this pledge, in favour of a whole Archipelago, reduced to a single island."[11] The emphasis of Buxton's attack was not the slave revolt threat. He believed that it was cowardice on the part of the government to yield to the West Indian clamor against the parent state's attempts to introduce slave laws in colonies with their own assemblies. When he finally mentioned revolts, he made the very valid point that the colonists were rejecting the very abolitionist measures that might have safeguarded Demerara from servile unrest. Considering the range of his reflections in this address, however, Buxton's focus on the issue of servile war in the colonies paled in comparison to Wilberforce's.

Wilberforce emphasized that Parliament ought to consider how its ac-

9. *Hansard's Parliamentary Debates,* new ser., 10 (March 16, 1824): 1112.

10. Buxton (1852), 123.

11. *Hansard's Parliamentary Debates,* new ser., 10 (March 16, 1824): 1115.

tions would affect not only the masters but also the slaves. He reiterated the argument that he and his friends used after the Barbados revolt of 1816 and, to a lesser extent, after Demerara. The colonists' thoughtless and inappropriate communication in their newspapers, at their dinner tables, and in the fields, Wilberforce believed, activated rumors of freedom granted but denied. The slaves' expectations consequently had risen to a feverish level that would brook no disappointment. In developing his argument, Wilberforce went beyond the need to deny that abolitionists had caused the revolt and that the colonists had sparked the rumor among the slaves. He sharpened his rhetoric and depicted the cataclysmic day of reckoning that was imminent. He stated solemnly that after serious deliberation he was convinced that the colonies were on the brink of a precipice. His language typified the caustic images conjured up in prophecies of doom and gloom. It was not the last time that abolitionists were to speak in such terms.

Wilberforce went on to assert that as slaves were in no mood to be disappointed, it was incumbent upon the British government to compel the colonial authorities to execute the 1823 measures of slave amelioration. Wilberforce struck a sensitive note here. He addressed the issue of parliamentary intervention in the colonies, which with the 1815 Slave Registration Bill had become a sore point. The three parties locked in the slavery debate each had a different concept of how best to regulate the relationship between Britain and her slave colonies, especially those with charters of self-government. The British government's position was one of compromise. Colonial secretary Canning had made it clear in 1823 that in embracing amelioration, the government's preferred policy was for a determined and persevering but judicious and temperate enforcement of the program.[12]

Time was to prove that the government was not so determined and persevering after all in seeking to improve the daily lives of the slaves. Until slavery was abolished by act of Parliament, the government generally maintained its old relationship with the self-ruling colonies. It left the whole of the regulation of actual government with the local institutions

---

12. *Hansard's Parliamentary Debates,* new ser., 9 (May 15, 1823): 286; D. J. Murray, *The West Indies and the Development of Colonial Government, 1801–1834* (Oxford: Clarendon, 1965), 127–128.

while relying upon the colonists' voluntary cooperation. In the nine years after 1823, the government reacted to abolitionist pressure by making frequent though insufficient attempts to obtain colonial consent to several variations of amelioration.[13] West Indian merchants and planters living in Britain and settlers in the colonies viewed the attempt to legislate on behalf of the slaves as a violation of their constitutional rights to make their own laws. They remonstrated against the slave legislation passed by three successive Secretaries of State for War and the Colonies from 1823 to 1828 and 1830 to 1831. During the antislavery era, they continually threatened to throw off their allegiance to Britain, establish their independence, or take protection under the former British colonies of North America.[14]

Taking their cue from their opponents, the abolitionists for a long time restricted their investigation of the need for reform to providing evidence of planters' contumacy and the obligation, consequently, to call on Parliament to fulfil Canning's pledge of 1823.[15] Wilberforce himself on March 16, 1824, did not completely avoid this approach. He argued that the late and respected statesmen Edmund Burke and Dundas reserved no qualms about legislating for the colonies and would be shocked that such a policy was objected to by those with colonial interests. From 1823 until abolition, abolitionists repeatedly argued that the right of Britain to legislate and enforce laws in her colonies had never been surrendered and was unquestioned.[16] When Wilberforce made the rebellion of the slaves the cen-

13. *Hansard's Parliamentary Debates,* new ser., 10 (March 16, 1824): 1069, 1165–1169; 14 (March 1, 1826): 968–982; 14 (March 3, 1826): 1080; *Hansard's Parliamentary Debates,* 3d ser., 3 (March 29, 1831): 1138; 3 (April 15, 1831): 142–145; Gross (1980), 63–85; Mathieson (1926), 162–163; Claude Levy, "Slavery and the Emancipation Movement in Barbados, 1650–1833," *Journal of Negro History* 55, no. 1 (January 1970): 1–14; W. L. Burn, *Emancipation and Apprenticeship in the British West Indies* (London: Jonathan Cape, 1937), 81.

14. *Hansard's Parliamentary Debates,* new ser., 9 (May 15, 1823): 327–328; *Hansard's Parliamentary Debates,* 3d ser., 11 (March 23, 1832): 815–832; 17 (May 14, 1833): 1197–1202; Williams (1852), 80; Andrew Thomson, *Substance of the Speech Delivered at the Meeting of the Edinburgh Society for the Abolition of Slavery, on October 19, 1830* (Edinburgh: William Whyte and Co., 1830), 12–13; Richard (1864), 76–77; *Jamaican Courant,* July 16, 1831; *Anti-Slavery Monthly Reporter* 1, no. 9 (February 28, 1826): 81.

15. *Anti-Slavery Monthly Reporter* 1, no. 6 (November 30, 1825): 51–53. Brougham MSS, Buxton to Brougham, October 3, 1827, Henry Brougham Papers.

16. Brougham (1857), 342–343; *Hansard's Parliamentary Debates,* new ser., 10 (March 16, 1824): 1152; 34 (June 19, 1816): 1175.

tral focus of his attempt to convince the government of the need to take more direct action in the colonies, he located the question of parliamentary intervention on another level. It was no longer merely a question of the right to intervene. Viewed from the perspective of the threat of servile war in the colonies, the crucial concern became the need to intervene to prevent calamity. Wilberforce argued that the rumors circulating among the slaves throughout the colonies made it imperative to ensure that promises of change were backed by actual enforcement. He considered it a dangerous misjudgment on the part of the government to respond to the Demerara rebellion by stepping back from slavery reform. Other abolitionists did take up and expand this argument.

Meanwhile, Wilberforce illustrated his point by reflecting on dire consequences occasioned by disillusioned slaves. He invited Parliament to contemplate the frustrations of slaves. The British government offered them a cup that was as soon dashed away as they brought it to their lips. He depicted the terror of slaves being reassigned to the state of darkness just when the light of dawn was about to break upon their gloom. Wilberforce warned the government that to avoid disaster inherent in a disillusioned slave population, instead of toying with the awakened aspirations of the slaves, it was mandatory to act decisively and without hesitation. He was convinced that since colonial cooperation in slave amelioration was not forthcoming, if the government also failed them the slaves would seize the initiative and attempt to achieve by violence what had been denied them by law.

To reinforce this argument, Wilberforce revisited the St. Domingue rebellion of 1791. Wilberforce likened the mixed signals conveyed from France to the slaves in St. Domingue to the reluctance of the ministers of the British Crown to follow through with its 1823 commitment. He regarded this circuitous approach as the real cause of the calamity that destroyed the wealth of the French colony. The slaves had just cause for their violent and destructive actions because they had been provoked beyond what was tolerable. Years of retrospection had led Wilberforce and his circle to reassess St. Domingue's notoriety as a bloody legend. In 1807 Wilberforce had referred to life in Haiti as "the wild licentiousness of a neighbouring kingdom."[17] By the early 1820s, with at least two slave rebellions in the British West Indies having occurred during an era of slave

17. Wilberforce (1807), 259.

reform promoted by the abolitionists, Wilberforce's perspective had changed. In his revised view, the government's hesitation was comparable to the blundering policy of the French towards its colonies. Colonial administrators and not the slaves were chiefly to be blamed for the upheaval. As a slavery reformer, Wilberforce was convicted that it was his responsibility to steer the British government from this dangerous path. The abolitionists presented not only the other side of nineteenth-century slave revolts in the British West Indies but also the other side of the St. Domingue slave revolt of 1791.[18] Wilberforce ended his contemplation by noting that the threat of slave rebellion was not to be ignored, for it impinged on the great question of the economic value of the colonies to the parent country. He did not agree with abolitionists who would challenge the alleged value of the colonies to Britain. He had, nevertheless, placed before the Parliament the dimensions of the slave rebellion argument fundamental to British antislavery ideology.

> Whatever parliament might think proper to do, he implored them to do it quickly and firmly. Let them not proceed with hesitating steps: let them not tamper with the feelings and the passions which they had themselves excited . . . Let every man present appeal to his own experience, nay, to his own feelings, for the truth of the position which he had just laid down . . . Now he was prepared to contend, that it was impossible this could be effected by the colonial assemblies; that it must be accomplished by the imperial parliament . . . By endeavouring to effect this object any other way, they were exciting irritation; and they would, perhaps, feel the effects of that despair, which all would lament, when it was too late, when they would vainly wish, that they had adopted a straighter, and a more direct course . . . a course which would not only be beneficial to the interest of humanity, but conducive to the wealth and prosperity of the country.[19]

It was a lengthy speech unique in its concentrated focus on the impact of rebellions on multiple aspects of the debates on slavery. Wilberforce had provided incontrovertible proof that slave rebellions were valuable to the antislavery position, for they questioned whether the bonds of slavery

---

18. See chap. 3.

19. *Hansard's Parliamentary Debates,* new ser., 10 (March 16, 1824): 1145–1155.

were to be broken by physical or moral and legal force. He had realized that slaves were active agents in the struggle. Wilberforce even went so far as to suggest the revolutionary notion that it was the right of the slaves to use force to ensure that the British government kept its promises to them. It was almost unimaginable that Wilberforce, who had insisted in 1807 that slaves were not yet fit for freedom and who had disavowed all association with the Barbados slave revolt of 1816, could be the author of such an excitable vision. However, Wilberforce's vision of apocalyptic doom was not consistent with the temporizing measures at which he aimed.

It was not until 1830 that the abolitionists rejected amelioration as impractical, and it was not till 1832 that Buxton presented to the House the first motion for the complete and immediate abolition of slavery.[20] By 1824 Wilberforce and his circle concentrated on such pastoral reforms as religious instruction, abolition of Sunday market, regulation of the flogging of males and the abolition of the flogging of females, prevention of separation of families and the sale of slaves, establishment of slave saving banks, removal of obstacles to manumission, encouragement of slave marriages, and admission of slaves' evidence in colonial courts of law.[21] Wilberforce gave limited force to a powerful argument. Nevertheless, he went a long way in clearly articulating and drawing together previous and later abolitionist deliberations on the race war factor in British abolitionism.

SAFETY IN EMANCIPATION

British abolitionists had realized that once they began to refer to slave violence in the antislavery deliberations, they could not ignore the great St. Domingue rebellion of 1791. Thomas Clarkson was in the forefront of addressing the St. Domingue question. While other abolitionists capitalized on the event to warn of the dangers of slavery, Clarkson was more preoccupied with the responsibility of showing that there was safety in emancipation. His treatment of Haiti, however, was the other side of the same coin. If colonists did not seize the safety that alone lay in eventual emancipation, they would suffer the ravages of the slavery system. By the 1820s

20. Committee on Slavery Minute Book, April 25, 1832, p. 138, MSS. Brit. Emp. S. 20 E 2/3, Anti-Slavery Society Papers; Richard (1864), 90; Mathieson (1926), 196.

21. *Hansard's Parliamentary Debates*, new ser., 10 (March 16, 1824): 1132.

the abolitionists had decided that emancipation and race war were not synonymous. Many thought quite the opposite however.[22] Clarkson was burdened with the need to erase from the public consciousness the idea that emancipation symbolized all the horrors of race war dramatized in St. Domingue. He was determined to prove that "the transition of the people of St. Domingo from bondage to freedom, has been accomplished with safety and ease."[23] He insisted that the Haitian slaves were freed "by virtue of the proclamation issued by Santhonax in the south and Polverel, the other French commissioner, in the north and west, with the almost unanimous consent of the planters . . . [the Negroes] did nothing to show they were incapable of enjoying this boon."[24] Clarkson went on to assert that the atrocities committed by the Negroes only took place when slavery reigned over them and when, from 1802 to 1804, Le Clerk took orders from Napoleon Bonaparte to reenslave the "Negroes," not when the law set them free.[25] The danger, then, was in slavery. Clarkson furnished six other examples of groups of slaves, who were immediately or gradually liberated or rescued from illegal shipments of slaves, to prove that it was erroneous to associate emancipation with slave rebellion.[26] Clarkson tried to prove that these blacks, like their Haitian counterparts, were peaceful and industrious once they had made the transition from bondage to freedom.

The most valued example to the British abolitionists was the experiment of Mr. Steele in Barbados. From 1782 to 1789, Steele had established on his three estates an arrangement resembling the manorial and copyholder system that operated in Britain. Steele's laborers were not set free but were managed in a state that prepared them for eventual freedom. Under his supervision, they settled their own disputes among themselves and worked for wages at daily assigned task work. Both in social and eco-

22. Robert Abzug, "The Influence of Garrisonian Abolitionist Fears of Slave Violence on the Anti-Slavery Argument," *Journal of Negro History* 55, no. 1 (January 1970): 15–28; D. B. Davis, "The Emergence of Immediatism in British and American Anti-Slavery Thought," *Mississippi Valley Historical Review* 44, no. 2 (September 1962): 215–216; Lewis (1978), 36.

23. *Edinburgh Review* 39, no. 77 (October 1823): 133; Clarkson (1824), 20, 24–26, 38.

24. *Edinburgh Review* 39, no. 77 (October 1823): 130.

25. Ibid. See also Richard (1864), 88–89. Sturge agreed with Clarkson that "the history of St Domingo from the commencement of its independence to the present time, may be considered a triumphant refutation of all those who say immediate emancipation is dangerous."

26. Clarkson (1824), 16–35.

nomic terms, Steele's Barbadian experiment was a great success. He tripled his investments, and the threat of slave discontent leading to violence was markedly absent from his plantations.[27] Clarkson's reflections on St. Domingue, though less explosive than those of other abolitionists, had come to the similar conclusion that the danger of slavery lay in the unmitigated continuation of the system. Elizabeth Heyrick also used events in St. Domingue to refute claims that emancipated slaves were dangerous and revengeful. Unlike Clarkson, however, she had decided that the lesson of the St. Domingue experience was that slavery should be abolished immediately not gradually.

DANGER IN SLAVERY

In spite of his cautious treatment of St Domingue, Clarkson did not completely refrain from the sharp rhetoric used to warn planters of the dangers that the slaves posed to an unreformed system. After the Demerara slave revolt, Clarkson was among those abolitionists who declared that one rebellion would lead to another if the lives of the slaves remained unchanged. He asserted that there was no novelty in the rebellion, nor was it unexpected. To the contrary, he observed with caustic candor, "it is only a mercy that such insurrections do not happen every month instead of only once in ten or twenty years."[28] Clarkson admitted also that the slave rebels of Demerara spoke directly to all three parties debating the slavery question. To the abolitionists and to the British government the slaves' rising was a mandate "not to delay or suspend but to renew and redouble our exertions."[29] To the advocates of slavery anxious about the threat to the peace and security of their property, Clarkson recommended, "Take away slavery and you take away insurrections, take away slavery and you give tranquillity to the islands."[30] In his opinion, the campaign of the "saints" was best calculated to achieve the very objectives sought after by

---

27. Ibid., 35; *Edinburgh Review* 39, no. 77 (October 1823): 35.

28. Address to gentlemen at Ipswich, December 5, 1823, Thomas Clarkson Papers; see also *Edinburgh Review* 40, no. 79 (March 1824): 243, for a similar abolitionist view on Demerara, and *Hansard's Parliamentary Debates*, 3d ser., 10 (March 7, 1832): 1262, for Buxton's view: "When he heard of insurrection [Jamaica], he was not surprised of it, and was convinced that nothing would be done to suppress it until the question of the extinction of slavery was set at rest."

29. Address to gentlemen at Ipswich, December 5, 1823, Thomas Clarkson Papers.

30. Ibid.

the proslavery forces. If they wanted peace in their colonies, they had to remove the motive that stimulated slave violence. It was a lesson that most colonists and their supporters in Britain never learned. Peace was not their first priority. Clarkson's examination of the slave revolt issue, however, led him to conclude, "We therefore, who are labouring to improve gradually the temporal and moral condition of the slaves and to bring them by degrees to the rank of a free peasantry are working in fact to prevent these insurrections, and we consider ourselves on that ground to be the best friends of the colonies."[31]

Henry Brougham elaborated on the fact that the British colonial slave society harbored combustible materials ready to explode with the least aggravation. He reinforced Wilberforce's initial reflections on the issue. Brougham warned in 1824 that slaves far outnumbered whites, a factor that made precarious the whites' safety. British West Indian slaves were surrounded by ex-slaves who had gained freedom by successfully defeating their former masters. Independent Haiti presented the spectacle of "Negroes" assuming the exalted position once held by vanquished whites. This was a dangerous example to slaves whose masters stubbornly refused to ease their oppressive existence. Furthermore, the geographical isolation of the colonies from the mother country on whose military support they were dependent in times of crisis, not least among which was servile warfare, underscored the fragility of an unreformed system of slavery. Brougham summarized the ever-present dangers that threatened to blow to pieces the slave colonial structure. "The frame of West Indian society . . . is so feeble in itself, and, at the same time, surrounded with such perils from without, that barely to support its demands, the most temperate judgment, the steadiest and the most skilful hand; and, with all our discretion, and firmness and dexterity, its continued existence seems little less than a miracle."[32] Although Brougham's speech was intended to support a motion against the treatment of Smith and other missionaries, he made

31. Ibid.

32. *The Missionary Smith,* 43. As early as 1804, during the slave-trade debates, Brougham had warned that the rebellion that had liberated the "Negroes" in St. Domingue served as an example to Jamaican slaves. See Henry Brougham, *A Concise Statement of The Question Regarding the Abolition of the Slave Trade* (London: J. Hatchard, T. N. Longman and O. Rees, 1804), 76, for his discussion on the threat that St. Domingue proved to slavery in neighboring Jamaica.

it his responsibility to draw to the attention of the colonists that the very composition of the slave West Indian society made it particularly prone to destruction.

A QUESTION OF PROPERTY

No planter in the British West Indies agreed with the abolitionists that "they . . . who should emancipate their Negroes there would promote their interests by so doing."[33] Planters assessed the antislavery campaign from a completely different perspective. With singularity of mind, they denounced every argument and proposal as an attempt to undermine their property. Mr. Baring's petition from the West India Committee of Merchants and Planters in London in 1823 typified their attitude: "The [slavery] question involved the security of property to an immense amount, belonging to the subjects of this country, as well as to the lives and means of subsistence of all the West India colonists . . . they considered . . . amelioration essential to the welfare of both parties; but it was another question whether property, which had been acquired under the sanction of that House, should be taken away . . . what improved morality and justice there was in the arbitrary deprivation of property, the acquisition of which the laws had allowed?"[34]

Planters lived in daily fear of slave rising but regarded the danger as a regular feature of the risks attendant upon possessions in the plantation system.[35] They believed that with rigorous policing measures and no outside interference, especially by abolitionists, the system could be kept under control. Fewer slaves would be inspired by promises of freedom to rise in arms against their masters. Uppermost in the minds of West Indian planters was their property. In their calculation, they would have more to lose if the "saints" succeeded ultimately in freeing the slaves than they would from the occasional revolt that could be quickly and brutally suppressed. Thus, they had no inclination to do anything that would appear to compromise the value of their slave property. They would not be so un-

33. Clarkson (1824), 50.

34. *Hansard's Parliamentary Debates,* new ser., 9 (May 15, 1823): 255–256. See also *Anti-Slavery Monthly Reporter* 1, no. 22 (March 31, 1827): 315, where abolitionists took note of the claims of the planters regarding the value of the colonies to Britain.

35. Craton (1980), 2; see also Northcott (1976), 41–42, where he comments that "slavery would need more than a revolution to shake it."

wise as to assist the abolitionists, whom they branded as misguided phil-anthropists, in destroying the plantocracy. The voice of caution meant lit-tle to them; economic interest meant everything.[36]

Throughout the campaign, the abolitionists tried to assure the slaving interests that they respected property rights and were prepared to take steps to protect them. One of the clearest indications of the abolitionists' sincerity on this point was their ready consent to the vital phrase in the amendment of Buxton's 1823 proposal. Abolitionists generally agreed that measures adopted for the mitigation and gradual abolition of slavery would be guided by "a fair and equitable consideration of the interests of private property."[37] In effect, this meant that whenever emancipation ar-rived, the planters could be certain that even the abolitionists would sup-port compensation for the loss of slave labor.[38] After the Demerara slave revolt, Buxton requested that the promised boon to the slaves be granted in such a manner so as to "injure no man's property, and wound no man's feelings."[39] Thomas Clarkson reinforced the abolitionists' sincere respect for the property rights of the planter class. "The emancipation that I de-sire is such an emancipation only as I firmly believe to be compatible not only with the due subordination and happiness of the labourer, but with the permanent interests of his employer."[40]

The West India interest was dogmatic that neither amelioration nor emancipation could be considered without compensation. Throughout their campaign, British abolitionists held to the position that improve-ments in the conditions of the slaves must not conflict with the interests

36. Memorial from the West India Planters and Merchants, November 22, 1823, p. 1, MS 725, Papers of the West India Planters and Merchants, Institute of Jamaica, Kingston; *Quarterly Review* 29, no. 58 (July 1823): 478; A. E. Furness, "George Hibbert and the De-fence of Slavery in the West Indies," *Jamaican Historical Review* 5, no. 1 (May 1965): 56–70; Northcott (1976), 44; Butler (1995), 10.

37. *Hansard's Parliamentary Debates,* new ser., 9 (May 15, 1823): 275. Abolitionists de-nied accusations that they were disinclined to compensate slave owners for their losses in the event of emancipation and insisted that the "people of England would rather pay £6,000,000 annually for the discontinuance than £3,000,000 for the continuance of slavery." *Anti-Slavery Monthly Reporter* 1, no. 12 (May 31, 1826): 177–178.

38. *Anti-Slavery Monthly Reporter* 1, no. 12 (May 31, 1826): 178, "Compensation, however unreasonable in principle, would readily be granted"; Butler (1995), 19, 24.

39. *Hansard's Parliamentary Debates,* new ser., 10 (March 16, 1824): 1133.

40. Clarkson (1824), 56 and preface.

of their masters. Some abolitionists did insist, nevertheless, that British law had erroneously protected slavery and that they rejected the principle of holding human property. In 1823, William Smith rose in the House of Commons to register his "strongest and most indignant protest against the doctrine of treating man as the property of other men."[41] While Smith made his opposition quite clear, he was also careful to note that the private ownership of legitimate property ought not to be trampled upon.[42] Henry Brougham by 1830 revisited the question and insisted that there was neither moral nor religious justification for the practice.[43] Buxton, who in 1823 had questioned the legality of the acquisition of slaves, returned to the subject in 1832. He settled on the compromising view that "the Negro . . . owed no compensation to the planter. Whatever the Government and the country might owe the planter as a compensation, the Negro did not owe the planter anything."[44]

Some abolitionists went so far as to challenge the planters' jealous regard for their property by questioning the value of colonial investments to Britain and to its individual investors. Abolitionist supporters with East Indian interests were in the vanguard of this challenge and included James Cropper, Emmanuel Sturge, Whitmore, Zachary Macaulay, and Henry Thornton.[45] Among their assertions was that the viability of the British West Indian economy was artificially boosted by "the enormous pecuniary sacrifices made by the people of this country in the shape of bounties and protections."[46] They also claimed that it was propped up by the accidental circumstances following the slave rebellion in St. Domingue in 1791. Abolitionists insisted too that after 1805, with competition in the sugar market from Brazil and Cuba, increased supply on British West Indian sugar glutted the market, causing the slump in sugar prices of 1806. The real gripe, however, was that higher import duties were paid on East

41. *Hansard's Parliamentary Debates*, new ser., 9 (May 15 1823): 311.
42. Ibid.
43. *Hansard's Parliamentary Debates*, new ser., 25 (July 13, 1830): 1176.
44. *Hansard's Parliamentary Debates*, 3d ser., 13 (May 24, 1832): 43.
45. For a discussion of East Indian cooperation in the antislavery attack, see Mathieson (1926), 29–32; Williams (1964), 183–188; Ragatz (1963), 363–371; Coupland (1933), 123–124; Burn (1937), 85–88; James (1938), 52–53.
46. James Cropper at Anti-Slavery Society Meeting in Liverpool on April 24, 1826, *Anti-Slavery Monthly Reporter* 1, no. 12 (May 31, 1826): 187.

Indian than on West Indian sugar. By 1813, the duty paid on importing one hundred weight of sugar from India increased from three to ten shillings. By 1821, the East Indians paid forty-five shillings to import one hundred weight of white or clayed sugar while the West Indians paid thirty. The East Indians argued that the favored position of the West Indians was unjustified.[47]

Anti-Slavery Society members with East Indian interests also claimed that should the West Indies be lost to the mother country, her contribution to Britain's economy could be easily replaced. Additionally, they viewed Britain's commercial connection with the colonies as a burden to the taxpayers in the metropolis. It was saddled with the expenses of civil and military establishments. Abolitionists regarded planter assertions that the colonial possessions benefited Britain's shipping and manufactures as a monstrous misrepresentation. The Anti-Slavery Society concluded by this period that on account of the monopoly of trade enjoyed by the British West Indian colonies, these possessions were a curse rather than a blessing. "We venture to say that Colonial Empire has been one of the greatest curses of Modern Europe . . . What have been its fruits? Wars of frequent occurrence and immense cost, fettered trade, lavish expenditure, clashing jurisdiction, corruption in governments and indigence among the people . . . This it is that has . . . led us to give subsidies which were never earned . . . what are the bounties and forced prices but an enormous poor rate in disguise?"[48]

The East India abolitionists, borrowing ideas from Adam Smith, also

47. James Cropper, *Letters Addressed to William Wilberforce, M. P. Recommending the Encouragement of the Cultivation of Sugar in Our Dominions in the East Indies, as the Natural and Certain Means of Effecting the General and Total Abolition of the Slave Trade* (Liverpool: Longman, Hurst and Co., 1822), iii; *Edinburgh Review* 38, no. 75 (February 1823): 210–211; *Anti-Slavery Monthly Reporter* 1, no. 17 (October 31, 1826): 243–244. This issue is entitled "On the Bounties and Protecting Duties, and the Restrictions on Trade, intended for the Support of the Slave System."

48. *Edinburgh Review* 41, no. 82 (January 1825): 483; Society for the Mitigation and Gradual Abolition of Slavery, *East and West India Sugar; or, A Refutation of the Claims of the West India Colonists to a Protecting Duty on East India Sugar* (London: J. Hatchard and Son, 1823), 63–65. (Hereafter this item is referred to as *East and West India Sugar.*) See also *Anti-Slavery Monthly Reporter* 1, no. 17 (October 31, 1831): 247–248; and 3, no. 57 (February 1830), article entitled "Cost of Negro Slavery—Army, Ordnance, Commissariat, Miscellaneous, Navy."

submitted that free labor was cheaper and more efficient than slave labor; a pragmatic justification for dismantling the system. James Cropper asserted that British consumers were paying 1.2 million pounds as a premium on slave cultivation and that by consuming free-grown as opposed to slave-grown produce, they would be doing themselves and the slaves a great service.[49] Joseph Sturge, a corn merchant from Birmingham, supported this idea by making free-grown or East Indian sugar available in London at a depot at No. 17 East Cheap. By September 1824, the Anti-Slavery Society formed a subcommittee for the use of sugar produced by free labor.[50]

Thomas Clarkson, who had no commercial connections in the East, was one of the more prominent abolitionists who lent some support to this position. In 1824 he had stated that free men in the East Indies were employed at a cheaper rate and that if the West Indians follow this example, they would spend less than they did to maintain their ineffective slave labor force. Clarkson observed that, "a Negro if he worked for himself, could do double the work."[51] Even Thomas Fowell Buxton referred occasionally to the argument that British West Indian slavery was not economically advantageous to the British Empire. In a meeting at Freemasons' Hall in 1828, Buxton explained that he could not understand how, "Britain professes herself the friend of freedom and the enemy of slavery, [but upholds] the gross inconsistency of that policy which gives premium, encouragement, protection and bounties to the produce of slave labour, denying all these to the produce of free labour."[52] At times, the abolitionists were able to marry economic arguments with positions founded upon the strong moral objections that typified their movement. The Anti-Slavery Society believed, for example, that it was an enormous injustice that "people of this country are made to contribute in bounties and protecting duties, to the maintenance of a system which they detest and reprobate."[53] In spite of negative assessments of the economic relationship be-

---

49. See Cropper (1822), v, 37–41, 48–50; *Anti-Slavery Monthly Reporter* 1, no. 9 (February 28, 1826): 83.

50. Committee on Slavery Minute Book, September 8 and 23, 1824, pp. 135–136, 138, MSS. Brit. Emp. S. 20 E 2/3, Anti-Slavery Society Papers.

51. Clarkson (1824), 44, 48–49.

52. *Anti-Slavery Monthly Reporter* 2, no. 36 (May 1828): 230.

53. *Anti-Slavery Monthly Reporter* 1, no. 14 (July 31, 1826): 198.

tween Britain and her colonies, the society noted that for the sakes of the slaves and for absentee proprietors, it would be grievous to witness the ruin of private property.[54]

The attacks on slavery as an economic institution give rise to the question whether the British West Indies was in economic decline during the period of the antislavery agitation. This is an ongoing debate sparked largely by Eric Williams's *Capitalism and Slavery* and Lowell Ragatz's *Fall of the Planter Class* and opposed particularly by Seymour Drescher and Roger Anstey.[55] The arguments, while focusing on the abolition of the slave trade, have spilled over to the campaign against slavery itself. While historians contend over the economic viability of the slave economies of the British West Indies, the abolitionists addressed the issue from a different perspective. They argued that the colonial system enriched the pockets of those with West India interests while it impoverished British manufacturers and consumers of colonial produce. They argued that the West Indian plantation system meant the underdevelopment of British India and seemed to support the strange view that the idea of colonizing was to purchase colonial produce at as dear a rate as possible. Abolitionists believed that Britain's support of the plantation economy of the West Indies also had the negative effect of aggravating the evils of slavery.[56] They also did not hesitate to point out that those with West Indian interests had been complaining for some time of the financial strain under which they were operating.[57]

The counterattack that went furthest toward displacing the formidable safeguard that planters secured in the property argument was found not in attempts to undermine the value of the colonies, however, but in the threat of slave revolts. The abolitionists logically reasoned that what-

54. Clarkson (1824), 44, 48–49.

55. See Seymour Drescher, *Econocide: British Slavery in the Era of Abolition* (Pittsburgh: University of Pittsburgh Press, 1977), chap. 1; Seymour Drescher, "Capitalism and Abolition: Values and Forces in Britain, 1783–1814," in *Liverpool, the African Slave Trade, and Abolition,* ed. Roger Anstey and P. E. H. Hair (Bristol: Historical Society of Lancashire and Chelshire Occasional Series, 1976), 167–195; Northcott (1976), 34–35, 38–39, for his discussion on the prosperity of Demerara proprietors in the pre-emancipation era.

56. *Anti-Slavery Monthly Reporter* 1, no. 14 (July 31, 1826): 204; 1, no. 22 (March 31, 1827): 316–323; 2, no. 32 (January 1828): 174.

57. *Anti-Slavery Monthly Reporter* 1, no. 12 (May 31, 1826): 178.

ever profits were to be gained through slavery were adversely affected when slaves resorted to war in the attempt to achieve their own emancipation. This position did not deny the planters' claim to the protection of their economic rights, nor did it question the value of the colonies to the parent body. It was a pragmatic call to the West India interest to take measures that would secure the safety of those rights and the value of the colonies.

NO SECURITY OF PROPERTY IN SLAVERY

In the course of the 1820s, the abolitionists learned and mastered the one argument capable of undermining the property claims put forward by the planters. Property interests might listen to reason only if it was clear that property was threatened by violence. One mode by which the society attempted to demonstrate the negative impact of slave rebellion on planters' property was by making a sharp distinction between owners of West Indian property resident in Britain and their dependents living in the colonies. The society insisted that the latter were the real obstacle to slavery reform and, thus, to West Indian prosperity. Their contumacy was not motivated by a desire to protect their property, for the slaves and the plantations did not belong to them. They had no self-interest in improving the management of the system, for if rebellion or any other disaster ruined the plantations, they had nothing to lose, and if compensation was granted when slavery was abolished, they had nothing to gain.[58] They clung to their posts as bookkeepers, managers, and overseers for the opportunity of exercising racial tyranny over the slaves. Their familiarity with oppression was responsible for their corruption.[59] The abolitionists claimed that the hired hands of the slavery system were ultimately responsible for putting at risk the property of others. The abolitionists noted, on the other hand, that the absentee planters, "the Ellises, the Hibberts, the Mannings, men of the most respectable characters and minds in the country" were the ones whose pecuniary interests would suffer in the event of unrest in the colonies.[60]

58. *Hansard's Parliamentary Debates,* new ser., 9 (May 15, 1823): 334–335; *Edinburgh Review* 41, no. 88: 480.

59. *Edinburgh Review* 41, no. 88; see also *Anti-Slavery Monthly Reporter* 1, no. 9 (February 28, 1826): 82.

60. Ibid.

The abolitionist leaders always tended to portray in a positive light West Indian proprietors living in England, many of whom were fellow M.P.s.[61] It was an attempt to appeal to the West Indians' regard for a reputation for fair-mindedness and consistency in principles. The abolitionists reminded the absentee planters that they had claimed to be "the strenuous advocates of popular rights, and the sworn enemies to oppression, at least in Europe."[62] The abolitionists were calling on colonial proprietors at home to demonstrate that their commitment to high ideals was not colored by geographical distance, race, and personal interests.[63] This was, of course, an attempt to persuade the absentees to urge their hirelings in the colonies to adopt amelioration measures that would protect their slave property. The abolitionists, however, did not quite achieve their objective with this tactic. It was perhaps true that the slaving interests at home were less cruelly disposed to the slaves than were those in the colonies. The abolitionists were also probably correct in asserting that the real power on the plantations lay in Britain and not in the West Indies. In the final analysis, however, it was the economic interests of the absentees more than the inhumanity of their managers on the plantations that firmly tied the slaves to slavery.

In a less cautious assessment, the abolitionists declared that the destruction to property that attended a slave revolt was more acceptable than the permanent existence of slavery. The society reiterated the abolitionists' respect for the rights of property but asserted that "such a revolution, violent as it would doubtless be, would be desirable, if it were the only possible means of subverting the present system."[64] The position was a restatement of the abolitionists' occasional assertion that the end justified the means. The rebellion of the slaves, if it should end in eventual emancipation, would be a worthwhile sacrifice. Many abolitionists shrank back from this radical view. It was a position that endorsed too closely Dr. Johnson's toast to the next rebellion in the West Indies.

A far more irrefutable and less contentious treatment was that the ris-

61. Wilberforce (1807), 248; *Hansard's Parliamentary Debates,* new ser., 9 (May 15, 1823): 335; Brougham (1804), 59.

62. *Anti-Slavery Monthly Reporter* 1, no. 9 (February 28, 1826), 52.

63. Ibid.

64. *Edinburgh Review* 41, no. 81 (October 1824): 213–214; 41, no. 82 (January 1825): 485.

ing of the slaves made slavery a precarious investment. It was a shrewd appeal to the commercial interest of the planters. The abolitionists pointed out that if protecting their interests was their principal concern, planters ought to be aware that in a servile war they would inevitably emerge as losers. The society cautioned, "We entreat these respectable persons to reflect on the precarious nature by which they hold their property . . . if the slavery debate ended, could they think themselves secure from ruin? . . . Property will be deprived of all its security. In a servile war, the master *must* be the loser—for his enemies are his chattels, whether the slave conquers or falls, he is alike lost to his owner. In the meantime, the soil lies uncultivated; the machinery is destroyed. And when the possessions of the planter are restored to him, they have been changed into a desert."[65]

The abolitionists attempted to persuade the colonists that protecting their property and reforming slavery were one and the same interest. In one sense, this was a reminder of the abolitionists' promise to keep in mind the well-being of the slaves and their masters' interests. The campaigners urged planters to stake their claims behind the struggle on behalf of slaves, for to sabotage the movement was to sabotage their own property. Abolitionists warned, "nothing short of a miracle can save the Whites, if they neglect any longer the performance of their promises, and the discharge of their imperative duty."[66] In the abolitionists' view, cooperation in amelioration was not suicidal for the colonists. It was the one insurance available against the rebellion of the slaves, which put their property on the line. The argument was a powerful abolitionist attack that ought to have hit its target dead in the center. It emphasized the far-reaching economic ruin that slave rebels inflicted on colonial property. It pulled from under their feet the main ground upon which planters objected to measures of slavery reform. Even in defeat, slave rebels were capable of hurting their masters at the point where it mattered most. The abolitionists, however, did not attempt to turn to much advantage the strength of this position. By 1825 they were still addicted to promoting pastoral measures of slavery reform, even when these were backed by explosive depiction of cataclysmic doom in the colonies. They were contented to request on be-

65. *Edinburgh Review* 41, no. 82 (January 1825): 487. James Cropper raised the same point at a Liverpool meeting that "if the slaves become worth nothing, then the masters' property is gone." *Anti-Slavery Monthly Reporter* 1, no. 12 (May 31, 1831): 187.

66. *Edinburgh Review* 41, no. 81 (October 1824): 214.

half of the slaves "institutions that they have no temptation to change."[67] Conservative as was this request, nevertheless, the West India interest and their supporters spurned abolitionists' grave advice to loosen their stranglehold on slavery.

PARLIAMENTARY INTERVENTION

The Anti-Slavery Society used slave revolts to elaborate on the danger of the defiance with which planters resisted the interference of the parent state in their colonial affairs. The society emphasized that intervention was necessary because the colonies were powerless. They were in no position to adequately protect themselves from the ravages to which they were periodically vulnerable. In times of crisis—European colonial war, drought, hurricane, and slave revolts—the colonists needed and depended on the protection of Britain to secure both their lives and their property.[68] The abolitionists accordingly warned planters that they should desist from their threats to throw off their allegiance to Britain and follow the pattern of independence set by the Americans. West Indian troops were small, and, divided as they were, they could not act in concert to either defeat the mother country or maintain independence with restless slave populations in their midst. Abolitionists warned the West Indians of the dreadful and real possibility that without Britain and her troops, their plantation possessions would be swept away in the wave of slave rising: "Are you, in point of fact, at this moment able to protect yourselves against your slaves without our assistance . . . can you still rise up and lie down in security? If we suspend our protection—if we recall our troops— in the week the knife is at your throats."[69]

Since the colonists were so dependent on British military might as well as financial assistance in times of crisis, it was inappropriate for them to reject as unconstitutional Britain's prerogative to superintend the government of the colonies. By depicting the relationship between the mother country and the colonies in this light, the colonists' defiance of the parent state appeared short-sighted, ungrateful, and a flirtation with danger. The abolitionists reiterated, "They [the colonies] are both defended from for-

67. Ibid.
68. See Mathieson (1926), 3.
69. *Edinburgh Review* 41, no. 82 (January 1825): 481.

eign attack, and protected from intestine trouble, by the forces of the mother country. Those planters who talk so largely of their rights could not hold their property four and twenty hours without the aid of those forces; they who deny the right of the parent state to protect the Black subjects from cruel usage, could not exist in the midst of those Blacks, but for the protection of her arm; left to themselves, they would suddenly experience a change indeed—the slave and his master would exchange places."[70]

This was a reminder of the unwritten pact between the colonial power and the colony. The parent body was responsible for protecting her dependent, while the dependent was obliged to submit itself to the parent's direction. All the colonists could hope to achieve by their foolhardy rejection of the advice of Britain was the end of forced labor and another black, liberated, and independent state (like Haiti) in the British West Indies.

The slave rebellion argument was used to persuade Parliament as well as absentee and resident colonists of the need for parliamentary intervention. As Wilberforce had done, the society compared the government's reluctance to take decisive measures in the colonies to the procrastination of the authorities in Demerara. The abolitionists had widened the discussion on parliamentary intervention in colonial affairs through its reference to the issue of slave rebellions. Slave violence made intervention a question of right and necessity as well as of responsibility. The abolitionists advised that the government should perform its rightful duty by the colonies, for, "an act commanding and ordaining them . . . will create over the whole British Islands less commotion by far than the very inconsiderable ferment which the worst possible management excited in Demerara."[71]

The obvious implication was that government was playing a danger-

70. *Edinburgh Review* 41, no. 81 (October 1824): 214–215. See also *East and West India Sugar,* 61–62, in which the author states that "slaves, outnumbering the white population in almost every colony by at least twenty to one, form the great object of their apprehensions, and it is against them they have to multiply precautions." The *Watchman and Jamaica Free Press* (June 15, 1832) similarly asserts that "it is nothing short of madness to talk about opposition to the Parent Government . . . men are . . . giving expressions to sentiments unsupported by reason, and formed without the slightest reflection."

71. *Edinburgh Review* 41, no. 81 (October 1824): 213.

ous game. Its failure to compel colonial compliance would unleash on a wider scale the kind of revolt that had taken place in Demerara. Henry Brougham dwelt on this point when on June 1, 1824, he discussed Rev. Smith's case in the House of Commons. Almost echoing Wilberforce, Brougham stated, "My opinion ever has been, that it is alike necessary to the security of our White brethren, and just, and even merciful, to the Negroes . . . to maintain firmly the legal authorities, and, with that view, to avoid, in our relations with the Slaves, a wavering uncertain policy, keeping them in a condition of doubt and solicitude, calculated to work their own discomfort, and the disquiet of their masters."[72] In 1826, the Anti-Slavery Society also insisted that the ministers of government were pursuing a dangerous policy in persisting in attempts to conciliate a manifestly contumacious body of colonists to adopt slave reform measures. "The course it was determined to adopt, must end in delay and disappointment, if not in insurrection, and all its concomitant evils."[73] The argument was sound. In the 1820s, however, enough parliamentarians were not convinced. As for the ministers of government, they believed that they were acting responsibly by pursuing the judicious and temperate enforcement of the measures of slave reform advocated by the abolitionists.

FROM GRADUALISM TO IMMEDIATE EMANCIPATION

It was not until 1830 that the abolitionists declared their determination to move away from their conservative program of mitigation and gradual abolition to demand the immediate emancipation of the slaves. The newer members of the Anti-Slavery Society took the lead in guiding the movement in this direction. At the 1830 annual general meeting held on May 15 at Freemason's Hall, leaders Denman, Lushington, Buxton, and Brougham, with Wilberforce in the chair, had expressed the usual cautious resolutions on the slavery question. The younger abolitionist Henry Pownall moved an amendment calling for the immediate emancipation of all slaves born in the colony by 1830.[74] The majority accepted the amendment. Thus, referring to the promise of eventual emancipation given in the 1823 resolutions by the government, Buxton had declared in the

72. *The Missionary Smith*, 6.

73. *Anti-Slavery Monthly Reporter* 1, no. 11 (April 30, 1826): 131; 1, no. 14 (July 31, 1826): 201.

74. *Anti-Slavery Monthly Reporter* 3, no. 61 (June 1830): 256–257; Richard (1864), 93.

House of Commons in 1830 that "slavery, not having been ameliorated by the colonial legislatures in accordance with the resolutions passed by the House of Commons on that day seven years ago, should, as soon as possible, be abolished."[75] Again on April 15, 1831, Buxton referred to the legislation of 1823 and called for the emancipation of infant slaves in the colonies.[76] Despite the steps that Buxton was taking towards immediate emancipation, radical abolitionists criticized that he was not going far enough. In 1831, he responded to a complaining letter from Sturge. The more radical supporters of the movement alleged that Buxton, as their leader, was retarding the cause by sticking to the 1823 proposals and seeking only immediate freedom for slave children.[77] It was not a very bold step, but Buxton at last believed that the time had come to begin the process that would lead to the eventual emancipation of the slaves.

The abolitionists forwarded two basic explanations to justify their shift in policy from gradual to immediate emancipation. They finally admitted that amelioration was a total failure. The evils of slavery could not be remedied; the system must be eradicated. Secondly, in spite of the failure of amelioration, the slaves had amply demonstrated that they were creolized and Christianized in the years following the abolition of the slave trade. Slaves were, therefore, fit for freedom. In changing their position, the abolitionists were forced to subject themselves to a considerable amount of self-reproach. Radical supporters of the antislavery movement had for some time criticized the conservative leaders of dragging their feet in pressing for freedom.[78] The leaders had replied that it would be a mockery and violation of justice and humanity to free slaves while they were unprepared for the responsibility of freedom. Slaves had first to be trained and educated for this perfect state of maturity. To free slaves without previous preparation would be ruinous both to the slaves and to their masters. Clarkson had gone so far as to state that if the slaves were "suddenly emancipated, nothing is more clear than they would not work

75. Committee on Slavery Minute Book, May 27, 1830, MSS. Brit. Emp. S. 20 E. 2/3, Anti-Slavery Society Papers; Mathieson (1926), 196.

76. Mathieson (1926), 196.

77. Letter from Buxton to Sturge, January 27, 1831, Northrepps Hall, Cromer, in Richard (1864), 98–99. See also Committee on Slavery Minute Book, MSS. Brit. Emp. S. 444, Vol. 3, p. 31, Thomas Fowell Buxton Papers.

78. See Heyrick (1824), 7, 9.

for their masters but would return into the woods and lead a savage life."[79] Brougham explained after the Demerara slave revolt that "it is for the sake of the blacks themselves, as subsidiary to their own improvement, that the present state of things must for a time be maintained."[80]

In making these statements, the abolitionists, no doubt, had their eyes set on the plantation society in the aftermath of slavery. They were anxious to ensure that the slaves would continue to labor on the estates, thereby making the right use of their freedom. Contrary to the economic views about the West Indian plantations that some abolitionists expressed, most of the leaders believed in and hoped that the colonies would continue to be a viable branch of the British economy when it was cultivated by ex-slaves.[81] While abolitionists sympathized with the plight of workers in industrialized Britain, they confined their attacks to slave labor and not free labor. Elizabeth Heyrick had criticized that the male leaders of the movement supported amelioration and gradual emancipation not only for economic reasons but also because they were over concerned about their public image. Their attitude was influenced by the fact that "every idea of immediate emancipation is still represented, . . . as impolitic, enthusiastic and visionary."[82]

Abolitionists' apologies for many of their conservative positions, however, were fairly regular by the 1820s. Abolitionists still maintained that slaves were expected to be industrious on the plantations after slavery was abolished. Even Heyrick was not opposed to the establishment of a free labor system in the British West Indies after emancipation.[83] The male leaders of British antislavery, nevertheless, admitted that the ideas on

79. Address to gentlemen at Ipswich, December 5, 1823, CN 33, Thomas Clarkson Papers.

80. *The Missionary Smith*, 7.

81. Wilberforce (1807), 249–250, 258–259; *Hansard's Parliamentary Debates,* new ser., 9 (May 15, 1823): 266; *Hansard's Parliamentary Debates,* new ser., 10 (March 24, 1824): 1133; Address to gentlemen at Ipswich, December 5, 1823, CN 33, Thomas Clarkson Papers; Committee on Slavery Minute Book, November 28, 1832, p. 179, MSS. Brit. Emp. S. 20 E 2/3, Anti-Slavery Society Papers; Richard (1864), 74; Davis (1962), 214; David Eltis, "Abolitionist Perceptions of Society After Slavery," in *Slavery and British Society, 1776–1846*, ed. James Walvin (London: Macmillan, 1982), 199.

82. Heyrick (1824), 10. See also Midgley (1992), 103–118, for her discussion on Heyrick's radical opposition to the relatively conservative attitude of the male antislavery leaders.

83. Midgley (1992), 108, 111.

which they forestalled emancipation were "slippery and dangerous and situated on the brink of the most fatal error."[84] Clarkson and, later, Joseph Sturge openly confessed, "We have to reproach ourselves with a long and most cruel delay of justice."[85] The Anti-Slavery Society stated a new position regarding the reputed laziness of the slaves; a reputation that they themselves had helped to shape. By 1827 the society, using the evidence provided by colonists regarding the thriving local provision markets in the colonies, came to the conclusion that "when facilities have been given them [slaves] of obtaining their freedom, their voluntary industry has been thereby greatly augmented."[86] As chairman of the annual meeting held at Freemasons' Hall in 1830, Wilberforce declared that "there was no longer . . . any time for delay or half measures."[87] Buxton also admitted that it was erroneous to place so much faith in the amelioration measures proposed in 1823.[88]

As a body, the society confessed that they were to be blamed for adopting gradualism: "They had been too indulgent towards the measures of Government, . . . too reluctant to embark in desperate councils [and] . . . too willing to avert the evils of collision."[89] The Anti-Slavery Society's analysis of the report of the House of Commons committee on slavery recanted the major views that abolitionists had expressed regarding the prospects of an emancipated slave society in the British colonies. They "unhesitatingly asserted" that the evidence showed "not only that the slaves will incur no risk of suffering want by emancipation, but that their speedy emancipation affords the only rational prospect of preserving the public peace, and of securing the permanent interests of the planters themselves."[90] When the Lords' committee of 1832 on the treatment and conditions of the slaves interviewed Buxton, he made it clear that the abolitionists were no longer convinced of the wisdom in delaying slavery. To

84. *Edinburgh Review* 39, no. 77 (October 1823): 120.

85. Ibid., 126; Richard (1864), 87–88.

86. *Anti-Slavery Monthly Reporter* 2, no. 27 (August 1827): 42.

87. *Anti-Slavery Monthly Reporter* 3, no. 61 (June 1830): 213–234.

88. Ibid., 239; *Hansard's Parliamentary Debates*, 3d ser., 13 (May 24, 1832): 96; Buxton (1852).

89. Extract from the *Morning Herald*, July 22, 1833, MSS. Brit. Emp. S. 444, vol. 12, reel 4, Thomas Fowell Buxton Papers.

90. *Analysis of The Report*, 210.

the contrary, he emphasized "the advantages of an early emancipation to masters as well as slaves and the dangers of delaying it."[91] Slaves in Jamaica rebelled in 1831–1832 just at the time when the activists adopted immediate abolition. Thus they abandoned amelioration altogether and maximized the opportunity for the danger of revolts to assume its place among the principles upon which they attacked the system of slavery.

THE ULTIMATUM

The Jamaican slave revolt pushed the abolitionists to a greater commitment to immediate emancipation than they had taken in 1830. The Anti-Slavery Society first met to discuss the rebellion on February 27, 1832. Secretary Thomas Pringle informed members that a letter of one Mr. Hilderbee referring to the rebellion had been passed to Buxton. "After much discussion on the subject of the disturbances in Jamaica, it was resolved that a deputation be appointed to confer with Mr. Buxton . . . to offer to the House their views on the late disturbances in Jamaica."[92] The society met again in April 1832. They were no longer inclined to limit their application of the obvious lesson that slave rebellion presented. In addition to the resolution that all children should be freed after the current session of Parliament, the society further resolved that "Parliament should proceed forthwith to adopt measures to secure immediate emancipation of all persons held in slavery in the British dominions . . . [and] that Mr. Buxton be respectfully requested to divide the House on his motion on 19 April."[93]

James Stephen was foremost in being vocal about linking the Jamaican slave revolt to the demand for complete and immediate emancipation for all slaves. On April 3, Stephen wrote to the society stating that he strongly advised "nothing short of immediate and general abolition of slavery in all the British colonies by direct parliamentary enactment."[94] Stephen made it clear that his views "have been strongly confirmed by . . . the late

91. *Abstract of the Report*, 117.

92. Committee on Slavery Minute Book, February 27, 1832, p. 123, April 4, 1832, p. 129, MSS. Brit. Emp. S. 20 E 2/3, Anti-Slavery Society Papers; Buxton (1852), 260.

93. Committee on Slavery Minute Book, April 4, 1832, p. 129, MSS. Brit. Emp. S. 20, E 2/3, Anti-Slavery Society Papers.

94. Committee on Slavery Minute Book, April 24, 1832, p. 135, MSS. Brit. Emp. S. 20, E 2/3, Anti-Slavery Society Papers.

insurrection in Jamaica, or the disorders so called."[95] The society did not deviate from Stephen's position. From that time on there was no looking back. Slave rebellion introduced a sharp edge to the tone of the society's reflections and resolutions. On four separate occasions in 1832, the Anti-Slavery Society used the threat of slave violence to lay before the British Parliament the grim state of the slavery question. The British public was also addressed. The following extracts demonstrate the direct manner in which the abolitionists were finally prepared to maximize the value of the slave violence argument.

> It is the duty of Parliament to proceed forthwith with the adoption of such measures as may accomplish the immediate and total abolition of slavery in the British Dominions . . . and . . . it is the conviction of this meeting that until this object shall have been effected, nothing can afford a security against the recurrence of such calamities as have recently afflicted the black and disgraced the white population of the island of Jamaica.[96]

> It is the duty of the Government and Parliament of this country to proceed without any further delay to fulfil their pledge and to adopt forthwith the necessary measures for the total abolition of slavery, it being now unquestionable that it is only by the interposition of Parliament any hope can be entertained of peacefully terminating its unnumbered evils or any security afforded against the recurrence of those bloody and calamitous scenes which have recently afflicted Jamaica.[97]

> Unless immediate measures are taken for the entire removal of this great national crime, it is to be feared that the natural hostility now existing between the slave and slave holder may lead to such an extermination of the system as will involve the oppressor and the oppressed in one common calamity.[98]

95. Ibid.

96. Committee on Slavery Minute Book, May 9, 1832, p. 144, MSS. Brit. Emp. S. 20 E 2/3, Anti-Slavery Society Papers.

97. Committee on Slavery Minute Book, May 12, 1832, p. 147, MSS. Brit. Emp. S. 20 E 2/3, Anti-Slavery Society Papers.

98. Committee on Slavery Minute Book, September 7, 1832, p. 163, MSS. Brit. Emp. S. 20 E 2/3, Anti-Slavery Society Papers.

The Committee anticipating the probability of emancipation being accomplished by violence, if the right of the slave to his freedom be not speedily established, call the attention of the public to the calamitous consequences which may attend further delay—consequences which all men of Christian principles will most deeply deplore; the blood which must be so profusely shed, the inevitable destruction of property in the colonies and the consequent injury to the commercial interests of Great Britain.[99]

The reflections and resolutions of the Anti-Slavery Society in this period were all very similar, and yet, no doubt to emphasize the increased sense of urgency and dread with which revolts now caused abolitionists to view the slavery question, they were repeatedly recorded in the minutes of their meetings. Although Eric Williams does not develop the point, he is correct in asserting that the rebellion of the slaves made the alternatives clear: emancipation from above or emancipation from below, but emancipation.[100] Abolitionists reiterated that it was imperative that Parliament enact legislation for emancipation. Failure to do so meant that the slaves, intent on having their freedom, would take matters in their own hands and continually turn to violence. Time was also of the essence. The colonies were no longer on the brink of a precipice, as Wilberforce had warned in 1824. They had gone over the precipice and the day of reckoning was at hand.

Additionally, it was evident that, despite the East India abolitionists' critical economic assessment of the colonies, as a body, antislavery agitators appreciated the value of the colonies to the mother country and were sincere in the intention to salvage colonial property from further destruction. They were no strangers to scenes of crowd violence attacking and destroying private property. They were living in an industrial age when workers in Britain were unleashing their economic frustrations on threshing machines and other property belonging to their employers. Although some abolitionists sympathized with workers' suffering, none supported their acts of vandalism.[101] It was no surprise, therefore, that the aboli-

99. Committee on Slavery Minute Book, September 19, 1832, p. 164, MSS. Brit. Emp. S. 20 E 2/3, Anti-Slavery Society Papers.

100. Williams (1964), 208.

101. Turner (1982), 32; see also the section of chap. 3 called "A Combination of European Workmen."

tionists reemphasized the argument that emancipation was necessary, for slave violence deprived property of all security. The abolitionists also recognized that they could no longer afford to muffle the slaves' ultimate aspirations. The time for pastoral measures in slavery had passed. The intensity of slave war made "total abolition" crucial. The letter that Stephen and Garrat wrote to the Anti-Slavery Society, which was included in the minutes of April 11, 1832, emphasized this wholehearted commitment. "We do not believe that in any middle course, or in the total rejection of the claims of justice and mercy, there would be greater safety. Only through measures brought forward and totally supported by the Government and in that way alone, a step towards the termination of slavery might be safely taken."[102]

Slavery advocates made a last ditch effort to sabotage the march to freedom. They reasoned that the Jamaican revolt was further proof that slaves were uncivilized barbarians. The revolt meant that the emancipation process should be interrupted. The abolitionists insisted on the contrary view. It was now unquestionable that slave rebellion should hasten not delay the abolition of slavery.[103]

Abolitionists maximized the extent to which they could convert the rebellion of the slaves into useful antislavery materials. They were convinced now more than ever that slave rebellion was the just retribution exacted on a nation guilty of the sin of upholding slavery. They reconciled the humanitarian struggle with the idea of justice in slave violence by reflecting that God is a just God and that his justice would not sleep forever. It was an old argument that had been raised as early as the second half of the sixteenth century, when John Hawkins became the first Englishman to engage in the slave trade. At that time, Queen Elizabeth II had declared (sincerely or otherwise) that if Hawkins was dealing in slave trading as opposed to the voluntary labour of Africans, "it would be detestable and call down the vengeance of heaven upon the undertakers."[104] Even Wilberforce, bent with age and retired from public life, had hinted in 1830 that he believed that a moral retribution was in store for Britain and her

---

102. Committee on Slavery Minute Book, April 11, 1832, p. 134, MSS. Brit. Emp. S. 20 E 2/3, Anti-Slavery Society Papers.

103. Letters to the secretaries of the missionary societies, MSS. Brit. Emp. S. 444, Vol. 3, p. 37, Thomas Fowell Buxton Papers.

104. "Sketch of the Life of William Wilberforce Esq. With a Review of the Present State of the Anti-Slavery Cause," Baptist Magazine, 3d ser., 3 (January 1833): 2.

colonies for persisting in the maintenance of slavery.[105] James Stephen Sr. was foremost among the abolitionists in propagating this ideology. "Servile wars were indicators of Divine wrath; and forerunners of approaching chastisement of the nations of Europe, for the grievous and impious oppression of the unfortunate African race."[106] Thus, Stephen regarded the Jamaican revolt as a confirmation of his predictions. He commented that slave violence and destruction ravaged Jamaica because colonists despised the warnings they received "and dreadful has been the consequences. The contumacy of the planters has been fully and fatally justified."[107]

Buxton expressed similar sentiments about the Jamaican slave rebellion. "Then indeed the storm seemed beginning, then the first whispers of that whirlwind seemed beginning which was to sweep off the white population. I thought indeed that the sword of eternal justice was unsheathed."[108] Buxton was persuaded that justice to the slaves would be done and that it would be visited on the property of the planters if not on their lives if slavery was not abolished. Slave rebellion led the abolitionists to adopt the radical concept that divine justice was on the side of the protest actions of the oppressed class.

It was only after the Jamaican rebellion that the abolitionists brought forward in the House of Commons their first motion for the complete and immediate emancipation of all slaves in the domains of Britain. Prior to presenting this motion, Buxton warned the House that "if the question respecting the West Indies were not speedily settled, it would settle itself in an alarming way."[109] In May 1832 Buxton finally rose in the House and called for a select committee to consider and report on measures for the extinction of slavery. He rested his motion on four points—decline of the slave population, the abuse of the whip, the neglect of the moral and re-

105. *Anti-Slavery Monthly Reporter* 2, no. 36 (May 1828): 217.

106. James Stephen (1830), 395.

107. Letter from James Stephen Sr. and Garrat, April 11, 1832, pp. 132–133, MSS. Brit. Emp. S. 20 E 2/3, Anti-Slavery Society Papers.

108. Notes and Drafts for Speeches, 1829–1839, Vol. 10, p. 64, MSS. Brit. Emp. S. 444, Thomas Fowell Buxton Papers; see also *Hansard's Parliamentary Debates*, 3d ser., 13 (May 24, 1832): 48; Mary Reckford, "The Jamaica Slave Rebellion of 1831," *Past and Present: A Journal of Historical Studies* 40 (1968): 123.

109. *Hansard's Parliamentary Debates*, 3d ser., 10 (March 7, 1832): 1262.

ligious instruction of the slaves, and slave rebellion. Buxton used the fear of rebellion to justify the demand for the eradication of slavery. He asked, "Did anyone doubt that a crisis was coming which would leave them no alternative but an immediate concession of freedom to the slaves, or a dreadful attempt to extort it through the horrors of a servile war?"[110]

This was neither mere rhetoric nor an attempt to use fear to control the government and people of Britain. Buxton was personally troubled by the dangers that he foresaw in the slave colonies. In February 1833 his prayer was that "almighty God would give these thy unhappy creatures their liberty—that liberty in peace and protect their masters from ruin and desolation."[111] Abolitionists corresponded with each other, expressing the same foreboding. Macaulay anxiously wrote to Brougham that "if we agree it [freeing the slaves] is safe, do so and do it at once."[112] The dread of recurrent servile warfare in the colonies was chiefly responsible for shaping Macaulay's view on the slavery issue. He stated, "above all I allude to the danger which it is admitted must arise from any long delay in the final adjustment . . . which must lead to anarchy and blood."[113] The Anti-Slavery Society by 1833 openly stated a similar viewpoint in an even more emphatic manner. Taking its cue from the 1832 House of Commons Committee appointed to inquire into slavery, the society asserted that "the evidence before us has most irrefragably and triumphantly established; that the danger of withholding freedom from the slaves is greater than that of granting it, and the controversy, therefore, as respects the expediency of an early emancipation, may be considered as decided."[114] It was unquestionable that by 1832, the slaves' rebellion was prominent among

110. *Hansard's Parliamentary Debates,* 3d ser., 13 (May 24, 1832): 46–48. See also *Journals of the House of Commons* 87 (1831–1832): 338. Buxton's motion rested on the question of safety but was amended with "in conformity with the Resolutions of this House on the 15th day of May 1823"; *Analysis of the Report,* 1.

111. Birthday/Anniversary Reflections, February 1832, Vol. 4, p. 233, MSS. Brit. Emp. S. 444, Thomas Fowell Buxton Papers.

112. Macaulay to Brougham, April 6, 1833 (13670), Henry Brougham Papers. Note that Macaulay was here reiterating the view of Lord Howick. See *Analysis of the Report,* 212.

113. Macaulay to Brougham, April 6, 1833 (13670), Henry Brougham Papers.

114. *Analysis of the Report,* 8; Agency Anti-Slavery Committee, *The Danger of Delay, and the Safety and Practicability of Immediate Emancipation, From the Evidence before the Parliamentary Committees on Colonial Slavery* (London: W. Johnston, 1833), 4.

the factors that fueled the last phase of the antislavery movement conducted in Britain.

PROLONGED APPREHENSIONS

A ministerial proposition for the emancipation of the slaves in the British West Indies was laid before the House of Commons for the first time in May 1833.[115] Its presentation, however, did not alleviate the abolitionists' fears of the threat of slave violence. To the contrary, the nature of its provisions intensified the impact of rebellion on the movement. Abolitionists were generally persuaded that its measures were unsafe and unsatisfactory. The proposal created divisions between radicals, intolerant of any compromise in emancipation, and conservatives, convinced that a degree of compromise was essential if the slaves were to gain their freedom.[116] Strangely enough, both radical and conservative abolitionists used the slave violence argument to justify their divergent positions. The conservatives, the leaders of the movement, won the day. Buxton, supported by leading Anti-Slavery Society members, had no doubt that his conservative parliamentary politics were better calculated to secure the ultimate objective of freedom for the slaves than the hard-line policy advocated by the radicals.

Pressure in the form of parliamentary petitions and Buxton's tactics to force the government to take the slavery question into its own hands, partly contributed to producing the 1833 antislavery legislation.[117] It was clear that, among other factors, parliamentarians accepted the abolitionist view that slave rebellion dictated emancipation. The House of Commons committee's 1832 report on slavery had explained that it restricted its investigation of the subject to two major considerations on account of the voluminous data that the slavery question was generating. One of these concerns was the rebellion of the slaves. The committee sought to determine whether "the dangers of convulsion are greater from freedom

115. *Journal of the House of Commons* 88 (1833): 389, 553. It became bill No. 482 on July 5, after the proposal's second reading. The full title of the bill was *A Bill for the Abolition of Slavery Throughout the British Colonies for Promoting the Industry of the Manumitted Slaves and for Indemnifying the Owners of Such Slaves.*

116. Buxton (1852), 274.

117. Committee on Slavery Minute Book, March 27, April 3, April 10, 1833, pp. 15, 19–20, 22, MSS. Brit. Emp. S. 20 E 2/4, Anti-Slavery Society Papers; Buxton (1852), 260, 321.

withheld, than from freedom granted to the slaves."[118] Just before he resigned from office, parliamentary undersecretary Lord Howick had no
doubts about the answer to such a reflection. He stated that delaying
emancipation would lead to great disasters.[119] Howick, as well as the head
of the West Indian desk at the Colonial Office, had prepared schemes of
emancipation.

Both plans concurred on the principle that planters should be compensated for the slave property they would lose after emancipation. In
spite of this provision, the plans were unacceptable to the West India
Committee and by 1833 both were discarded.[120] Stanley, the successor of
Lord Goderich as Secretary of State for War and the Colonies, drew up
the emancipation plan that was finally brought before Parliament in May
1833. These ensured that slaves were retained on the estates for as long as
possible, provided planters with a large compensation package in the form
of a loan, protected West Indian sugar on the British market, and left to
the local legislatures the details of emancipation. Stanley's scheme almost
totally disregarded the demands of the abolitionists. It mentioned nothing, for example, concerning the religious and moral instructions of the
ex-slaves. Both the abolitionists and the West Indians rejected it. It was
published in the *Times* on May 11 but was received with hostility.

With the assistance of James Stephen Jr., legal counsel to the Colonial
Office from 1813 to 1834, Stanley's plan was reexamined, and by May 14,
a modified version was published. Stanley prefaced his emancipation proposals on three principles; the dangers of servile war, the immorality of
slavery and the contumacy of the colonists. Its five clauses stipulated that
when emancipation was proclaimed children under six were to be entirely
free if they were maintained by their parents. If not, they were to be subjected to certain restrictions. All other slaves were free in all other spheres
except labor. For twelve years, they were to work for their former masters as apprentices for three-quarters of the day, equal to ten hours, and
could work for themselves in the remaining quarter of the day. If they
worked in all their free time, in twelve years they would have saved
enough to buy their freedom. Planters were obligated to supply food,

118. *Analysis of the Report*, 2.
119. *Hansard's Parliamentary Debates*, 3d ser., 11 (March 23, 1832): 815.
120. Gross (1980), 67.

clothes, and allowances to their apprentices. For the loss of their private property, planters were to receive compensation in the form of a loan totaling 15 million pounds to be provided either by Britain or the "Negroes." Stanley preferred the latter. Stipendiary magistrates would superintend the apprenticeship system. The debate over the emancipation bill spanned fifteen weeks. During this time, no doubt because of both pro- and antislavery objections, two major changes were adopted. Buxton was relieved to note that slaves would no longer be considered liable to pay for their own emancipation.[121] The loan was converted to a gift of 20 million pounds. Secondly, the proposed apprenticeship was reduced almost by half.[122]

THE MONEY BATTLE

The abolitionists' early assessment of the whole scheme was that it was a disaster. In an article entitled *Remarks on the Proposed Bill for the Abolition of Colonial Slavery,* the Anti-Slavery Society asserted that "it cannot for a single moment be expected that all this will pass—that the twenty millions and the apprenticeship will go down smoothly together— still less that this confidence in Transatlantic assemblies will not be abused, or that a handful of half paid magistrates will do justice between 800,000 slaves and slave owners. On the other hand, it is certain, that when the seeds of discord are thus sown, and anger and discontent scattered with a profuse hand, all must terminate in bloodshed and confusion."[123]

The two clauses of Stanley's emancipation scheme that most irked the abolitionists were compensation for former masters and apprenticeship for would-be ex-slaves. They objected to compensation because it left intact and sanctioned the principle of holding human property.[124] Buxton had even gone so far as to argue that "if compensation were to be made, the compensation was due from them [the planters] to the Negro—com-

---

121. *Hansard's Parliamentary Debates,* 3d ser., 18 (May 14, 1833): 1260.

122. Ibid., 1221–1231; *Journals of the House of Commons* 88 (1833): 482, 553, 592, 599–600, 602, 611–612, 614, 617–618; Burn (1937), 62–70; Gross (1980), 70–74.

123. Committee on Slavery Minute Book, British West Indies General, 1795–1835, p. 8, MSS. Brit. Emp. S. 22, G. 44, Anti-Slavery Society Papers.

124. Extract from the *Morning Herald,* July 22, 1833, MSS. Brit. Emp. S. 444, vol. 12, reel 4, Thomas Fowell Buxton Papers; Richard (1864), 104; Buxton (1852), 265; Committee on Slavery Minute Book, p. 1, MSS. Brit. Emp. S. 22, G. 44, Anti-Slavery Society Papers.

pensation for evils without number and for years of unrewarded toil."[125] Abolitionist leaders, however, soon regarded compensation as a worthwhile sacrifice for immediate emancipation.[126] Compensation would help to pacify the planters, thus making slavery safer for all parties. The thinking of the leaders was, of course, that "while the Negroes were set at liberty, the planters should not be exposed to ruinous loss."[127]

Buxton felt it was wiser and safer to attempt to modify rather than to reject the bill. He said to his sister Mrs. Foster that he would prefer to give up the 20 million pounds than have bloodshed in the colonies.[128] Thomas Pringle concurred: he would "give twenty millions with the utmost satisfaction, if it accomplished the entire, complete and satisfactory performance of the annihilation of this great crime."[129] By adopting this conservative position on the money issue, Buxton and others were only adhering to the earlier position taken by the Anti-Slavery Society.[130] Nevertheless, Buxton and his conservative band came under considerable attack for the compromise. Joseph Sturge complained to Buxton, "If you had stood firm, the planters would have got no compensation." Buxton replied, "Perhaps so . . . they no compensation and we no extinction of slavery: or rather it would have been extinguished by a rebellion."[131] Buxton also explained to Sturge, George Stephen, and others who also wanted him to fight the money battle, that had he done so Stanley might have carried out his threat to throw up the whole bill.[132] Buxton believed that by allowing Stanley's proposal to go through its first and seconding readings with its irksome compensation clause, the abolitionists would strengthen their ability to eliminate or at least shorten the proposed period of apprenticeship.

125. *Anti-Slavery Monthly Reporter* 3, no. 61 (June 1830): 240.

126. Richard (1864), 107–108.

127. Buxton (1852), 263.

128. Ibid., 279.

129. Extract from the *Morning Herald*, July 22, 1833, MSS. Brit. Emp. S. 444, vol. 12, reel 4, Thomas Fowell Buxton Papers.

130. *Anti-Slavery Monthly Reporter* 1, no. 12 (May 31, 1826): 178. The society had stated here that "compensation, however unreasonable in principle, would readily be granted."

131. Buxton (1852), 278.

132. Ibid., 279.

APPRENTICESHIP: THE FEARFUL EXPERIMENT

Neither conservative nor radical abolitionists were able to reconcile themselves completely to the apprenticeship scheme proposed by Stanley. Up
to a point, Buxton was willing to accept the plan as an expedient for the
continued productivity of the colonies. He considered that it was a necessary training ground for ushering the slaves from forced to free labor.
He positively supported the principle of making the "Negroes" industrious since idle ex-slave populations would present the unattractive prospect that the property of the planters would fall to ruin. The abolitionists
had always intended that the British West Indian system would move from
a slave- to a free-labor economy. As David Brion Davis has observed,
"Abolitionists were not considering the upward mobility of workers but
rather the rise of the Negroes to the level of humanity . . . they combined
the ideal of emancipation with an insistence on duty and subordination
. . . the anti slavery movement reflected the needs and values of the emerging capitalist order."[133]

Buxton was persuaded that emancipation must be only as immediate
as it would ensure safety, peace, and continued productivity in the
colonies. He was appalled to realize, however, that the West Indians did
not regard apprenticeship as a beneficial measure that would prepare the
slaves to continue to work diligently when freed. They regarded it as a
part of their compensation package. Consequently, Buxton feared that the
colonists would use the period of labor without wages as a valuable
respite during which they could squeeze the last juice out of their apprentices. He was persuaded that such an attitude would lead to great conflict in the colonies, for he was persuaded that the slaves were determined
not to work unless they were paid. On that ground, Buxton objected to
apprenticeship, calling it slavery by another name. Having come to that
conclusion, he warned, "to compel the slaves to become apprentices . . .
we have reason exceedingly to dread will cause insurrection and bloodshed in the colonies."[134] In the House of Commons, Buxton reiterated that

    133. David B. Davis, *The Problem of Slavery in the Age of Revolution, 1770–1823*
(Ithaca: Cornell University Press, 1975), 466–467.
    134. Extract from the *Morning Herald,* July 22, 1833, MSS. Brit. Emp. S. 444, vol. 12,
reel 4, Thomas Fowell Buxton Papers; Miscellaneous letters and letters from Joseph Gur-
ney, October 29, 1832, vol. 3, p. 34, MSS. Brit. Emp. S. 444, Thomas Fowell Buxton Papers.

"he could not help saying this—from all the facts that had come to his knowledge, and from the communication he received, both public and private, his mind was deeply impressed with a conviction that a servile war would be the inevitable consequence of deferring emancipation."[135]

During the House of Commons debate on the ministerial plan for the abolition of slavery Buxton again objected to the apprenticeship scheme on the grounds that delaying emancipation would result in bloodshed in the colonies. "If you did not determine to do justice to the Negro, and to pay them wages, and that forthwith, you would have an insurrection of the blacks in that colony. What, he would ask, was the main cause of the late insurrection of the blacks in Jamaica? It was the determination of the Negroes not to work without remuneration."[136] Other abolitionists supported Buxton in warning that apprenticeship, by prolonging the servile regime, was destined to end in cataclysmic upheaval. Thomas Pringle remonstrated that "when he opened the Bill, he found that it was not for the abolition of slavery, but for the substitution of one species of slavery for another. It did not promote the industry of the slaves but it prevented all possibility of industry . . . he could only describe the Bill as the worst of all possible things under the best of all possible titles . . . the consequence of this measure if carried into effect, would be . . . servile insurrection."[137]

Slave violence was central to the debates regarding the clauses that would direct the slaves to freedom. Having compromised in order to secure in principle a bill for abolition, the antislavery leaders persisted for some time in their opposition to apprenticeship. On July 12, 1833, a group of abolitionists waited on Stanley to discuss the apprenticeship issue. Stanley reiterated that apprenticeship must stand or the whole bill would go with it.[138] On July 24, 1833, Buxton rose in the House of Commons and

135. *Hansard's Parliamentary Debates,* new ser., 17 (May 14, 1833): 161, 163. Buxton stated that he "saw no alternative in the rejection of this measure but the precipitation of emancipation by bloodshed and violence." He opposed property in slaves but supported the proposition (of apprenticeship) of the right gentleman (p. 163). Buxton was also opposed to apprenticeship because he was convinced that slaves would not work without wages (p. 162).

136. *Hansard's Parliamentary Debates,* 3d ser., 19 (July 24, 1833): 1190.

137. Extract from the *Morning Herald,* July 22, 1833, MSS. Brit. Emp. S. 444, vol. 12, reel 4, Thomas Fowell Buxton Papers.

138. Buxton (1852), 330; George Stephen (1971), 230–234; Gross (1980), 81.

made another bid to have apprenticeship shortened. He reasoned, "If they [apprentices] were not paid, insurrection would be the consequence and that would be the termination of British authority in those islands . . . it was his intention to move . . . to limit apprenticeship to the shortest period which could be sufficient for introducing the necessary regulations; and that no money should be paid to the planters until slavery should have been extinguished."[139]

Buxton's motion was defeated. The abolitionists finally conceded defeat on the apprenticeship issue as they had done on compensation. In a memorial to Lord Glenelg, the Anti-Slavery Society voiced its general disapproval and distrust of apprenticeship. They reluctantly conceded to the scheme, nevertheless, believing that its unsatisfactory measures were still safer than the perpetuation of the present system. The memorialists wrote,

> Any attempt to combine freedom with slavery must fail, and they earnestly deprecate any partial, imperfect or protracted measure which continued the violation of the great principle of justice, which afford, in their opinion, little relief to the slave and be attended with equal expense and danger to the community . . . The Apprenticeship System, [is] neither safe nor satisfactory, but on the contrary, fraught with evils of such magnitude as to endanger the success of the whole experiment . . . they submit ultimately to the term, not from any conviction of its necessity or utility, but principally from an apprehension of those direful consequences which must have ensued from the rejection or abandonment of the whole measure.[140]

Buxton, Denman, Brougham, and Lushington eventually voted with those who accepted Stanley's bill on August 7, 1833, after its third reading and hoped for the best in the colonies.[141] They judged that a compromise on freedom was less dangerous than no freedom at all. Thomas Clarkson endorsed the decision. He seems to have been similarly persuaded that the compromise was a vital sacrifice to safeguard the colonies from servile war. "I tremble to think what might have been the consequences, if you

139. Extract from the *Morning Herald*, July 22, 1833, MSS. Brit. Emp. S. 444, vol. 12, reel 4, Thomas Fowell Buxton Papers.
140. Committee on Slavery Minute Book, MSS. Brit. Emp. S. 22, G. 44, 1795–1839, pp. 2–3, Anti-Slavery Society Papers.
141. *Journals of the House of Commons* 88 (1833): 647.

had refused the proposals of the Government."[142] Wilberforce rejoiced that he had lived to see the day that Britain was willing to pay 20 million pounds to set its slaves free. He died on July 29.[143] On August 28 the bill received the royal assent.[144]

AFTER EMANCIPATION

With fearful apprehension Buxton awaited the initial outcome of slave emancipation. He was skeptical that the experiment as designed by the ministers of government could be peacefully implemented. Even before government laid out its plan for emancipation, Buxton outlined the precautionary measures he would take in pursuing freedom for the slaves. He imagined that had he the opportunity to speak directly to the slaves, "I would implore them to do their part towards the peaceful termination of their bondage. I would say to them 'The time of your deliverance is at hand; let that period be sacred, let it be defiled by no outrage, let it be stained by no blood, let not the hair of the head of a single planter be touched. Make any sacrifice . . . rather than raise your hand against any white man . . . Preserve peace and order to the utmost of your power.'"[145]

Buxton also wrote to several missionary societies pledging them to send out more ministers to the colonies in anticipation of abolition. He wrote to the Moravians, the Church Missionary Society, the Baptists, and the Wesleyans, requesting written answers to specific questions. He believed that the presence of the missionaries would "tranquilize the minds of the emancipated Negroes through the medium and by the influence of religion."[146] Buxton made it clear to his radical abolitionists critics that he was not willing to entertain emancipation without some form of police regulations. The precautions that Buxton advocated to prepare for emancipation suggest that he was the last of the abolitionists to reassess earlier abolitionists' ideas that immediate emancipation would ruin the

142. Clarkson to Buxton, September 25, 1833, from Playford Hall in Buxton (1852), 283.

143. Liz Deverell and Gareth Watkins, *Wilberforce and Hull* (Hull: Kingston Press, 2000), 65.

144. *Journals of the House of Commons* 88 (August 28, 1833): 726.

145. Buxton (1852), 278–279.

146. Letter to the Secretaries of Missionary Societies, November 2, 1832, vol. 3, pp. 37–39, MSS. Brit. Emp. S. 444, Thomas Fowell Buxton Papers.

colonies. Buxton believed that, like a strong religious force in the colonies, a form of regimentation was essential to keep the labor force under control of white managers. He explained that "in the reform of the greatest abuses, we are bound as legislators to effect them without convulsions . . . the line of our duty, therefore, in this case, as it appears to me, lies in the instant adoption of those Police Regulations which are necessary to secure a peaceable liberation of our slaves."[147]

It was only when the first reports regarding the slaves' immediate reception of the emancipation decree streamed into Britain that Buxton experienced some thankful relief that his worst fears on the slave revolt issue were over. He gave thanks to God that slaves were emancipated and that the abolitionist predictions of imminent apocalyptic doom in the colonies did not materialize. Buxton wrote, "I prayed for the slavery cause—I turn to the prayer of last year—I cannot but acknowledge that it has been most signally and surprisingly fulfilled—liberty in peace and peaceful liberty to the slaves has been accomplished . . . I prayed that those concerns which have caused much prolonged anxiety might be permitted to prosper—and so they have—the burden has greatly ceased. I have been signally relieved."[148]

There is no doubt that soon after the Demerara slave revolt of 1823 until slavery was declared abolished in 1834, British abolitionists exploited the slave rebellion argument even though they subordinated its dynamic potential to serve only the objectives that they were willing to embrace at any given time. In the 1820s, this explosive vision of doom and retribution was used merely to call for the implementation of pastoral measures of slave reform. After 1830 it was used to demand complete and immediate abolition. The abolitionists' slave rebellion discourse reflected a blend of some revolutionary doctrines and concepts and the needs and values of the emerging capitalist orders. Nevertheless, even from the earlier period, the issue of slave violence was alone capable of attacking the West India interest where it was most vulnerable. Abolitionists demonstrated that to maintain a system of unmitigated slavery was to undermine

147. Letter to Mr. Sturge, October 29, 1832, vol. 3, p. 34, MSS. Brit. Emp. S. 444, Thomas Fowell Buxton Papers. Buxton also recommended to the Lords' committee of 1832 the need for a strong police force in the West Indies after slavery abolition.

148. Birthday Anniversary Reflections, December 28, 1834, vol. 4, p. 288, MSS. Brit. Emp. S. 444, Thomas Fowell Buxton Papers.

the very property for which those with West India interests, and the British nation as a whole, had so much regard. Furthermore, the abolitionists used the rebellion of the slaves to widen the controversy over the colonial relationship between the parent state and her colonies. It was incontrovertible that in times of rebellion the colonists owed their trade, their bounties, and their lives, as well as their property, to the protection of the mother country. Objection to intervention was thus not only absurd but also suicidal. The laws of the mother country, like its military resources, were framed to protect the domains and people of his majesty's subjects.

Right down to the very last phase of the slavery struggle, the rebellion of the slaves featured strongly. It was upon this issue that abolitionists objected to the emancipation bill in general and to apprenticeship in particular. The conservative leaders of the movement were willing to concede the 20 million pound compensation to planters to buy their cooperation for peaceful emancipation. They held out longer against apprenticeship because, more than any other clause, it seemed destined to produce servile upheaval. Abolitionists pointed to rebellion to insist not only that emancipation must be granted but also that its measures must be safe and satisfactory. The abolitionists argued that slaves would respond to an unsatisfactory emancipation decree by taking matters in their own hands and forcing freedom by war. The British emancipation bill passed into law, however, without satisfying fully either conservative or radical abolitionists. Buxton's fearful apprehensions in the penultimate years of slavery, which in part led him to advocate precautionary measures of control, were finally converted to thankful relief only when the first reports from the colonies confirmed that slaves received the frightful experiment of apprenticeship in peace. Buxton had great difficulty in exercising the faith of such abolitionists as Clarkson that emancipation, however much it compromised the rights of the "Negroes," could be safe and practicable.

6

CONCLUSION

British antislavery discourse on the major nineteenth-century slave revolts in the Caribbean colonies was, in a sense, a defensive one. By taking the initiative to rise in rebellion immediately after each wave of abolitionist-sponsored programs, the slaves enabled proslavery advocates to make a strong case about the incendiary effect of antislavery activities on the servile population. Thus abolitionists were forced to counter the allegations of the planters. This counterdiscourse vacillated between blunt rejection of the allegations and acceptance of limited responsibility for the conduct of rebellious slaves. The abolitionists also took the opportunity in this defensive discourse to emphasize that their campaign was a noble humanitarian undertaking well worth the risk of servile warfare. Their defensive arguments proved that the mass protest action of the slaves engendered an extensive deliberation on slave revolts and that the antislavery leaders did not flinch in their commitment to the cause even when the rebellions reduced the strength of their support.

British abolitionists' commentary on slave rebellions, however, did not consist entirely of a self-defensive position. Antislavery activists did not seek merely to contradict the claim that they were instigating slave violence. They were particularly intent in proving that proslavery descriptions of nineteenth-century slave rebellions were outdated and inaccurate. Planters and their supporters had failed to appreciate or chose to overlook that the rebellions of the last years of slavery in the English Caribbean were devoid of the bloody terror with which they were wont to imagine the conduct of rebellious slaves. Abolitionist commentary focused on and presented an opposing perspective of the slaves' rebellion. They refused to dwell on the economic devastation that planters violently denounced in St. Domingue in 1791, Barbados in 1816, and Jamaica in 1831–1832. Instead, the abolitionists exulted that not one piece of plantation property was destroyed in the Demerara rising in 1823. In shaping their analysis of what constituted a slave revolt, British abolitionists also

CONCLUSION 181

laid great emphasis on the fact that nineteenth-century slave rebels without exception demonstrated no intention whatever to take their masters' lives. They did admit that a few whites lost their lives at the hands of rising slave populations but were keen to point out that cold-blooded murder formed no part of the rebels' aims.

The abolitionists' scrutiny of the tactics and objectives of slave rebels captured the multidimensional features of these rebellions. The revolts represented action against unfair treatment. They were processes in labor bargaining. They were holy wars against an unholy regime. They were decisive actions against procrastinating colonial and metropolitan authorities. They were, above all, conscious political movements of an oppressed people staking personal claims for their freedom. Abolitionist depiction of British West Indian slave revolts in the nineteenth century demonstrated how the rising of the slaves led a band of conservative reformers to adopt some of the revolutionary concepts of the protest actions of working-class people. Abolitionists used the rebels' forceful methods to demand first slavery reform and later abolition.

As citizens, slaves too were entitled to inquire about and protest against poor working conditions without being denied their share of even-handed British justice. Nineteenth-century slaves in the British West Indies caused abolitionists in metropolitan Britain to abandon some of the negative attitudes they had held toward the egalitarian ideologies that emerged in the age of the American and French revolutions. Abolitionists' slave rebellion commentaries contradicted the common assumption that slave rebellions were nothing but counterproductive and violent reactions that ought to be brutally and swiftly suppressed. Abolitionist were largely sympathetic to the rebels and positively conceptualized and gave esteem to a process that was otherwise readily condemned and dismissed. It was remarkable that to a degree worthy of significant attention, British abolitionists justified the active resistance of slaves in the last phase of British West Indian slavery.

Abolitionists managed the information on slave rebellions so as to make it useful to the cause. This was particularly apparent in their indictment of the suppression of slave revolts. Paradoxically, abolitionists rescued defeated slave rebels from being passive objects of a cruel and dehumanizing system and transformed them into agents or martyrs. The victimization of slaves in rebellion provided the abolitionists with the ammunition they needed to present to the British people and Parliament a stinging denunciation of a corrupt and corrupting judicial regime desperately in need of change. The abolitionists demonstrated that the injury that slaves unleashed during rebellion was mild in comparison to the vindictive spirit that dominated the colonists' crushing of slave rebellions. The abolitionists went so far as to examine the suffering of persecuted sectarian missionaries alongside that of defeated slave rebels. The experiences of both slaves and missionaries demanded alterations to the servile regime. The interaction between slave rebellion and antislavery in this respect reinforces the solid humanitarian framework that significantly shaped British abolitionism.

The slave rebellion argument also served to heighten the economic dimensions from which the campaigners sought to undermine the servile regime. Most abolitionists did not embrace the view that the colonies in themselves were a liability to the mother country but that the slave revolts undermined the colonies' continued prosperity. After the 1823 rebellion in Demerara, antislavery activists repeatedly emphasized the way in which servile war threatened the very property that made the plantation economies of the colonies so valuable to their stakeholders. Emphasizing the danger of rebellion provided the campaigners with a definition of their mission. It was a mission to warn West Indian property holders, absentee and resident, that it was in their interest to support the antislavery initiative in an effort to stave of the destruction of their colonial possessions and possibly even their lives. This warning was directed as well to the government and Parliament of Britain. Abolitionists insisted that slave rebellion made it glaringly apparent that Britain ought to implement a more authoritative mode of directing affairs in her colonies in order to maintain possession of them. The abolitionists also used the rebellions to alert the mother country that despite the objections of the colonists, the survival of the colonies was dependent on the intervention of Britain.

The open resistance by nineteenth-century slaves in the British West Indies provided humanitarian reformers on the other side of the Atlantic with the abolitionists' slave rebellion discourse. Although this discourse has hitherto remained hidden from history, it was extensive and varied. It took shape before abolitionists demanded emancipation, and when emancipation ultimately became their objective it was used as a significant reinforcement. It shifted its focus from being a defensive abolitionist instrument to being a medium through which plantocratic descriptions of slave revolts were challenged and replaced by a more positive interpretation of the slaves' overt resistance. The slaves' conduct had so challenged the outlook of conservative humanitarian reformers that some of the very revolutionary doctrines that the abolitionists had rejected in Europe were employed to expand their attack against slavery. In the final analysis, the abolitionists' slave rebellion discourse was a propaganda tool used to justify different stages of abolitionist demands.

This study of how the experience of nineteenth-century rebel slaves traveled with the currents of the Atlantic from the shores of the colonies to the hallowed hall of Westminster is by no means the definitive study on slave resistance history. It is outside its range to investigate fully two important issues that it has raised. A satisfactory articulation of abolitionists' comparative assessment of the value of persecuted missionaries and punished slaves in the aftermath of these rebellions to the metropolitan antislavery campaign, begun in this study, needs further development. Secondly, this book strongly suggests the need to establish one way or the other whether these rebellions were influenced by factors external to the slaves. Nevertheless, this work has illustrated that historians like Craton are not justified in the skepticism they reserve regarding the integration of the study of slave revolts within the broader framework of British antislavery. This study complements the scholarship of Hilary Beckles, James Walvin, Mary Turner, and Eugene Genovese, who have made the crucial observation that slaves fed off the work of the metropolitan humanitarians. While they explained how British antislavery impacted on slave revolts, this work explains how slave revolts impacted on British antislavery. By providing a full-length study of how slave revolts shaped antislavery commentary, this book expands the limited treatment of the themes by Mary Turner, Phillip Curtin, Gad Heuman, and Barry Higman. Slave revolts and the British abolitionist discourse have hitherto been treated as independent themes of British West Indian slavery. This tendency prevailed even after Beckles and others proved that the slaves made themselves allies of the metropolitan reformers. This study reinforces the linking of the two themes and has provided the basis for its inclusion in the growing study of Atlantic history.

BIBLIOGRAPHY

PRIMARY SOURCES

Agency Anti-Slavery Committee. *The Danger of Delay, and the Safety and Practicability of Immediate Emancipation, From the Evidence Before the Parliamentary Committees on Colonial Slavery.* London: W. Johnston, 1833.

Anonymous. *An Epistle to William Wilberforce Esq. Written During the Disturbances in the West Indies.* London: Darton and Harvey, 1792.

Anonymous. *Remarks on the Insurrection in Barbados and the Bill for the Registration of Slaves.* London: Ellerton and Henderson, 1816.

Anti-Slavery Monthly Reporter, 1825–1831. London: J. Hatchard. (The issues from vol. 3, no. 63 [July 1830] were renamed the *Anti-Slavery Reporter.*)

Anti-Slavery Society. Papers. Rhodes House Library, Oxford, England. Baptist Missionary Society. *Colonial Slavery—Defense of the Baptist Missionaries From the Charge of Inciting the Late Rebellion in Jamaica; in a Discussion between the Reverend William Knibb and Mr. P. Borthwick at the Assembly Rooms on Saturday 15 December 1832.* London: Tourist Office, Paternoster Row, 1832.

———. *Facts and Documents Connected With the Late Insurrection in Jamaica and the Violations of Civil and Religious Liberty Arising Out of It.* London: Holsworth and Ball, 1832.

———. *A Narrative of Recent Events Connected with the Baptist Mission in This Island Comprising also a Sketch of the Mission from Its Commencement in 1814 to the End of 1831.* Jamaica: Edward Jordan and Robert Osborn, 1833.

Barbados Mercury and Bridgetown Gazette, 1816.

British Parliamentary Papers. Vol. 47. *Papers Relating to the Slave Trade 1831–1834, Slave Trade 80. Jamaica: A Report from the House of Assembly on the Injury Sustained During the Recent Rebellion, 1831–1832(561).* Shannon, Ireland: Irish University Press, 1969.

British Parliamentary Papers. Vol. 66. *Demerara Minutes of Evidence on the Trial of John Smith a Missionary 1824(158),* vol. 23. Shannon, Ireland: Irish University Press, 1969.

British Parliamentary Papers. Report from the Select Committee on the Extinction of Slavery Throughout the British Dominions with the Minutes of Evi-

dence, Appendix and Index, August 11, 1832. London: Hatchard and Son, 1832.

Brougham, Henry. Papers. University College London Library, London.

Buxton, Sir Thomas Fowell. Papers. Rhodes House Library, Oxford.

Clarkson, Thomas. Papers. In *Abolition and Emancipation,* part 1. Huntington Library, San Marino, CA; Wiltshire: Adam Matthew Publications, 1997. Microfilm, reels 1 and 1a.

Cobbett's Parliamentary Debates. London: T. C. Hansard, 1795.

Colonial Office. Papers. Public Record Office, Kew Gardens, London.

Cornwall Courier, 1832.

Cropper, James. *Letters Addressed to William Wilberforce, M. P. Recommending the Encouragement of the Cultivation of Sugar in our Dominions in the East Indies, as the Natural and Certain Means of Effecting the General and Total Abolition of the Slave* Trade. Liverpool: Longman, Hurst and Co., 1822.

Edinburgh Review, 1823–1825.

Hansard's Parliamentary Debates. London: T. C. Hansard, 1816–1833.

Jamaican Courant, 1824–1832.

Journal of the House of Commons 88(1833).

The London Missionary Society's Report of the Proceedings against the Late Reverend John Smith of Demerara, Minister of the Gospel . . . and Including the Documentary Evidence Omitted in the Parliamentary Copy With an Appendix; Containing the Letters and Statements of Mr. and Mrs. Smith, Mrs. Elliot, Mr. Arrindell, &C and Also, the Society's Petitions to the House of Commons. The whole published under the authority of the directors of the said society. London: F. Westley, 1824.

London Times, 1816–1832.

Macaulay, Zachary. Papers. In *Abolition and Emancipation,* part 1. Huntington Library, San Marino, CA; Wiltshire: Adam Matthew Publications, 1997. Microfilm, reel 4.

The Missionary Smith — Substance of the Debate in the House of Commons on Tuesday the 1st and Friday the 11th of June 1824 on a Motion of Henry Brougham, Esq. Respecting the Trial and Condemnation to Death by a Court Martial to the Rev. John Smith, Late Missionary in the Colony of Demerara With a Preface Containing Some New Facts Illustrative of the Subject. London: J. Hatchard and Son, 1824.

Parliamentary History of England. London: T. C. Hansard, n.d.

Ramsay, James. *An Essay on the Treatment and Conversion of African Slaves in the British Sugar Colonies.* London: James Phillips, George Yard, Lombard Street, 1786.

The Report from A Select Committee to the House of Assembly, Appointed to Inquire into the Origins, Causes and Progress of the Late Insurrection. Barbados: W. Walker, Mercury and Gazette Office, 1818.

"Sketch of the Life of William Wilberforce Esq. With a Review of the Present State of the Anti-Slavery Cause." *Baptist Magazine*, 3d ser., 3 (January 1833).

Society for the Mitigation and Gradual Abolition of Slavery Throughout the British Dominions. *East and West India Sugar; or, A Refutation of the Claims of the West India Colonists to a Protecting Duty on East India Sugar*. London: J. Hatchard and Son, 1823.

———. "Negro Slavery No. 7. Insurrection of Slaves in the West Indies particularly in Demerara." In *Tracts of the Anti-Slavery Society*. London: J. Hatchard and Son, 1823.

———. "Negro Slavery No. 8. Insurrection in the West Indies; St. Lucia, Trinidad, Dominica and Demerara." In *Tracts of the Anti-Slavery Society*. London: J. Hatchard and Son, 1823.

———. *Negro Slavery or A View of the More Prominent Features of That State of Society as it Exists in the United States of America and in the Colonies of the West Indies Especially in Jamaica*. London: J. Hatchard and Son, 1823.

———. *A Review of Some of the Arguments Which Are Commonly Advanced Against Parliamentary Interference in Behalf of the Negro Slaves, With a Statement of Opinions Which Have Been Expressed on That Subject by Many of Our Most Distinguished Statesmen*. London: J. Hatchard and Son, 1824.

———. "Barbados—New Slave Law." In *The Slave Colonies of Great Britain; or A Picture of Negro Slavery Drawn by the Colonists Themselves; Being an Abstract of the Various Papers Recently Laid Before Parliament on That Subject*. 2d ed. Corrected. London: J. Hatchard and Son, 1826.

———. *Abstract of the Report of the Lords Committee on the Condition and Treatment of the Colonial Slaves, and of the Evidence Taken by Them on That Subject; With Notes by the Editor*. London: J. Hatchard and Son, 1833.

———. *Analysis of the Report of a Committee of the House of Commons on the Extinction of Slavery*. London: J. Hatchard, 1833.

Stephen, James. *The Slavery of the British West India Colonies Delineated, As It Exists Both in Law and Practice, and Compared with the Slavery of Other Colonies, Ancient and Modern*. Vol. 1. Aberdeen: A. Constable and Co., 1824.

———. *The Slavery of the British West India Colonies Delineated, As it Exists Both in Law and Practice, and Compared with the Slavery of Other Colonies, Ancient and Modern*. Vol. 2. Being a Delineation of the State in Point of Practice. London: J. Hatchard and Son, 1830.

Stockdale, Percival. *A Letter from Percival Stockdale to Granville Sharp Esquire*

Suggested to the Author by the Present Insurrection of the Negroes in the Island of St. Domingo. N.p., n.d.

"Substance of the Debate in the House of Commons on the Motion for the Mitigation and Gradual Abolition of Slavery Throughout the British Dominions." *Quarterly Review* 29, no. 58 (July 1823): 475–508.

Tweedie Estate Records. Jamaica Archives, Spanish Town.

Watchman and Jamaica Free Press, 1830.

West India Planters and Merchants. Papers. Institute of Jamaica, Kingston.

Wilberforce, William. *A Letter on the Abolition of the Slave Trade; Addressed to the Freeholders and Other Inhabitants of Yorkshire.* London: T. Cadell and W. Davies, Strand; and J. H. Piccadilly, 1807.

———. *An Appeal to Religion, Justice and Humanity of the Inhabitants of the British Empire, in Behalf of the Negro Slaves in the West Indies.* London: J. Hatchard and Son, 1823.

———, ed. *Tracts of the Anti-Slavery Society.* London: J. Hatchard and Son, 1823.

SECONDARY SOURCES

Abzug, Robert. "The Influence of Garrisonian Abolitionist Fears of Slave Violence on the Anti-Slavery Argument." *Journal of Negro History* 55, no. 1 (January 1970).

Anstey, Roger. "Capitalism and Slavery: A Critique." *Economic History Review* 21 (1968).

Argosah, Kofi, ed. *Maroon Heritage: Archaeological, Ethnographic and Historical Perspectives.* Barbados: Canoe Press, 1994.

Barclay, Alexander. *Practical View of the Present State of Slavery in the West Indies or An Examination of Mr. Stephen's "Slavery of the British West India Colonies."* 2d ed. London: Smith Elder and Co., 1827.

Beckles, Hilary. "The Two Hundred Year War: Slave Resistance in the British West Indies. An Overview of the Historiography." *Jamaican Historical Review* 13 (1982).

———. "Inside Bussa's Rebellion: Letters of Colonel John Rycroft Best." *Journal of the Barbados Museum and Historical Society* 37, no. 2 (1984).

———. *Black Rebellion in Barbados: The Struggle Against Slavery, 1627–1838.* Bridgetown, Barbados: Carib Research and Publications, 1987.

———. *A History of Barbados from Amerindian Settlement to Nation State.* Cambridge: Cambridge University Press, 1990.

———. "Caribbean Anti-Slavery: The Self-Liberation Ethos of Enslaved Blacks." *Journal of Caribbean History* 22, nos. 1 and 2 (1990). Reprinted in *Caribbean Slavery in the Atlantic World.* Ed. Verene Shepherd and Hilary Beckles. Jamaica: Ian Randle Publishers, 2001.

Blackburn, Robin. *The Overthrow of Colonial Slavery, 1776–1848*. London: Verso, 1988.

Bleby, Henry. *Death Struggles of Slavery*. London, 1853.

Boubacar, Barry. *Senegambia and the Atlantic Slave Trade*. Cambridge: Cambridge University Press, 1998.

Bradley, Ian. "Wilberforce the Saint." In *Out of Slavery: Abolition and After*. Ed. Jack Hayward. London: Frank Cass and Co., 1985.

Brizan, George. *Grenada, Island of Conflict: From Amerindians to People's Revolution, 1498–1979*. London: Zed Books, 1984.

Brougham, Henry. *A Concise Statement of the Question Regarding the Abolition of the Slave Trade*. London: J. Hatchard, T. N. Longman, and O. Rees, 1804.

———. *The Speeches of Henry, Lord Brougham, Upon Questions Relating to Public Rights, Duties and Interests With Historical Introduction and A Critical Dissertation Upon the Eloquence of the Ancients*. Vol. 2 of 4. Edinburgh: Adam and Charles Black, 1838.

———. *Works of Henry, Lord Brougham*. Vol. 10. *Speeches on Social and Political Subjects*. London: Richard Griffin and Company, 1857.

Brown, C. L. "Empire Without Slaves: British Concepts of Emancipation in the Age of the American Revolution." *William and Mary Quarterly*, 3d ser., 61, no. 2 (1999).

Bryant, Joshua. *An Account of the Insurrection of the Negro Slaves in the Colony of Demerara Which Broke out on the 18th of August, 1823*. Demerara: Guiana Chronicle Office, Georgetown, 1824.

Burn, W. L. *Emancipation and Apprenticeship in the British West Indies*. London: Jonathan Cape, 1937.

———. *History of the British West Indies*. 2d ed. London: George Allen and Unwin, 1965.

Burns, Sir Alan. *History of the British West Indies*. Rev. 2d ed. London: George Allen and Unwin, 1965.

Bush, Barbara. "Toward Emancipation: Slave Women and Resistance to Coercive Labour Regimes in the British West Indian Colonies, 1790–1838." In *Abolition and Its Aftermath*. Ed. David Richardson. London: Frank Cass and Co., 1985.

———. *Slave Women in Caribbean Society, 1650–1838*. Kingston: Ian Randle Publishers, 1990.

Butler, Kathleen Mary. *The Economics of Emancipation: Jamaica and Barbados, 1823–1843*. Chapel Hill: University of North Carolina Press, 1995.

Buxton, Charles, ed. *Memoirs of Sir Thomas Fowell Buxton*. 5th ed. London: John Murray, 1852.

Campbell, John. "Reassessing the Consciousness of Labour and the Role of the

'Confidentials' in Slave Society: Jamaica, 1750–1834." *Jamaican Historical Review* 21 (2001).

Carrion, I. P., ed. *Freedom Road*. Cuba: Jose Marti, 1998.

Clarkson, Thomas. *Thoughts on the Necessity of Improving the Condition of the Slaves in the British Colonies; With a View to Ultimate Emancipation; and on the Practicability, the Safety and the Advantage of the Latter Measure*. London: J. Hatchard and Son, 1824.

Coupland, Reginald. *Wilberforce: A Narrative*. Oxford: Clarendon, 1923.

———. *The British Anti-Slavery Movement*. London: Thorton Butterworth, 1933.

Cormack, P. *Wilberforce: The Nation's Conscience*. England: Pickering Paperbacks, 1983.

Craton, Michael. *Sinews of Empire: A Short History of British Slavery*. New York, Anchor, 1974.

———. "Proto-Peasant Revolts? The Late Slave Rebellions in the British West Indies, 1816–1832." *Past and Present* 85 (November 1979).

———. "The Passion to Exist: Slave Rebellions in the British West Indies, 1650–1832." *Journal of Caribbean History* 13 (1980).

———. *Testing the Chains: Resistance to Slavery in the British West Indies*. London: Cornell University Press, 1982.

———. *Empire, Enslavement and Freedom in the Caribbean*. Jamaica: Ian Randle Publishers, 1997.

Craton, Michael, James Walvin, and David Wright. *Slavery, Abolition and Emancipation—Black Slaves and the British Empire. A Thematic Documentary*. London: Longman, 1976.

Curtin, Philip. *Two Jamaicas: The Role of Ideas in a Tropical Colony, 1830–1865*. New York: Greenwood, 1968.

Da Costa, Emilia. *Crowns of Glory, Tears of Blood: The Demerara Slave Rebellion of 1823*. Oxford: Oxford University Press, 1994.

Davis, David B. "The Emergence of Immediatism in British and American Anti-Slavery Thought." *Mississippi Valley Historical Review* 44, no. 2 (September 1962).

———. *The Problem of Slavery in the Age of Revolution, 1770–1823*. Ithaca: Cornell University Press. 1974.

———. *Slavery and Human Progress*. Oxford: Oxford University Press, 1984.

———. "Capitalism, Abolitionism and Hegemony." In *British Capitalism and Caribbean Slavery: The Legacy of Eric Williams*. Ed. Barbara Solow and Stanley Engerman. Cambridge: Cambridge University Press, 1987.

Dookhan, I. *A Pre-Emancipation History of the West Indies*. London: Collins, 1971.

Drescher, Seymour. "Capitalism and Abolition: Values and Forces in Britain, 1783–1814." In *Liverpool, the African Slave Trade, and Abolition.* Ed. Roger Anstey and P. E. H. Hair. Bristol: Historical Society of Lancashire and Chelshire Occasional Series, 1976.

———. *Econocide: British Slavery in the Era of Abolition.* Pittsburgh: University of Pittsburgh Press, 1977.

———. "The Historical Context of British Abolitionism." In *Abolition and Its Aftermath: The Historical Context, 1790–1816.* Ed. David Richardson. London: Frank Cass and Co., 1985.

Dresser, Madge. *Slavery Obscured: The Social History of the Slave Trade in an English Provincial Port.* London: Continuum, 2001.

Eltis, David. "Dr. Lushington and the Campaign to Abolish Slavery in the British Empire." *Journal of Caribbean History* 1 (1970): 41–56.

Evans, Eric. *Britain Before the Reform Act: Politics and Society, 1815–1832.* New York: Longman, 1989.

Finalson, W. F. *The History of the Jamaican Case Being an Account Founded upon Official Documents of the Rebellion of the Negroes in Jamaica the Cause Which led to it and the Measures Taken for Its Suppression, the Agitation Excited on the Subject Its Causes and Its Character and the Debates in Parliament, and the Criminal Persecution, Arising out of It.* London: Chapman and Hall, 1869.

Findlay, George. *The History of the Wesleyan Methodist Missionary Society.* London: Epsworth, 1921.

Furness, A. E. "George Hibbert and the Defence of Slavery in the West Indies." *Jamaican Historical Review* 5, no. 1 (May 1965).

Gardner, W. J. *A History of Jamaica: From its Discovery by Christopher Columbus to the Year 1872.* London: Frank Cass and Co., 1971.

Gaspar, David Barry. "The Antiguan Slave Conspiracy of 1736—A Case Study of the Origins of Collective Resistance." *William and Mary Quarterly,* 3d ser., 35 (April 1978).

Gaspar, David Barry, and David Geggus, eds. *A Turbulent Time: The French Revolution and the Greater Caribbean.* Bloomington: Indiana University Press, 1997.

Geggus, David. *Slavery, War and Revolution. The British Occupation of Saint Domingue, 1793–1798.* Oxford: Clarendon, 1982.

———. "Haiti and the Abolitionists: Opinion, Propaganda and International Politics in Britain and France, 1804–1838." In *Abolition and Its Aftermath: The Historical Context, 1790–1916.* Ed. David Richardson. London: Frank Cass and Co., 1985.

Genovese, Eugene. *From Rebellion to Revolution: Afro-American Slave Revolts in the Making of the Modern World.* Baton Rouge: Louisiana State University Press, 1979.

Godwin, B. *The Substance of a Course of Lectures on British Colonial Slavery.* London: J. Hatchard and Son, 1830.

Goodridge, S. *Facing the Challenge of Emancipation: A Study of the Ministry of William Hart Coleridge, First Bishop of Barbados, 1824–1842.* Barbados: Cedar Press, 1981.

Goveia, Elsa. *Amelioration and Emancipation in the British Caribbean.* St. Augustine: University of the West Indies, 1977.

Gratus, Jack. *The Great White Lie: Slavery, Emancipation and Changing Racial Attitudes.* New York: Monthly Review Press, 1973.

Green, W. L. *British Slave Emancipation, 1830–1865.* Oxford: Clarendon, 1976.

Gross, Izhak. "The Abolition of Negro Slavery and British Parliamentary Politics, 1832–1833." *Historical Journal* 23, no. 1 (1980).

Harris, J. *Slavery or Sacred Trust?* London: Williams and Norgate, 1926.

Hart, Richard. *Slaves Who Abolished Slavery—Blacks in Rebellion.* Vol. 2. Jamaica: Institute of Social and Economic Research, 1985.

Hayward, Jack. *Out of Slavery: Abolition and After.* London: Frank Cass and Co., 1985.

Herskovits, Melville. *The Myth of the Negro Past.* Boston: Beacon, 1958.

Heuman, Gad. "A Tale of Two Jamaican Rebellions." *Jamaican Historical Review* 19 (1996).

———, ed. *Out of the House of Bondage: Runaways, Resistance and Marronage in Africa and the New World.* London: Frank Cass and Co., 1986.

Heyrick, Elizabeth. *Immediate Not Gradual Abolition or an Enquiry into the Shortest, Safest and Most Effectual Means of Getting Rid of West Indian Slavery.* London: J. Hatchard and Son, 1824.

Higman, Barry. "The West India 'Interest' in Parliament, 1807–1833." *Historical Studies* 13 (October 1967).

———. *Slave Population and Economy in Jamaica, 1807–1834.* Manchester: Manchester University Press, 1976.

Hinton, John Howard. *Memoir of William Knibb, Missionary in Jamaica.* London: Houlston and Stoneman, 1847.

Hobsbawm, Eric J., and George Rude. *Captain Swing.* London: Lawrence and Wishart, 1969.

Hollis, Patricia. "Anti-Slavery and British Working Class Radicalism in the Years of Reform." In *Anti-Slavery, Religion, and Reform: Essays in Memory of Roger Anstey.* Ed. Christine Bolt and Seymour Drescher. England: Wm. Dawson and Sons, 1980.

Ifill, Max. *Social Death or Communal Victory? A Critical Appraisal of Slavery and*

Social Death by Orlando Patterson. Trinidad: Economic and Business Research, 1990.

Jakobsson, Stiv. *Am I Not A Man and A Brother? British Missions and the Abolition of the Slave Trade and Slavery in West Africa and the West Indies, 1786–1838.* Uppsala: Gleerup, 1972.

James, C. L. R. *The Black Jacobins: Toussaint L'Ouverture and the San Domingo Revolution.* London: Allison and Busby, 1938.

———. *A History of Negro Revolt.* New York: Haskell House Publishers, 1969.

Johnson, Elizabeth. "The Historiography of Slave Rebellion: Cuba in a Hemispheric Perspective." *Journal of Caribbean History* 31, nos. 1 and 2 (1977).

Klein, M. "The International Labour Market and the Emancipation of Slaves in the Nineteenth Century." In *Unfree Labour in the Development of the Atlantic World.* Ed. Paul Lovejoy and Nicholas Rogers. London: Frank Cass and Co., 1994.

Klinberg, Frank J. *The Anti-Slavery Movement in England: A Study in English Humanitarianism.* New Haven: Yale University Press, 1926.

Knight, F. K. *The Disintegration of the Caribbean Slave Systems, 1772–1886.* UNESCO Publishing, 1997.

Kopytoff, Barbara. "The Early Political Development of Jamaican Maroon Societies." *William and Mary Quarterly,* 3d ser., 35 (April 1978).

Laurence, Keith O. *Tobago in Wartime — 1793–1815.* Jamaica: University of the West Indies, 1995.

Levy, Claude. "Slavery and the Emancipation Movement in Barbados, 1650–1833." *Journal of Negro History* 55, no. 1 (January 1970).

———. *Emancipation, Sugar, and Federalism: Barbados and the West Indies, 1833–1876.* Gainesville: University Presses of Florida, 1980.

Lewis, Andrew. "An Incendiary Press: British West Indian Newspapers During the Struggle for Abolition." *Slavery and Abolition* 16, no. 3 (Dec. 1995).

Lewis, Gordon. *Slavery, Imperialism, and Freedom: Studies in English Radical Thought.* New York: Monthly Review Press, 1978.

———. *Main Currents in Caribbean Thought: The Historical Evolution of Caribbean Society in Its Ideological Aspects, 1492–1900.* Baltimore: John Hopkins University Press, 1983.

Luster, R. *The Amelioration of the Slaves in the British Empire, 1790–1833.* New York: Peter Lang, 1995.

Marshall, Bernard. "Maroons in Slave Plantation Societies: A Case Study of Dominica, 1785–1815." *Caribbean Quarterly* 22, nos. 2 and 3 (1976).

Mathieson, William Law. *British Slavery and Its Abolition, 1823–1838.* New York: Longman's, Green and Co., 1926.

McGowan, Winston. "Christianity and Slavery." *History Gazette* (Guyana History Society), no. 24 (September 1990).

Mellor, George R. *British Imperial Trusteeship, 1783–1850*. London: Faber and Faber, 1951.

Midgley, Clare. *Women Against Slavery: The British Campaigns, 1780–1870*. London: Routledge, 1992.

Molesworth, William. *History of England from the Year 1830–1874*. Vol. 1. London: Chapman and Hall, 1877.

Mullin, Gerald. *Flight and Rebellion: Slave Resistance in Eighteenth-Century Virginia*. New York: Oxford University Press, 1974.

Murray, D. J. *The West Indies and the Development of Colonial Government, 1801–1834*. Oxford: Clarendon, 1965.

New, Chester. *The Life of Henry Brougham to 1830*. Oxford: Clarendon, 1967.

Northcott, Cecil. *Slavery's Martyr: John Smith of Demerara and the Emancipation Movement, 1817–1824*. London: Epsworth, 1976.

Patterson, Orlando. "Slavery and Slave Revolts: A Socio-Historical Analysis of the First Maroon War, Jamaica, 1655–1740." *Social and Economic Studies* 19, no. 1 (1970). Reprinted in *Maroon Societies: Rebel Slave Communities in the Americas,* ed. Richard Price, New York: Anchor, 1973.

Price, Richard, ed. *Maroon Societies: Rebel Slave Communities in the Americas*. New York: Anchor, 1973.

Ragatz, Lowell. *The Fall of the Planter Class in the British Caribbean, 1776–1833: A Social and Economic History*. New York: Octagon Books, 1977.

Reckford, Mary. "The Colonial Office and the Abolition of Slavery." *Historical Journal* 14, no. 4 (1971).

———. "The Jamaica Slave Rebellion of 1831." *Past and Present: A Journal of Historical Studies* 40 (1968).

Richard, Henry. *Memoirs of Joseph Sturge*. London: Patridge and Bennet, 1864.

Richardson, Ronald Kent. *Moral Imperium: Afro Caribbeans and the Transformation of British Rule, 1776–1838*. New York: Greenwood, 1987.

Rodway, James. *History of British Guiana from the Year 1682 to the Present Time*. Vol. 2, 1782–1833. Demerara: J. Thompson, 1893.

Schomburgk, Robert Hermann. *The History of Barbados*. London: Frank Cass and Co., 1971.

Schuler, Monica. "Ethnic Slave Rebellion in the Caribbean and the Guianas." *Journal of Social History* 3, no. 4 (1970).

Sheridan, R. *Sugar and Slavery: An Economic History of the British West Indies, 1625–1775*. Barbados: Caribbean University Press, 1974.

Short, K. R. M. "Jamaican Christian Missions and the Great Slave Rebellion of 1831–1832." *Journal of Ecclesiastical History* 27, no. 1 (1976).

Simon, Kathleen. *Slavery*. London: Hodder and Stoughton, 1929.

Stanley Brian. *The History of the Baptist Missionary Society, 1792–1992*. Edinburgh: T&T Clark, 1992.

Stephen, George. *Anti-Slavery Recollections in A Series of Letters Addressed to Mrs. Beecher Stowe.* 2d ed. 1854. Reprint, London: Frank Cass and Co. 1971.

Temperley, Howard. *British Antislavery, 1833–1870.* London: Longman, 1972.

Thompson, Bakpetu. *The Making of the African Diaspora in the Americas, 1442–1900.* Harlow, Essex: Longman, 1987.

Thomson, Andrew. *Substance of the Speech Delivered at the Meeting of The Edinburgh Society for the Abolition of Slavery, on October 19, 1830.* Edinburgh: William Whyte and Co., 1830.

Tibbles, Anthony, ed. *Transatlantic Slavery: Against Human Dignity.* London: National Museum and Galleries, HUSO, 1994.

Turley, David. *The Culture of English Anti-Slavery, 1780–1860.* London: Routledge, 1991.

Turner, Mary. "The Baptist War and Abolition." *Jamaican Historical Review,* Sam Sharpe Rebellion 150th Anniversary Issue, 13 (1982).

———. *Slaves and Missionaries: The Disintegration of Jamaican Society, 1787–1834.* London: University of Illinois Press, 1982.

Turner, S. "The Bishop of Jamaica and Slave Instruction." *Journal of Ecclesiastical History* 34, no. 4 (1975).

Waddell, Rev. Hope Masterston. *Twenty-Nine Years in the West Indies and Central Africa: A Review of Missionary Work and Adventure, 1829–1858.* 2d ed. London: Frank Cass and Co., 1970.

Wallbridge, Edwin A. *The Demerara Martyr: Memoirs of the Reverend John Smith, Missionary to Demerara.* Demerara: Charles Gilpin, 1848.

Walvin, James. *Questioning Slavery.* Kingston: Ian Randle Publishers, 1977.

———. "The Rise of British Popular Sentiment for Abolition, 1781–1832." In *Anti-Slavery, Religion, and Reform: Essays in Memory of Roger Anstey.* Ed. Christine Bolt and Seymour Drescher. England: Wm. Dawson and Sons, 1980.

———. *Slavery and the Slave Trade: A Short Illustrated History.* London: Macmillan, 1983.

———. *England, Slaves and Freedom, 1776–1835.* London: Macmillan, 1986.

———. *Slaves and Slavery: The British Colonial Experience.* Manchester: Manchester University Press, 1992.

———, ed. *Slavery and British Society, 1776–1846.* London: Macmillan, 1982.

Warner, Oliver. *William Wilberforce and His Times.* London: B. T. Batsford, 1962.

Webber, R. F. *Centenary History and Handbook of British Guiana.* British Guiana: Argosy Co., 1931.

Wilberforce, Robert I., and Samuel Wilberforce. *The Life of William Wilberforce.* 5 vols. London: John Murray, 1838.

Wilberforce, William. *The Correspondence of William Wilberforce.* 2 vols. London, 1840.

Williams, Eric. *Capitalism and Slavery.* London: Andre Deutsch, 1944.

————. *British Historians and the West Indies*. London: Andre Deutsch, 1966.

————. *From Columbus to Castro: The History of the Caribbean, 1492–1969*. London: Andre Deutsch, 1970.

————. *The March to Liberty Through Jesus Christ: A Discourse On Slavery and Emancipation*. Trinidad: Citadel Publishing Service, 1977.

————, ed. *Documents on British West Indian History, 1807–1833 (Select Documents from the P.R.O., London, England, Relating to the Colonies of Barbados, Jamaica and Trinidad)*. Port-of-Spain: Trinidad Publishing Co., 1952.

————, ed. *The British West Indies at Westminster, Part 1: 1789–1823—Extracts from the Debates in Parliament*. Westport, CT: Negro University Press, 1975.

Wiltshire, Anthony. "The Reaction of the Barbadian Plantocracy to Amelioration, 1823–1833." M.A. thesis, University of the West Indies, Cave Hill Campus, Barbados, 1983.

Wright, Philip. *Knibb "the Notorious": Slaves' Missionary, 1803–1845*. London: Sidgwick and Jackson, 1973.

www.spartacus.schoolnet.co.uk (accessed March 14, 2002)

SOURCES ON HISTORICAL PHILOSOPHY

Bloch, Marc. *The Historian's Craft*. Trans. Peter Putnam. Intro. by Joseph R. Strayer. Manchester: Manchester University Press, 1954.

Carr, Edward Hallett. *What is History?* New York: Vintage, 1961.

Dunne, T. "The Writer as Witness." *Historical Studies* 16 (1987).

Elton, Geoffrey Rudolph. *The Practice of History*. London: Sydney University Press, 1967.

Elton, Geoffrey, and Robert Fogel. *Which Road to the Past? Two Views of History*. New Haven: Yale University Press, 1983.

Evans, J. L. *The Foundations of Empiricism*. Cardiff: University of Wales Press, 1985.

Fay, B. "Nothing But History: Reconstruction and Extremity after Metaphysicalism." *History and Theory* 37 (1998).

Finley, Moses I. *Ancient History: Evidence and Models*. London: Chatto and Windus, 1985.

Jenkins, Keith. *Re-Thinking History*. London: Routledge, 1991.

Kearns, Katherine. *Psychoanalysis, Historiography and Feminist Theory: The Search for Critical Method*. Cambridge: Cambridge University Press, 1997.

Lorenz, C. "Can Histories be True?" *History and Theory* 37 (1978).

Martin, R. "On Telling the Truth about History." *History and Theory* 34 (1995).

Partner, N. "Hayden White: The Form of the Content." *History and Theory* 37 (1998).

Samuel, R. "Grand Narratives." *History Workshop Journal* 29 (1990).

White, Hayden. *The Tropics of Discourse: Essays in Cultural Criticism*. Baltimore: Johns Hopkins University Press, 1978.

———. "The Question of Narrative in Contemporary Historical Theory." *History and Theory* 23 (1984).

———. *The Content of the Form: Narrative Discourse and Historical Representation*. Baltimore: Johns Hopkins University Press, 1987.